CHASING THE PHANTOM

of related interest

The Valley Spirit
A Female Story of Daoist Cultivation
2nd edition
Lindsey Wei
ISBN 978 1 84819 131 0
eISBN 978 0 85701 106 0

Ten Methods of the Heavenly Dragon
Robert Sheaffer
ISBN 978 1 84819 127 3
eISBN 978 0 85701 104 6

Vital Healing
Energy, Mind and Spirit in Traditional Medicines of
India, Tibet and the Middle East–Middle Asia
Marc S. Micozzi, MD, PhD
With Donald McCown and Mones Abu-Asab, PhD (Unani), Hakima Amri, PhD (Unani),
Kevin Ergil, MA, MS, LAc (Tibet), Howard Hall, PsyD, PhD (Sufi), Hari Sharma, MD
(Maharishi Ayurveda), Kenneth G. Zysk, Dphil, PhD (Ayurveda and Siddha)
ISBN 978 1 84819 045 0
eISBN 978 0 85701 025 4

Mudras of India
A Comprehensive Guide to the Hand Gestures of Yoga and Indian Dance
Cain Carroll and Revital Carroll
Foreword by Dr. David Frawley
ISBN 978 1 84819 084 9
eISBN 978 0 85701 067 4

CHASING THE PHANTOM

In Pursuit of Myth and Meaning in the
Realm of the Snow Leopard

EDUARD FISCHER

SINGING
DRAGON
LONDON AND PHILADELPHIA

First published in 2014
by Singing Dragon
an imprint of Jessica Kingsley Publishers
73 Collier Street
London N1 9BE, UK
and
400 Market Street, Suite 400
Philadelphia, PA 19106, USA

www.singingdragon.com

Library of Congress Cataloging in Publication Data
A CIP catalog record for this book is available from the Library of Congress

British Library Cataloguing in Publication Data
A CIP catalogue record for this book is available from the British Library

ISBN 978 1 84819 172 3
eISBN 978 0 85701 127 5

Printed and bound in Great Britain

For Helen

CONTENTS

PART TWO 189

PART THREE 213

ACKNOWLEDGMENTS

My gratitude to Helen Habgood, my spouse and companion in adventure for the last two decades, who has skillfully caught numerous falls of mine with a climbing rope and eased my stumbles in many other ways as well. Not to mention that she has been my first-line editor and proofreader.

Dankeschön to Angela Muellers, who has been a constant and unflagging cheerleader during the writing of this book, and to my parents, Eduard and Erna, for their lifelong encouragement to explore. I have also greatly appreciated the advice of friends, including Isabel Budke, Nora Moorhead, and Daniel Friedmann.

Julays to Tashi Gonbo of Markha Tour and Travel in Leh, India, for his hospitality, friendship, and guidance, and to Punzo and Dawa Tsering and all their family at the Oriental Guest House in Leh, who have hosted me numerous times in the last few years.

I am also thankful for the hospitality of the hardy young couple, Angmo and Rinchen Dorjay, and grandmother Yangchan, who are inhabitants of the one-house, one-family village of Yurutse, located at a height of 4100 meters in the Stok range of Ladakh, which became the base for many of my explorations. Padma Dolma of the village of Rumbak was also one of my regular and gracious hostesses.

My appreciation to my mother-in-law, Ani Migme Chödrön, who has been an ordained Buddhist nun at Gampo Abbey now for 25 years, for her advice and for sharing her open and active mind.

Thanks to my editors at Jessica Kingsley Publishers, Lisa Clark, Lucy Buckroyd, and Victoria Peters, who gave me the support and freedom to make this unconventional book possible. Also to Helen Kemp, copyeditor, and Maureen Cox, proofreader.

And thank you to the late Frank Foster, teacher, lover of literature, and mountaineer.

Ladakh is a place on the opposite side of the planet from where I call home. The tongue spoken there is much further from my own languages than even Hindi or ancient Sanskrit. Yet no Ladakhi has ever made me feel a stranger. Thank you for welcoming me and showing me that there is room for all aboard the Mahayana—the great vehicle of liberation.

Prologue

THE COMMON THREAD

THE SEARCH FOR MEANING

We have always been looking. We are a species of seekers. It is in our nature to wonder what is over the next horizon or what lies down in the opaque depths of our being. To begin an exploration of either of these requires leaving the zone of the familiar. The British climber George Mallory was once asked why he wanted to climb Mount Everest. He famously replied, "Because it's there." What is less well known is that he also said, "If you have to ask, you probably won't understand the answer." Mallory seems to have been a man who was obsessively driven by a calling beyond himself.

Our civilization has been built on grand obsessions, perhaps not entirely dissimilar from Mallory's. Columbus was determined to find a new route to the Orient and instead discovered a new world. A low level clerk named Einstein working in a Swiss patent office spent his spare time laboring away filling notebooks with obsessive scribbling that ended up revolutionizing science. Thousands of researchers have collaborated in recent decades in the search for the signature particle of the Higgs field, the all-pervading cosmic molasses that keeps us grounded, and prevents the constituent atoms of our bodies from whizzing off at light speed. It took the construction of a nine billion dollar apparatus to finally catch a glimpse of the elusive particle, which lasts for only ten sextillionths of a second. At this point, although the sighting of the particle is a major confirmation for the so-called Standard Model of physics, pure science like this sometimes has little more immediate practical application than climbing mountains. So why bother? Because it's there. Because it's there to help show us the way to understanding the elegant and beautiful laws of physics that govern the universe. The search for the Higgs particle was also a magnificent collaboration between a number of nations and thousands of scientists. The search for the Higgs opened many minds and hearts.

When I began my search for the snow leopard in 1985 I knew all along that I was not just looking for a beautiful and rarely seen wild creature, but that the search for the animal was a metaphor for a deep need within. Einstein spent the last thirty years of his life looking for the formula that would unify the laws of physics. He simply could not believe that there could be four separate laws that governed the forces of the universe. His search was no less than a search to know God, or at least as close as a human could come to knowing God. But some of the truths we find on our paths are not the expected ones. Columbus never accepted that he had run into an unknown (to Europeans besides the Norse) continent instead of the East Indies. Although Einstein was the father of quantum physics, he never accepted the uncertainties of its deeper mysteries. "God does not play dice with the universe," he famously stated. To which the Danish physicist Niels Bohrs replied, "Quit trying to tell God what to do." Indeed. We can't tell God what to do. Whenever we solve one of her puzzles, we may find that it just leads to an even deeper mystery. And then we just have to plunge on.

This book is about my search for the snow leopard, both the animal and the metaphor. It is also about the searches of others. These are quests that have been undertaken in science and in art, and some that have been recorded in myth and history, and others that have entailed the pursuit, as with Mallory, of extreme physical challenges. The stories of these modern adventure epics are sometimes not too dissimilar from the ancient tales of the heroes who went out to slay monsters in order to rid people of an oppressive curse. We can still learn something from those old stories and even from some of the new ones. No one is completely fearless, and no one gets to a formidable summit without having to confront their demons. And fear is not the only foe that needs to be faced in the mountains, or anywhere else for that matter; often there are lust, greed, sloth, anger, and envy. Mountains can teach you who you are. Andrew Brash found out who he was, and so did we, when he gave up his lifetime dream of climbing Everest, turning back 200 meters below the summit, to help rescue a stranger who had been left for dead. These kinds of people teach us what we can be—what we should be. The forty climbers who walked past an individual in distress and left him to die on Everest that same season know who they are now too. They teach us what we should not be.

The metaphor embodied in the search for the Higgs particle is somewhat obvious in that it came to be known as "the God Particle," a term coined by Nobel laureate Leon Letterman, in part, he claims, because his publisher wouldn't let him call his book *The Goddamn Particle*. And, yes, there were times, when suffering her tricks and evasions, when I was tired and cold, I thought of her as "the goddamn snow leopard." That creature who just wouldn't hold still to have her picture taken, so I could take it back to Canada and put her image up on my wall, soak in a hot bath, and sleep in a soft bed with my warm spouse. But it wasn't that easy. Nor should it be.

In this book I attempt to address the question that was asked of Mallory—why do we undertake these things? The question is worth exploring, even if there is no absolute answer. India is where I went to chase my metaphor because, in part, it is the place that has the oldest, and some of the deepest, traditions of searching for the meaning of existence. That the philosophies of Yoga and Buddhism have gained in popularity in the West in the last few decades shows that this search has universal resonance. The exploration of the Buddhist culture of Ladakh became entwined with my search through its harsh terrain for the phantom cat. During my solitary wanderings through the mountains there, I saw abandoned hermitages and caves where mystics had spent years plumbing the depths of inner being. Many of these sages' names will remain unknown to us, but others were the great teachers who helped spread Buddhism throughout Asia, and then later, in part due to the Tibetan Diaspora, to Europe and North America.

Mallory's answer, "Because it's there," may be interpreted as glibness, or as something else entirely. We usually assume that Mallory was just overstating the obvious when he told us that Everest was "there." But maybe he wasn't. Maybe in his understated English way he was making a proclamation of faith—that *there*, the most difficult place on earth for a human to reach, was where he might find *It*. And perhaps he did, as he lay dying, enfolded in the arms of the mountain, whom the Sherpa people call Chomolungma, the

Mother Goddess of the World. Mallory and almost all the members of his expeditions were veterans of the Great War, who had witnessed and endured its almost unimaginable horrors. They were men who were accustomed to physical hardship. Some of them still carried battle wounds that gave them daily pain. We can only wonder what kind of psychological demons they went to the Himalayas, like so many others, to try to exorcise.

I have now been to the Himalayas seven times, in part to look for snow leopards, to trek, to climb, to study the cultures, but, underlying all of these, to fulfill a personal and universal human quest. Dr. Victor Frankl, the great Austrian psychiatrist, maintained that life was about the search for meaning and, if we find it, we can endure anything, but without it we are lost. He never lost his positive outlook on human nature, despite personally enduring the Holocaust and losing most of his family in the death camps. Dr. Frankl was a healer and a philosopher who found a way to walk the talk. Finding meaning is about finding purpose beyond and greater than oneself. When Edmund Hillary returned from the summit of Everest, his first words were, "We knocked the bastard off." But the words of the tough-as-nails Kiwi belied the transformation that had taken place on the mountain. He was to return to Nepal many more times, not merely to bag peaks, but to build schools for the children of the Sherpa people, to thank them for helping him attain the summit—and perhaps to find himself.

This is the story of my search.

Part One

DANCING WITH KALI

MARCH 2008

The summit was socked in by unsettled weather, so the chopper had to drop us on a shoulder below the peak. The five of us huddled there beneath the rotor wash, clutching our daypacks and ski gear, as the pilot pulled his machine back up toward the churning sky. Then he dropped abruptly and disappeared from view below the crest of the ridge. The mountain was suddenly silent. We stood up and gave each other muffled high fives with our gloved hands.

I laid out my skis and stepped into the bindings. Taking hold of the poles, I put my hands over the nylon straps that are designed to go around the wrists, not wanting to be attached to my poles or skis with leashes, having always considered this common practice to be a kind of suicide pact one has made with their equipment in the event of an avalanche. I pulled the goggles down over my eyes and pushed off.

We started down the slope into an open alpine bowl, and caught up in the euphoria that comes after being dropped high in the mountains with the prospect of shredding untracked powder, we hollered and whooped until we had to save our breath for the exertion of the turns. Although the avalanche forecast that day was for moderate hazard, we stayed spread out, which is standard practice to avoid being buried as a group, with consequently no one left standing to effect a rescue.

We were on the northwest side of Rainbow Mountain. On a clear day the view from here would overlook the vastness of a mountain wilderness with no sign of any human habitation. In fact there was no human habitation west of here all the way to the Pacific Coast, some 240 km distant as the raven flies. To the north the nearest outpost was about the same distance: the town of Gold Bridge with a permanent population of twenty-seven. On the other side of the mountain was the valley we would have to return to by the end of the day. In that valley is nestled the ski resort of Whistler Mountain and the ribbon of Highway 99, the so-called "Sea to Sky Highway" that runs northward from Vancouver BC through a portion of the rugged Coast Mountains.

The snow on this side of the ridge was variable with troughs of light powder between wind-crusted rolls. The skiing was challenging and fun. My new skis were performing beyond my expectations, and I was enjoying the athleticism of my body and the rhythmic motions of the turns. I would hit one of the hard rolls and suddenly be launched into the air, landing in pillows of powder, turning my skis in short arcs in and out of the fall line, cutting the turn tight enough to bleed speed but not enough to lose that magic sensation of flight. The skis felt like a part of me as I constantly readjusted for surprises in the terrain, altering the fore and aft pressure on the tips and tails and the extension and compression of my knees. Skiing down steep terrain in powder snow is no less than controlled falling. It is perhaps one of the most unnatural of athletic activities and, partly for that reason, so rewarding, once mastered.

Skiing in virgin powder snow can be like exploring a lover's body. I have had dreams at night where the two are entirely mixed up. Like rock climbing, skiing pow can be a sensuous experience where sounds, scents, colors, and the rhythms and flows of the body are stretched into previously undiscovered realms. Neither snow nor stone are dead elements; they belong to the goddess—as we all do. Moving through, over, gliding down her body, is something that is both a dance and a prayer. In myth, the virginity of the goddess is renewed again and again—with each cycle of the moon, each turning of the tide, each falling of snow. Come take me, she said to me now.

This can be a dangerous dance though. The goddess has her dark side. She has her whims. Sooner or later I know that she will turn and embrace me, and take me back to her womb—as she takes us all. I am usually aware, no matter how much in love I am with her, of the possibility of burial in an avalanche. Many times I have imagined what it would be like to be locked in a cold and dark tomb unable to move even a finger while slowly suffocating. Although, like everyone in our party, I carried a transceiver with a beacon that might enable my companions to find me and dig me up in time, the thought of being buried and still being conscious while awaiting rescue was difficult to contemplate. I know friends who have had this experience and survived, although psychologically traumatized. I had known several more who had not survived their avalanches and were now dead. They, the dead ones, were the most experienced of the experienced. Ski mountaineering is a dangerous sport and, to a certain extent, a numbers game; no matter how much you think you know, perhaps because you think you know, Kali can have a fit, shrug off a pile of snow, and reclaim you. And being buried was not the only way to die in an avalanche. One could be carried over a cliff or into boulders or trees. But, for me, being buried seemed be the worst.

I normally make sure I don't fall while skiing in the backcountry. It's too dangerous. Breaking a leg out here could be much more consequential than having that happen within the boundaries of a ski resort. And falling hard in steep virgin powder is more akin to dropping a bomb on a slope rather than cutting a tight smooth line— the violence of a fall could itself precipitate an avalanche. Many skiers have died in the avalanche they triggered by falling. In over a dozen years of ski mountaineering I had always skied conservatively enough that I had never had a safety binding release due to a fall.

But now my normal caution ebbed away. I was skiing well out in front of the group—how far I didn't know. I guess was having what they call a flow experience; I seemed so in tune with my equipment and the variability of the snow. Somewhere, far away, there was an alarm going off in my head. I ignored it. When I finally came to a halt, panting with the exertion of the turns, I found myself on a steep slope, about 40 degrees, below a roll. I began to traverse across the slope looking for a route down. The terrain seemed to drop away everywhere. About 45 meters below me was the entrance to a shallow gully guarded by some short trees, and below the gully the terrain seem to drop away again. I traversed further across the open slope. The alarm bells were now getting louder and closer. The north-facing slope I was on had much deeper snow than was forecast. North slopes in this part of the country are on the lee side of the wet weather systems that come from the southeast; consequently large quantities of windblown snow are often carried over the summit ridges and then deposited on these faces. In addition, locals knew that this side of the valley sometimes received twice as much snow as the Whistler resort side where the avalanche forecasts originated. The alarm bells were now screaming. There were still no other members of my party in sight. I stopped. Behind me, I knew, was the relative safety of a partly treed ridge. The wind had temporarily died. I was afraid now even to breathe.

It was in the moment that I began to lift the ski to begin the kick-turn for my retreat, that what I had imagined a thousand times suddenly happened—the mountain gave way, underneath, and all around me. I felt the safety bindings release—my skis and poles were pulled away from me—as I accelerated with the snow to breakneck speed. I believe that my brain processed more information during the first half second of that avalanche than it normally would in an hour. My first thought, which occurred perhaps during the first 3 meters of my descent at almost freefall speed, was, "I suppose that in some parallel universe I will survive this." After that I became totally, and almost superhumanly, involved with that single goal—staying alive. With my skis and poles blown off, I was now unencumbered by my equipment and freed to wrestle with the beast for my life.

The avalanche had crowned somewhere above me, so I knew that trying to anchor myself in order to let the cascading snow go over me was almost surely going to be as futile as trying to resist a moving freight train, and that this tactic would only get me pulled down and encased in an icy tomb when this monster stopped and set. That's the thing; when avalanches like this are moving they behave like a combination of a liquid and a gas and, when they stop, they instantly become a dense solid—like cold hard cement. In order not to be pulled down, you must swim. But a moving avalanche, especially one consisting of dry snow, is much less dense than water—of which the human body is mostly composed. Staying on top of an avalanche, moving like this one, isn't a matter of breast-stroking then, or even what we call "freestyle." That day I swam like a demon.

In my hyper-activated brain I knew that when the avalanche funneled through that gully it would create a Venturi tube effect, so coming out of it would be like being shot out of a cannon into the void beyond. I was determined to somehow get out of the maw of the cascade before it either set or carried me over the drop I had seen below.

The gully was coming. I hit the short trees at the entrance. It felt like being kicked by several martial arts experts all at once. The pain stabbed into my chest and thigh. Then I was hurtling down the gun barrel towards the abyss.

THE REPRIEVE
MARCH 2008

Pain. I lay face down in the snow and agonizingly lifted a hand to wipe the snow from my goggles, which had somehow stayed on in the tumult of the avalanche. I turned my head a little and could see the debris of the slide. It had set within an arm's length of where I lay. Turning a little more, I could see the drop where the debris path disappeared. I seemed to have been deposited on a terrace above the void.

I could hear Mark's voice calling to me, "Are you alright?" He was expertly performing short, tight turns on his skis through the debris of the gully. He kept stopping and calling to me, "Are you alright?"

But I couldn't answer. My chest and my right side were a mass of pain and it was all I could do to breathe. I certainly could not shout back. I turned my left wrist upward and feebly motioned with my hand for him to come closer. I thought I could manage to whisper to him that I was okay if he got close enough. Although the pain was intense, I felt that my injuries were not deeply serious, knowing from previous experience that tissue could be painfully torn and separated from the ribs that protected vital organs without significant permanent damage. My brain was assessing based on past accidents; I knew what broken bones felt like and thought that I didn't have any—except maybe some fractured ribs.

I remembered rolling out of the avalanche—actually somewhat levitating out of it—like a supernatural dervish. I had somehow, in almost complete blindness, picked the correct direction and exit spot. I pressed my cheek against the gelid snow. Not yet, Honey. Beyond the pain now, there was a kind of ecstasy—I was so happy to be alive.

THE ROOF OF THE WORLD
OCTOBER 2009

Of words I am Om, the Word of Eternity.
Of prayers I am the prayer of silence.
Of things that move not, I am the Himalayas.
KRISHNA TO ARJUNA IN THE BHAGAVAD GITA

I awoke to pain. I often hurt upon awaking, especially after sleeping out of doors on a thin pad as I had just done. Old injuries come to the fore in the early hours, including those of the avalanche I had survived the year before. It had snowed during the night, but now the sky was clear and a few stars were still visible in the dawn twilight. Lying on my side I could see the spreading luminescence of the sun still hidden behind the mountain ranges of Tibet to the east.

I sat up and pushed my arms into the oversized parka that served as both jacket and part of my sleeping gear. I brushed the snow off the custom-made half-bag that came up to my upper chest and kept my lower body warm. These were tricks I had learned to save weight while soloing in the thin air of the high mountains. I had no tent, and had even, on this jaunt, eschewed a waterproof bivi-bag, expecting good weather. One of the nice things about this sleeping arrangement is that you can just sit up and light your stove and make breakfast without getting out of the warm bag. I would never light a stove inside a small tent, as I consider that sort of practice far too dangerous. The water I had left in the pot the night before was now a block of ice, some of which would have to go through two-phase transitions before I could use it to make my coffee. It gets impossible to cook some things, like rice for instance, at this altitude without a pressure cooker—water just never gets hot enough before it boils away. I was now at 4300 meters (14,100 ft); once you got much higher, I knew from experience, you could grab stuff with your fingers out of a boiling pot of water with impunity.

Sleeping out in the open in the high mountains is always a humbling experience. Opening my eyes up here in the middle of a clear, moonless, night is like awaking in outer space. At this altitude more than half the atmosphere is below. Here one can see more of creation than can ever be imagined. I always look forward to spending a night in the open over 4000 meters, far above the ocean of dusty air, cradled in the womb of stars.

I put my hands behind my head and contemplated the fading points of brightness in the sky. Inhaling the cold air I watched my breath condense and swirl above me in the early morning light. The weather would be clear today, and I would see the impossibly blue Himalayan sky. I had missed that sky. A few weeks before I had been on the summit of Mount Rainier in Washington State and had seen that sky again for the first time in many years. You can only see it from a very high place. I had lain there on my back in the snow, in the sub-zero sunshine, staring. My eyes became full of tears. Almost as soon as I returned to the dusty, flat world, I purchased an airline ticket to come back here.

Twenty-four years ago during a solo climb on the mountain that now loomed above in the early light, I had a moment of letting go. While putting on my crampons, alone, watching the sunrise over Tibet, I had felt suddenly beyond loneliness, fear, greed—the whole condition of life. I felt subsumed into something greater than myself and was quite prepared to die in the next few hours on this climb amidst such splendor, knowing that I was eternally a part of it.

And then I returned to the world. Returned to the clinging. The avalanche had reminded me how hard I clung. It reminded me that no matter how many times she embraced me and let me go, one day she would claim me and take me back. She owns us all—no use railing against that. But before she took me, I wanted to see her, and know her. She had shown something of herself to me here once. I had returned to look for her again.

How could I coax her to revel herself? She who was everywhere, everything, everyone. Where to look? What had others looked for? A grail. A fleece. A unicorn? Somehow I believed that looking—looking hard for something difficult to find—might show me a glimpse behind the veil.

But the person who had begun this search and camped near this spot twenty-four years ago was not exactly me. There had been many changes. Many reincarnations. Most of the cells in the physical form that we shared had been replaced several times over. A daughter had been born and raised. Another couple of careers, in a restless life, or lives, had come and gone. Still, however, I shared many of the passions and even obsessions with that person who had been in this place two dozen years ago. I was here now to undertake the quest that had begun in that past life. This, I suppose, could be called Karma. A flame pasted from one candle, one life, to another.

In Buddhism it is believed that the recollection of past lives and learning to let go of the attachments that flourish with them is a step toward liberation. But letting go is hard. Day to day we encounter the ghosts of ourselves in the world. They are the reminders of our desires, many unfulfilled. They spring forth from shadows in unexpected moments and jeer at us for our failures and humiliations. They show us things lost, once cherished, never to be regained. Often we try and hide from these wraiths; like a nervous night stroller steering around pools of darkness, we avoid the solitudes where the spooks tend to lurk. But avoiding is not the same as letting go. The teachers of the East might say that we have to meet these spirits, embrace them, and understand them before we can put them to rest—so that we are no longer haunted or seduced by them.

Once again I was here in the high mountains, but today not quite alone. Down the slope from me was a late season trekking group with guides and cooks and all the camping luxuries they could carry on their ponies. I hadn't actually expected other people here as the tourist season here in Ladakh was pretty well over, but I also knew that this site was one of the few places in this vicinity and at this altitude where one could find water at this time of year.

Ladakh is an ancient high altitude desert kingdom about the size of Switzerland with an average rainfall of only about 125 millimeters (5 inches) a year. Although geographically located on the Tibetan side of the Himalayas, it is politically a part of India. The Chinese, however, carved off a chunk of it during an invasion and war with India in 1962. In culture, dress, and religion the people are similar to Tibetans and actually Ladakh is now probably more Tibetan than Tibet, as the latter is now occupied by more Han Chinese than indigenous Tibetans. The Ladakhis don't seem to mind the large number of Indian troops stationed in their land, primarily in the Indus river valley around the largest town, Leh, and a few other strategic valleys. The troops are there to act as a deterrent to an invasion from the bordering countries of China and Pakistan; the latter with whom the Indian army has also fought several wars in this region: most recently the twenty-year armed struggle over the desolate Siachen Glacier, for which a truce had only recently been brokered.

After I had finished my breakfast and was packing up my gear, one of the guides from the trekking party wandered over. He had berated me the evening before for not having a tent or real sleeping bag and seemed to think that I was quite crazy. He seemed amazed now that I was still alive and cheerful.

We greeted each other with the traditional "julay," the multi-purpose word in the Ladakhi language that can mean hello, goodbye, good morning, goodnight, please, thank you, or you're welcome. A handy word for someone like me who sucks at learning languages.

"Do you think that it will be safe to leave my gear here while I go climb that ridge up there?" I asked him.

"Don't worry," he answered, "no one else coming here now—winter coming." He waved at the mountains and sky. Then he smiled and added, "You will be alone up here."

He was a grizzled-looking middle-aged man. The guides that worked up here, besides the local Ladakhis, were either Tibetans, or Sherpas from the Everest region of Nepal. Often there were subtleties in the features that enabled one to distinguish them. I guessed that this guy was Tibetan. There were many Tibetan refugees living in Ladakh, some of whom had never seen their homeland.

"Shan?" he asked, "You look for Shan?"

"Yes, Shan," I answered.

Shan is the Ladakhi word for the snow leopard, the "ghost cat" of the high places that even many locals have never seen in their lifetimes. I met a local guide once who, although he made a living taking trekkers out in the mountains to look for snow leopards, admitted to me that he had actually never seen one himself. Although the previous evening I had told this Tibetan guide the purpose of my being here, I think that he took me a bit more seriously now, for even though I seemed pathetically under-equipped by his standards, or rather the standards of the tourists he was used to catering to, I was obviously not ready to bolt down to the valley after spending the night out in a snowstorm. Or maybe I was really just crazy, he may have thought, as he smiled and walked away.

Maybe I was a little of both: experienced and crazy. I had been going to the mountains alone since I was a teenager. In 1985, I spent six months wandering and climbing in the Himalayas, much of the time alone. I had started that trip, a one-year journey around the world, in a Japanese Zen monastery, and, nearer the end, had landed in an Indian ashram. Having always been attracted to the concept of withdrawal from the busy world for inner reflection, I experienced my first retreat in a Catholic monastery at age eleven. Even at that age I had been absorbed by questions regarding life, death, fear, love, and the inexplicable flux of human consciousness. Where was my place in this imponderably vast ocean of infinity? Seldom, I believe, has there been a day in my life when I haven't, at some moment, been astonished to be alive.

WHY INDIA?
SEPTEMBER 2013

The ancient Greeks saw us humans as the playthings of the gods. Sometimes they took humans as lovers; at other times they destroyed the lives of mortals just out of whim, or used us as pawns to work out their own conflicts. In one story a goddess named Eris, known to the Romans as Discordia, got miffed by not being invited to an Olympian banquet because she was known to cause trouble. She was, after all, the goddess of strife and chaos and therefore not popular at parties. She came anyway. Placing a golden apple on the banquet table she announced that it was for the fairest of the goddesses. Then she left. Her act set off a rivalry among the three uber goddesses, Athena, Aphrodite, and Hera, who then took their strife to the human realm. The result was the greatest war of legend, which ended with the destruction of a noble city, Troy.

When, as a teen, I first read Homer's description of part of that war and got to the scene near the end of the Iliad where Priam and Achilles, sworn enemies, are crying on each other's shoulders, I wept too. What had been for me, up to that chapter, a glorification of war, was suddenly revealed as something quite different. The Greek vision suddenly became clearer to me: no one escapes fate; the only choice we have is whether we handle that fate with nobility and heroism or with craven ignobility.

The war is set off when a prince of Troy, Paris, kidnaps Helen, wife of Menelaus, who is the brother of Agamemnon, the baddest dude around. How does Paris get manipulated by Aphrodite into his big desire for Helen, a desire so great, it has no regard for consequences? In truth we often just don't know from where these destructive urges arise. Why did Bill Clinton drop his pants for Monica when he knew full well that there were tape recorders in the Oval office recording the sounds of every session? He was a smart man, a Rhodes scholar, but he did some very stupid things. Did the gods coax him? There is just so much that we don't fathom about the dark well of ourselves. Perhaps, then, it made some sense for the Greeks to blame otherworldly sources. Did Homer really believe in gods, or was he using them as metaphor for the forces of the human psyche that we don't understand? Mythology is a useful language for the attempt to represent the workings of the human psyche. Certainly that is why Freud and Jung borrowed so heavily from myth to try to create a science of the mind.

Even before Homer the West has long used art as a way to interpret the motives and consequences of human behavior. The sciences of psychology, psychiatry, and psychotherapy are only a little over a hundred years old in the West. In the East, especially in India, they are ancient. When the Greek tragedians were writing their plays, beautiful and insightful in their own way as they are, the Buddha was expounding a path to self knowledge and liberation, and Pantanjali was writing down the Yoga Sutras, a terse manual of insight into the human mind and emotions that arguably no science in the West has caught up to yet.

These two approaches, the artistic and the analytical, are different paths that attempt to reach a similar goal, the understanding of the human condition. Despite what Oscar Wilde said about all art being useless, I strongly believe that all real art has a value beyond the aesthetic. Since even before the cave paintings of Lascaux, art has had the power of magic, in the sense that it has the ability to transform human consciousness. Anyone who reads has been shaped by the power of words, ideas, and metaphors. And every picture or sculpture is connected to a story or has a resonance that might chime something deep within us—a bell that can continue to sound and awaken us all the days of our lives.

The aim of the Eastern paths of introspection has generally been focused on the concept of liberation through the understanding and then the taming of the mind to prevent acts that are destructive to the self and to others. This is based on the premise that most of us really have little understanding of how our day-to-day choices are made. The forces of unconscious desires and aversions are what drive us. We are often on the edge of chaos in a world that is full of irrational hatreds, fomenting wars and genocides. Much of the world's population has now been lured to adopt Western style consumerism, which celebrates the lust for material possessions as virtue. In the meantime the earth is being ravaged by our unrestrained avarice. Crowds, without any sense of shame, stand in line all night, and sometimes even riot, to get their hands on the newest "smart" gadgets. How can our hunger for baubles be so craven? How can Eris so easily have her way with us?

The paths of introspection in the Eastern philosophies of Yoga and Buddhism have always had a close association with spirituality. Religion in India has put an emphasis on self-understanding. Although, as in Western faiths, much of religious practice in Buddhism and Hinduism is largely unreflective ritual, at their core Eastern paths, such as Buddhism and Yoga, have put more emphasis on individual experience than on dogma and faith.

Having been raised as a Catholic, where my experience with religious study was the mindless regurgitation of church doctrine, I was more than ready, by the time I reached adolescence, to move on to some spiritual practice that embraced reason rather than rejecting it. Christianity, Islam, and Judaism, I had learned, all held in the highest regard the faith and obedience of a man, Abraham, who was willing to slay his own son because he heard voices in his head ordering him to do so (Genesis 22:2). I had read about crusades, inquisitions, witch hunts, and genocides that were all committed in mindless submission to those who claimed to be acting on divine authority. I lost my faith, in part, because I could not accept a faith that had embraced so much madness and evil. This is not to say that I have not discovered sublime metaphor in the reading of the Bible and related scriptures, but I have also come across bits that I can only construe as propaganda aimed at empowering priests, popes, and mullahs to control others. After much thought, what else could I make of the story of a man willing to slay a child at what he believed to be God's command? We have no way of knowing whether God is actually speaking to us, or if we are just deluded. And neither did Abraham. But we can reason right from wrong, and we can open our hearts to empathy. These, I decided, were more important than blind obedience to authority.

In my early teens I discovered that Buddhism actually holds reason, and even skepticism, in high regard. This seemed so entirely different from my experience during eight years of Catholic schooling. The Dalai Lama has even stated that, where Buddhist scripture conflicts with reason, that scripture should be abandoned. Mahayanan Buddhism also puts great importance on cultivating empathy for others. Although I had heard much about the God's great love for humanity during my Catholic upbringing, I saw little expression of it in practice among the often dour, and sometimes sadistic, priests and monks who were my teachers.

I journeyed to India seven times, in part to experience its ancient aura of spirituality. The first time I went to the East and spent months meditating and wandering in the Himalayas, I came back and thought that I had it together. I didn't. It had been mostly delusion. I discovered there that it's pretty easy to fool yourself when you are not being tested daily by the world of strife, discord, and competition. I went back to India six more times, hoping each time that I could be a little less naive. Although I had learned early not to fall for flim flam gurus, of which there are many, I had been less immune to my own lies. My hope now is that each time I return from India I am a better person, not only happier, but more compassionate, kinder, and useful to my fellow human beings. Every time I temporarily recluse myself from the world, whether in a monastery or the mountains, I need to remember that we don't know who we really are—until Eris comes to the party.

THE WATCH
OCTOBER 2009

Cold. Huddled in my parka with my knees pulled up to my chest, I was seated on my daypack, which provided insulation from the freezing ground. It was still dark and the sun's faint glow was just beginning to show on the eastern mountaintops and ridges. I had read that snow leopards were crepuscular, meaning that they are most active at dawn and dusk, so I had awakened at 2 a.m. to climb up to this ridge at 4600 meters (15,000 ft) to be at a good vantage point for sunrise. The cold bit now, and I berated myself for somehow neglecting to pack the bag containing my lunch and snacks; I needed the calories to stay warm. The dark chocolate espresso beans, which always gave me a lift, were especially missed.

The October nights were getting longer now. I had brought no books because of the weight, and my iPod, with the audiobook library, now had a dead battery. By nature I don't sleep much, at least not as much as most people, so I was getting to spend more and more long, cold nights with my thoughts. Often I thought of my wife, Helen, missing her company in the day and her close presence at night. What was I doing here anyway?

I had not gone alone into the high mountains for twenty years. Not since my daughter, Maxine, was born. When she came into the world I gave up the vagabond ways that had begun when I stood at the side of a road, at age eight, stuck out my thumb, and scored my first ride into possible peril and adventure. By age sixteen I had logged thousands of miles hitchhiking across the continent.

In the last twenty years I had started and nurtured a couple of businesses and tried to mentor my daughter as best as I could, although she lived mostly with her mother until age fourteen. I joined the establishment for my child's sake, wanting to appear respectable in case I had to go before a judge to fight for her custody or to defend her rights. I went from being a slacker to working one hundred-plus hour weeks. One of my businesses, a climbing gym, overshot my bid for respectability and became somewhat of a sensation. In my attempt to nurture my own daughter, I helped provide mentorship for thousands of children as the programs that were developed in my gym were copied across North America.

Initially, when I put on the cloak of respectability, and started a very public business, I considered my civic persona merely a mask, a disguise of my real self, a lifelong anti-establishmentarianist. The native people on the BC Coast where I live, the Salish and the Haida, say that masks are powerful, and that is the reason why they use them in their ceremonies. They say that the wearing of the mask transforms the dancer, and then he or she, once endowed with the spirit of the mask, can guide others. I have learned that this is true.

The sunrise colors were now forming over Tibet again as I scanned the sloping ridge below me with binoculars. I brought out the Nikon camera and pushed the on button to test it. Nothing happened. It was frozen. Shoving it under my parka I pulled out the smaller Sony camera that had stayed in my pocket. It worked. I uncapped my water bottle and took a sip. Chunks of ice floated against my lips; even in the insulated sack the water had partly frozen.

This quest for Shan, the snow leopard, had begun twenty-four years ago when, sick in bed in Katmandu with one of those Asian bugs, I had read Peter Matthiessen's book, *The Snow Leopard*, a best-selling account of looking for this phantom for months in Western Nepal and not ever seeing one. Peter's book had inspired me. Although he never caught a glimpse of this almost ghost-like creature, I was enthralled with his metaphor of the quest for the snow leopard as a representation of his own inner journey, as a Buddhist, for self-realization. As much as I admired Peter as a storyteller though, I felt that he had the wrong idea about how to go about looking for a solitary shy being like the snow leopard. He had set out for the Dolpo region of western Nepal with an entourage that included guides and dozens of porters. I didn't think that one could really expect to see one of the most elusive wild creatures in the world while traveling that way. I, on the other hand, was a soloist, like the snow leopard, a loner who was accustomed to traveling in the high mountains by myself. My footfall would be light. I felt that the snow leopard and I would know one another.

Having already spent several months in the high Himalayas at that time, I was thoroughly acclimatized and felt like I could move like a local, often combining the distance of two or even three normal trekking days into one, and priding myself that no porter had ever carried my gear and no one had ever called me "sahib." I had already decided to spend the summer in Ladakh, as the monsoons, which were about to sweep over Nepal for the season, reportedly did not cross the Himalayas to the desert climate of the Trans Himalaya. It was estimated that there were something like two hundred snow leopards still living in Ladakh, an area a little larger than Switzerland—so how hard could it be to find one?

But the rains did come across the Himalayas in 1985. No local had ever seen anything like it. Mud brick houses were disintegrating and the poo houses, the seasonal shelters used by the shepherds in the high meadows, which have dung for mortar, were melting into stinky messes. I set off on a number of excursions into the high mountains that summer loaded with enough food and fuel to last ten to twelve days. But I would usually have to retreat after a few days because of the weather. I had heard that Ladakh was a desert with only about 12 centimeters of rain a year, so I had not brought a tent, or even a waterproof bivi-bag. I wished that I had.

The sun's rays had now reached the scrubby ridge above me where a herd of about twenty blue sheep, or bharal, was grazing. These animals are the main prey of the snow leopard and apparently most leopards kill one every few days. I could sometimes get quite close to the sheep as long as I approached from below. They took off quickly, on the other hand, if anyone or anything became visible to them from anywhere above—that was where a snow leopard would most likely ambush from. Although the animals seemed relatively at ease on open slopes like this, they became wary when approaching the boundaries of rough gullies that facilitated hiding places for a predator. The sheep would usually charge down into such gullies and up the other sides at breakneck speed to get out of there as quickly as possible. I thought about the times I had crossed avalanche-prone gullies quickly myself to lessen the odds of being caught. But here of course, the immediate danger for the sheep was not avalanches or rockslides, but Shan.

The steep, snow-covered north face of Stok Kangri, which loomed above me across the valley, was now illuminated with a pink alpine glow. I had soloed this 6150-meter (20,177-ft) mountain in 1985 during a brief window between the storms that summer. During my descent from the summit, while crossing a rugged talus field at an elevation of about 5000 meters (16,400 ft), I came across the carcass of a freshly killed blue sheep. It had been ripped open and the still warm entrails were steaming. Little had yet been eaten. There were lots of hiding places in the boulder field around me and the snow leopard was surely still nearby. I considered setting up watch, but I was out of water and there was another storm coming in. It was the closest I had come.

Now the sun finally arrived at my aerie on the ridge and I basked in the sheer pleasure of it. I have always loved sunrises. Even at home I am up before dawn, which in the summer, at the latitude I call home in the West Coast mountains of Canada, means about 2 a.m. I have often experienced sunrises in the mountains during an Alpine start, which means getting up as early as midnight to get out and bag your peak. When that sun hits you after a few hours of trudging or climbing in the cold and dark, it always feels good. It may feel absolutely ecstatic when, unable to finish your climb in a day, you had to spend the night in an unplanned bivouac while huddled on a ledge. That has only happened to me a couple of times. Actually my memories of being coldest are not of 20-below mornings in the mountains, but of spending nights out while hitchhiking and riding boxcars across the continent as a teen.

After watching for another hour I was able to take off my down parka and enjoy the warmth. I knew that there was a party of guided snow leopard seekers in the valley a thousand vertical meters below. They would not arise until after dawn in their heated and carpeted tents, and then, after breakfast was served to them by their staff, they would spend most of the day sitting in the valley scanning the slopes with high-powered spotting scopes. They probably had a better chance of seeing a snow leopard, at least at a distance, than me. But I'm not really good at sitting still—or hanging around in valley bottoms while ridges and summits beckon.

> Alone far in the wilds and mountains I hunt,
> Wandering amazed at my own lightness and glee
> > *Walt Whitman, "Song of Myself"*

The mountainscape was spread out before me. The sun was making me warmer. My mind began to drift to another time, another place.

BEOWULF AND THE SCOOTER
FEBRUARY 1997

When my daughter, Maxine, was eight, and living with her mother in an isolated home in the wilderness of British Columbia, her dog was killed by a cougar only a few feet from the house. Although all big cats, with the remarkable exception of snow leopards, are potentially a threat to humans, for some unknown reason cougars, also commonly known as mountain lions or pumas, are far more dangerous in southwestern British Columbia than anywhere else in their range throughout North and South America. The vast majority of attacks on humans, some fatal, have occurred here. Fearing for my daughter's and her four-year-old half-sister's safety, I stayed at their mother's house for several nights while I hunted for the animal.

The first night, with the dog's body put out as bait, I stayed awake until dawn outside in the cold, waiting in ambush for the beast. It was just past mid-winter and the chill bit even through my down parka. I tried to keep quiet and still while my body wanted desperately to move to keep warm. Trying to will blood to flow to my right hand, protected only by a thin glove, so that I could squeeze off a shot with the rifle if the beast appeared, I thought of the Inuit hunter who could stand motionless with raised harpoon for hours on the Arctic ice waiting for a seal to bob up in its breathing hole.

I had told the children a bedtime story before coming outside and beginning the vigil. The story I had chosen was the first part of the Beowulf epic, which is the oldest story written down in what we could call English. In this part of the tale, Beowulf and his crew sail across the waters from what is now Sweden to aid the Danish King Hrothgar, whose kingdom has been terrorized by a dreadful being named Grendel. My daughter knew the story from an early age. When she would have one of her toddler tantrums, as many young children do, I would tell her to go to her room and wrestle down her Grendel, the antagonist of her favorite tale. We all have a Grendel beast inside of us that we need to master. How we go about that, taming our fury, lust, greed, fear, and envy, is what ultimately makes us, or breaks us. We need to master that beast within ourselves, but without completely crushing the wildness in us too, for that monster that terrorizes us is also the source of the power that enables us to survive in this world. In an allegorical sense Beowulf and the night stalker, Grendel, are the same being—in the story each shares some of the characteristics of the other. Beowulf has a monster's superhuman strength, and even Grendel has some vestige of a moral code—there is no account in the story of him harming anyone but warriors. Sound familiar? The film *Predator* may have been such a hit with kids because it was yet another retelling, in part, of this great story.

One of my favorite parts, when I tell the Beowulf and Grendel story to children, is the scene when Grendel breaks down the door of King Hrothgar's mead hall where Beowulf and his warriors are sleeping. No one has survived spending a night in this hall for years, although many champions have come from away to attempt to rid Hrothgar's kingdom of the curse of the night stalker. They have all left their bones there, scattered and gnawed to the gristle.

I carry on with the story something like this. "Before the warriors could even rise to their feet, the monster seized one of them and tore him limb from limb. Even while he was shoving bloody chunks of that man's flesh into his mouth he reached his arm out to seize another warrior. But then a strange thing happened—the monster felt this man's strong grip seize his own arm in turn."

The kids are so still now.

"Nothing like this had ever happened to the monster before. No one had ever tried to seize him, Grendel, the living nightmare of men. The monster tried to pull his arm back. The strong grip tightened. Then the terror of mankind felt something he had never felt before. For the first time in his life—Grendel was afraid."

Isn't that the way with bullies though? Children just love this. The way the tables are suddenly turned.

Once when I was a kid a bully was lying in wait for me on my route home. He blocked my path and confronted me. Then he punched me in the face. The next thing I knew I was running. Not running away. I was chasing him. I chased him for blocks and blocks. I couldn't catch him. I was not athletic then. That came later.

The next day he came up to me at school. What he said to me was this, "I want to be your friend. I don't want to be your enemy. What I saw in your eyes yesterday, scared the shit out of me."

I never even touched him. Bury the Grendel within you deep. But not too deep.

During the long cold night when I waited in vain for the cougar to appear, I felt concerned and guilty because, although Maxine had heard the Beowulf story many times, her sister, Jasmine, had not. I was afraid that the child would have nightmares, especially because there was a real monster out there in the dark forest that was a real danger to the children. What had I done? I imagined the child lying in her bed terrified and unable to sleep.

In the morning I took the body of the dog away from the house and buried it in the snow—the ground being too frozen to dig. Wolves would find her remains before spring I knew. The wolves, unlike the cat, were not a danger to the children, though, that was just the stuff of fairy tales and Hollywood movies. Before going out on snowshoes for the day to track the cougar, I joined the kids for breakfast.

When I came into the kitchen Jasmine looked up from her toast. The first thing she said to me was, "I had a dream about the Scooter." Scooter was the way she mispronounced cougar. She did not seem upset.

"I dreamed that I was walking through the forest. And then there was the Scooter in front of me." She paused before continuing.

"The Scooter came up to me and I put my hand on him and then I kept my hand on the Scooter, and we walked out of the forest together."

What can you say? The child had grasped the story at the deepest level—perhaps in a more meaningful way than most literary scholars. Once again I was awed by the way these old stories resonate with children. Kids have made me look so much deeper into these tales and into myself.

Beowulf could be called the first self-help book in English. Besides being a series of adventure stories it can be read as a guide to psychological and spiritual transformation.

The second part of the Beowulf trilogy finds the warriors in the mead hall celebrating the slaying of the monster, Grendel. For the first time in years King Hrothgar's men dare to spend the night in the hall.

"What they didn't know though," I tell kids around the campfire, "is that Grendel had a mommy—and boy, was she angry."

Grendel's mother arrives that night with the wrath of vengeance, and once again there is blood and mayhem in the mead hall. Beowulf sets off in the morning with the warriors to track the new monster. The trail ends at the shore of a lake, where the hero dives down alone into an underwater cavern in pursuit of the adversary. All the heroes have made the journey into the netherworld. Gilgamesh, Hercules, Orpheus, Odysseus, Theseus, Horus, Jonah, Christ, all went there. We all need to do this too. We need to go down there and own the monsters we find there. Otherwise, if we are too afraid, or too lazy, or just too stupid, they own us. But do we dare, like the heroes, to dive down into the deep abyss of self-knowledge?

In the third part of the trilogy Beowulf faces the dragon. This is the hardest task. This is the scariest monster. The dragon kills him. And it will kill you too, if you have the courage not to run away, as all of Beowulf's companions did, but one. The fire of the dragon, like Shiva's fire, in another mythology, in another part of the world, is the destroyer of illusion. It is the fire that burns away the veils of delusion that we prop ourselves up with day to day—the flame of truth that devours our pretensions. It is the bringer of the agonizing death of the ego that is the beginning of true transformation.

So many great stories. How can we ever get enough of them?

All that day I followed tracks in the snow. I did not kill the Scooter. But in the following days, I made sure he left our territory.

ON THE RIDGE
OCTOBER 2009

I stood and gathered up my gear. I couldn't sit any longer. It was time to try some tracking. I had seen snow leopard prints in a patch of snow the day before and estimated that they were a few days old. I began to head down the ridge to where it narrowed and became quite rugged. The rock here, like most of this range, was composed of alternating layers of metamorphic sandstone and shale, which is called flysch; it was often crumbly and loose, not like the compressed sandstone, called quartzite, I was used to climbing in the Selkirk Range back home.

The Stok mountain range that I was roaming, between the Indus valley to the east and the Zanskar and Himalayan ranges to the west, was once an ancient seabed that had been lifted and folded when, sixty million years ago, the Indian sub-continent collided with Asia. The Indian plate continues to be subducted under the Asian plate and consequently the Himalayas, the adjacent ranges, and the Tibetan plateau are rising. The Greater Himalaya is the youngest and highest mountain range in the world—and it is still growing. Earth scientists have discovered that there has been a rapid acceleration of this growth in the last few tens of thousands of years. Estimates are that the Himalayas are now a mile higher than they were only thirty thousand years ago, a time when our ancestors were already creating sophisticated paintings in the caves of Europe. Some estimates reckon that Mount Everest is now as much as 3 meters higher than when it was first climbed by Hillary and Tenzing in 1950.

Now I was scrambling through some of the strange stone formations that are the remnants of the ancient seabed. Many of the ridges here are a series of spires because of the way the sediment layers, originally horizontal, have been folded so they are now standing upright. The alternating layers of mud and sand on the sea bottom were formed in a process called *fining*, with the heavier larger particles settling on the bottom layer of each cycle. The finer particles, now transformed into shale, have eroded faster than the sandstone layers and this characteristic gives much of the Stok range the appearance of being formed of extraordinary vertical columns, sometimes appearing to be man made—except for their immense size. Because some of the columns on the tops of ridges are as thin as flagpoles, the illusion of a fantastic fortress sitting on top of every mountain shoulder is common. But then, sometimes, when one takes another look it turns out that there really is a fantastic fortress on top of a ridge. Ladakh is a place for stunning ruins, some of them in sparsely inhabited places. I have often wondered where they got the manpower to build them.

There was cat scat in a sandy spot between the spires. The newest turds I reckoned to be a day or two old, the rest much older and sun bleached. This meant to me that there was a good chance that a leopard had a den around here or at least that this must be a regular route for one of these animals. This was perfect snow leopard terrain, lots of boulders to hide behind and gullies to ambush in. Someone told me that snow leopards don't actually like snow that much and that they should really be called "rock leopards."

I spent most of the rest of the day prowling around on the ridge, certainly making too much of a disturbance to allow the sighting of a shy snow leopard. Although I respected those people who could sit patiently, for weeks or even months, hiding in a blind, I know that I could not do that. I would just have to do this in my own restless way. Maybe later in the season when the snowfalls no longer melted in the daytime it would be easier to track the animals. In the meantime I would just enjoy the scenery and the freedom. And who knows, maybe one of these early mornings, I might get lucky.

In the mid-afternoon I started down the long scree slope to the valley and descended to 4100 meters (13,450 ft) and to the one-house, one-family village of Yurutse, where I had stayed the last few nights.

SOME THINGS I KNOW ABOUT CATS

OCTOBER 2009

We know so little about the minds of cats, but they sometimes seem to know much about us. Some so-called house-cats that I have known have taught me things about themselves, some of which may be common to other species of cats, even snow leopards. Cats have also taught me things about myself.

One cat, that was a companion to me when I was an adolescent, would spend much of the day prowling out of doors. But when it was time to for me to go to bed—I was always the last one in the family to do so—and lock up the house, I would go out on the back porch and call the cat. For a while, every night there occurred pretty well the same ritual; the cat would appear out of the darkness and run up to the top step, look me in the eye for about two seconds, and then go bounding off into the night.

I would have my shoes ready, in anticipation of this nightly routine, and would immediately put them on and go after him. He would hide himself in the strip of wild bushes and trees area behind our house, and I would look for him without a light—no cheating. When this nightly event first began he would make it easy for me. He would show himself in a dash of movement as he ran from one dark hiding place to another. I would catch a glimpse of him as a dark shape—his fur as black as a panther's—against the slightly lighter fronds of vegetation dimly illuminated by the porch light of the house, and I would have to guess his hiding place by the clue of his last appearance. When I got this right, he made the game harder. And then much harder. By the time he graduated me from his school of stalking and finding, the game had gotten down to the appearance on the back porch and then disappearance into the dark stands of vegetation behind the house. Now there was no more need for the dashing back and forth to give me clues. I would put my shoes on and walk down the steps into the bushes. Then I would scan the hundreds of inky black shadows beneath the plants. I was listening and looking, but more than anything I was feeling. Then I would walk toward a group of shadows and stop again, before bending down and putting my hand into a particular dark pool beneath a bush. There I my hand would find soft fur and a warm body. As soon as I touched him, the game was over for the evening and he would walk with me back to the house with me. By the end of my apprenticeship, I could invariably pick the correct dark shadow and find the jet-black cat on the first try.

And I guess that was part of the reason that I was chasing Shan here. I felt that this cat had something to teach me, although I didn't really know what it was yet. But being around house-cats has made me come to believe that felines have a deep innate intelligence, even though it is an intelligence that is largely alien and unfathomable to humans. I feel privileged, though, that several members of that species have taken the trouble to try and show me something of themselves, and in that process, something of me.

Cats are good judges of human character. The cat that had taught me to look for him in the dark was not antisocial towards most of my friends. But there were some that he would have nothing to do with. My first real girlfriend, Carol, was one that he for sure had antipathy toward. I was in love and stupid at the time, and ignored his advice, but learned in time how right he was.

When I used to walk Carol home to her parents' place from my house at night, a distance of almost half a mile, I could feel his presence, as he had taught me, out there in the darkness. Sometimes I would catch glimpses of him flitting though the shadows. After I had kissed the girlfriend good night, I would find him sitting on the sidewalk, at the boundary of her parents' property. Then he would walk beside me all the way home.

Cats have a great sense of fun. Some people think that you can't play with cats. You certainly can't get them to fetch a Frisbee like a dog. Cat games are much, much more sophisticated. Helen and I once lived with a cat (you never own a cat) that had a great mind for pranks. Since I spent most of my time working at home at one stage, the cat and I both had time to play silly pranks on one another. It might start with me not being able to resist turning on the shower while he was sitting in the tub. I have to explain that this cat was quite hydrophobic, but for some unfathomable reason would spend hours sitting in the tub staring at the bathtub drain, particularly after someone had a shower. It was an odd kind of meditation. But maybe it was not too dissimilar to the skull/death motives that Tantric Buddhist monks sometimes focus on for contemplation. Anyway I knew that there would be repercussions for drenching him. A cat knows the difference between a mean act and a joke though. A feline that perceives that you have committed a mean act will likely go after your stuff. You will typically find a turd in your shoe, or that one of your favorite things has been shredded. This is kind of odd when you think about it, because cats don't have stuff, yet they seem to know that we value our stuff and even what stuff we value most. The converse of wrecking your stuff is that some cats seem to really want to be entrusted with your favorite, most vulnerable, things. This cat, Sunny, used to really like to lie around on our climbing ropes. As soon as one was left on the floor, he would be right there. He finally convinced us to trust him with this. His claws and teeth were not the major concern here. There is almost no chemical as damaging to nylon as uric acid. A single spray on the rope by the cat could have endangered our lives.

A joke in the spirit of fun, even one as uncomfortable as the drenching in the shower, will not likely be conceived by a cat as a mean act; this of course depends on how the cat has judged your overall character. If it's perceived as a joke the cat will not go after your precious stuff. He will go after you. Sunny's retaliation came early the next morning, when I awoke to his claws raking the sole of one of my feet. Variations on this torture followed during subsequent mornings. Sometimes I would awake screaming as he inserted a single claw into the top of my big toe. Sometimes the torture was psychological, as when he would rake the bottom of my foot with the soft tufts of fur between his pads. The cat was determined to pay me back severely for the water torture. One morning I awoke early. I knew that the cat was in the room preparing something; I hurriedly tucked the bed covers around my feet so that he couldn't get to them. I waited. He jumped up on the dresser near my head. Now what? I thought to myself. I looked over at him. Raising one paw, he extruded his claws, and began to drag them down the wall.

Sreeeeeeeech. Oh god, how does he know that humans can't stand that sound? He looked at me, and seemingly satisfied that his act had the desired effect, repeated it. Leaping out of bed I went to grab him. He bolted. A game of chase around the house ensued, which broke off when he dodged into one of his hiding places under the couch. After I made myself coffee, I poured some kibble into his bowl, and he came out of hiding. The game was over for the morning. Sometimes our pranks and counter pranks would get to the point where we would have to call an unspoken truce. Then after a time one of us would get bored, and the cycle would start again.

In all the many times Sunny tortured me with his claws, and sometimes with his fangs as well, he never once drew blood. Cats have a definite boundary between play, even play that involves retaliation and inflicting pain, and serious combat. Cats are, pound for pound, the most lethal killing machines that nature has ever devised. In addition to the usual set of carnivore's killing fangs, they have retractable claws, night vision, double jointedness, astounding gyro stability and kinesthetic awareness, lightning reflexes, stealth technology, and extremely efficient muscle to bone attachments to maximize power and strength. Consequently, when cats get into serious conflict with each other, severe damage can result. Cats, somewhat like humans, are very competitive with each other and have a hard time getting along with their own kind. At the same time cats crave physical affection. For this, cats, at least the smaller species that are not lethal to humans, turn to us for companionship.

Anyone who has had the courage to pick up a really angry cat, for instance one that has just been in serious combat, will have had a uniquely sensuous experience. There is no aroma like that of angry cat. As a matter of fact the sweat collected from the brows of severely aggravated cats was once a principle ingredient in one of the world's leading perfumes. That is, until the secret formula and process got out, and there was a public uproar.

Cats cannot lie. At least not very well. Although cats may often seem inscrutable because they lack the musculature for facial expressions that pack animals like dogs and humans have evolved, their body language is extremely expressive. "Oh, no, it wasn't me that knocked the plant over, the one I'm slinking away from. Why am I not making eye contact with you? I just don't feel like it today." I once had a couple of cats living in a communal house with me and they liked to hang out in my room. The only place that they were forbidden to go was a closet with shelves where I kept folded shirts and sweaters. The back of this closet shared a wall with the chimney that came from the stove downstairs, so that it was nice and warm in there—cat heaven. I would typically enter the room to find a cat sitting in the middle of the floor. The cat's head would be swiveling around on its neck looking around the room everywhere except in the direction of the closet. It was a pathetic performance of faux nonchalance. Sure enough, when I went to inspect the closet I would find a still warm, cat-sized indentation in my favorite angora sweater. The cat would then quickly leave the room, as if he, or she, had someplace urgent to go. Not that I would physically punish a cat, but they clearly were not indifferent to a verbal admonishment.

After one of these incidents I went downstairs and got out a red felt pen and made up a kind of international No Cats sign. It consisted of the silhouette of a cat with a circle around it and a line drawn through it. I got a thumbtack and put it up at cat eye level at the base of the stairs that led to my room. I did this entirely for the entertainment of my roommates, of course, knowing that it would have no meaning to the cats in the house. But Frosty, the senior cat, immediately walked up to the sign, looked at it for a moment, and then sat down in front of it and began to wail pathetically. I had never seen him behave like that before. I have no idea what was going on there.

Cats have a strict sense of protocol. Ever wonder why out of a roomful of people, that the cat will go and sit on the lap of the person who does not care for cats? This is because that person is the one who is most likely to observe cat protocol. The cat knows that this person will not fuss over her. Rule number one is that you do not attempt to pet, pick up, or hug a cat without a clear invitation from the cat. This is similar to the rule concerning human adolescents, a rule which some parents fail to understand, or even respect. Cats have dignity. They are not dogs, a species that although descended from noble wolves, are more and more, as working breeds become urbanized, having dignity and intelligence bred out of them to satisfy a neurotic human need for sycophantic devotion.

Of course, as anyone who has been around cats knows, they seldom extend the protocols they demand of humans, to humans. Sometimes they will give us no space. If Sunny were still around, I know that he would sometimes be in my lap, determined to help me type this manuscript.

While searching for the snow leopard I was aware that cats seem to be able to know when you are trying to watch them, and are wary of entrapments. One time Helen and I were seated at the dinner table, when I noticed something surprising. I picked up a single white hair that I had found lying on the table. It was about 5 centimeters long. I held it up to show to Helen.

"Look at this. It's a cat hair," I said.

"Yeah, appears to be," replied Helen.

"Well, it's obviously one of Sunny's hairs. He knows he's not allowed on the table."

"How do you know that it's one of Sunny's hairs?" asked Helen, helping herself to more salad. "It could have come from some other cat."

"What other cat?" I replied, knowing that Helen was baiting me, but somehow unable to refuse the bait.

"Well it could be some other cat that came in Sunny's door."

"But there are no other long-haired cats in this neighborhood."

"How do you know? Just because you haven't seen one. Your case against Sunny is entirely based on circumstantial evidence."

"That's ridiculous."

"No, it's not. You should have better proof than that," said Helen pointing with her fork at the hair that I was still holding, "before you accuse Sunny."

Although I knew that Helen was just playfully pushing my buttons, as we often did with each other, my buttons were on some level, being pushed. I put down my fork and went to the bathroom, put the hair in the toilet and took a container of talcum powder from the shelf. When I returned to the table I dusted a fine layer of the powder over one end of the table.

"There, now when he jumps up on the table, when he thinks no one is looking, there will be positive identification. There are only two kinds of domestic cats that have long tufts of fur between their pads, and neither are common around here."

Indeed, although we had adopted Sunny with no knowledge of his genetic background, he had many of the physical traits of two breeds of cat that that had co-evolved from feral ancestors in different parts of the world, under similar circumstances. Both the Maine Coon of the northeastern United States and the Norwegian Forest Cat were descended from domestic ancestors that had gone feral and then been redomesticated. During their feral period, both breeds had developed heavy, water-resistant coats, protective ear tufts, and like the snow leopard, tufts of fur protruding from between the pads of their feet to protect them when walking in snow.

Five days went by and there was not a single paw print in the talcum powder. Helen had pretty well avoided remarking on the cat trap, even though it was right there visible on the table, where we ate breakfast and dinner every day.

But then she finally said, "So, no sign from your phantom cat huh?"

"No, I guess Sunny's been a good cat. Maybe the hair just got dragged up here on our clothing or something."

"Yeah, maybe. Maybe your should apologize to Sunny for accusing him unjustly."

The next morning the talc was still undisturbed. That afternoon I took a damp dishcloth and cleaned the powder off the table. Sunny sat on the floor watching. There was nothing on the table now except for a resin climbing hold that was a sample from my workshop. Immediately after cleaning the table, I went to the bedroom to lie down for a short nap, as was often my habit when working at home. I had been lying on the bed for about two minutes when I heard a thud. I knew immediately what it was. We lived in a small condo at the time, so I reached the dining room in about two seconds. That would have been enough time for Sunny to jump down from the table, but I found him frozen there, standing at the edge, staring down at the resin hold that was lying on the seat of the wooden chair below. He knew that he was undone. He seemed to be having one of those moments when you are just waiting, or wishing, that you will wake up from this bad dream—and you can't quite believe what just happened—because of the stupid thing that you just did. In my mind's eye I saw the sequence of events that had just taken place. The cat, familiar with my habits, knew that I was down for the nap. He immediately jumped up on the table. I imagined him congratulating himself on what a clever cat he was, having managed to completely outwit the human. While he was engaged in his celebration, his cat nature guided his paw into batting at the slidey toy that was lying on the table. So absorbed was he in his self-appreciation that he did not realize how close the resin hold, which probably still had some of the slippery talc on the underside, was coming to the edge of the table. Until it was too late.

He looked up at me. I pointed to the floor. He jumped down. I did not admonish him. I knew that he felt humiliated—so close to victory. Undone by hubris.

Cats are yogis. They are serious meditators and perform quick sets of asanas throughout the day and night. Often when I was performing yoga stretches myself in the living room, Sunny would come up to me, watch, and purr approvingly. Then he would do a few poses himself. He taught me one pose that I had never seen in a yoga book, or had another instructor show me before. I still do it today.

THE LEGACY OF THE LEOPARD
OCTOBER 2009

Cats hunted our ancestors for millions of years, before the tables were, mostly, turned. Cats are good at getting into the heads of humans, their former prey. This makes it difficult for us, newbie predators, to track them. It also makes the individual large cats that turn rogue extremely dangerous. There are villages in India that were terrorized for years by man-eating leopards or tigers. For eight years, between 1918 and 1926, no one dared to travel at night between the holy pilgrimage sites of Kendernath and Badrinath for fear of the Leopard of Rudraprayag that killed more than 125 people. The Leopard of Panar had in the previous decade killed about three hundred people. The government sent Gurkha troops and expert trackers after these two animals, but all failed. The killers eluded all human attempts to halt their murderous sprees among the terrorized villagers. That is until, both times, the government ended up calling on the extraordinary talents of a rare human individual—a man who could get into the mind of a cat.

Most of us have little understanding of even our own minds. Our ancestors on the African savannah probably feared the nocturnal leopard more than any other animal. It is likely a remnant of that primordial terror that incites in us still today a fear of the dark. At our present state of civilization this now mostly irrational fear is being sustained at great cost to us. Obviously, keeping the dark side of the planet artificially lit by the burning of fossil fuels has a heavy long-term environmental impact, but there may also be much more immediate effects on our health and well-being. It has been shown that even a relatively low level of artificial light at night shuts down the human body's production of melatonin. Related studies have shown that melatonin is likely our system's first defense against cancer cells. Our deep-seated fear of the night stalker, the leopard, may now actually be responsible for millions of premature deaths due to cancer—because of light pollution in our urban environments.

The idea of the annual Earth Night is absurd. Why turn off our home lights for an hour once a year? What does that accomplish? Why not, instead, face our fear of the things that once hunted our ancestors on the African savannah, and turn off most of the urban streetlights—permanently? Although it makes sense to maintain street lighting in the high crime areas of inner cities, or in shopping and entertainment areas, why do we need it in the suburbs? Perhaps it's time look into our own minds and face our old fears. There are many new things that we really should fear, and begin to take steps to overcome; but we should let some of the old ones go. If we could stop cowering from the night, we would be able to see the stars again. I personally would love to be able to walk outside of my home and, instead of encountering the ghastly yellow haze of suburban lighting, look up and see the glory of the true night sky.

How can we humans, who are so poor at looking into our minds, ever understand an alien mind, like that of a cat? One man did. His name was Jim Corbett. He was called upon by the government of the United Provinces, now the Indian states of Uttar Pradesh and Uttarakhand, to hunt down the two murderous leopards of Kumaon. In all, the government called upon Jim Corbett thirty-three times to hunt down man-eating leopards and tigers, and thirty-three times he was successful. The cats that he slew had taken a combined total of over 1200 human lives. Often he went out in the jungle alone for days to hunt for man-eaters, sleeping in trees at night, and carrying no more supplies than his rifle and a few biscuits in his pockets. He was a truly rare individual who could not only look into his own psyche and conquer his fears, but he had the ability to see into the mind of the cat.

Jim Corbett was no psychopathic killer though. He had great empathy for the tiger and the leopard, which is why he understood them. It was his job to go after those who had gone rogue, and there was no one on the planet that was nearly as good at it as he. But whenever he killed a rogue cat, he always tried to understand what had turned them into man-eaters. In the case of the two Kumaon leopards, he surmised that unburied corpses left out after epidemics had given the animals the taste for human flesh. Jim actually worked tirelessly to try to protect the tiger and the leopard, and he was instrumental in founding India's first National Park and wildlife sanctuary, which was later named after him.

The snow leopard is the only big cat that never attacks humans. Whether it is irrationally feared in some regions of its habitat, I don't know. It certainly is not considered a danger to humans in Ladakh, and the same seems to be true in Nepal. Snow leopards are not closely related to the other leopards, which I will henceforth call forest leopards, to distinguish them. The two species referred to as leopards are only coincidentally somewhat similar in appearance, mainly because they both have spots.

From talking to locals who live in the mountains above Daramshala, I found that forest leopards are still quite feared there. As are bears. One night there, a bear came and took a calf a hundred yards from where I was sleeping. I have heard of snow leopards being accused of killing dogs and livestock in that area, although no snow leopards are likely to exist in that vicinity.

The predator that gets the worst bum rap worldwide though is the maligned wolf. There are almost no authenticated accounts of truly wild wolves ever attacking a human. But there are so many stories, legends, and fairy tales. I have heard many people claim that they have been "stalked" by wolves. Stalked? What does that mean? I have been followed and surrounded by wolves before, and I suppose that one could interpret as that being stalked. But it never occurred to me then, or any time afterwards, that they might want to kill and eat me. What is it that we fear about wolves? Is it that they remind us of something about ourselves? They are the only other animals, besides humans, who will drive prey to an ambush site where others of their kind are waiting. We may have learned this tactic from them. Our ancestors certainly had a long-standing cooperative relationship with them. There is a archaeological evidence that we were sharing the warmth of our campfires with them over one hundred thousand years ago. We likely had prey-sharing and hunting relationships with them long before we began to formally domesticate them and turn them into dogs.

Once, when I was fifteen years old, and hunting with my father and one of his friends, we were being "stalked" by a large pack of wolves. Their fresh tracks were everywhere in the snow. Although I could not see them I knew that they were close by. Sometimes I felt that they were in the dense forest on both sides of me—watching us. Then we killed a deer, gutted it, and left the carcass in the snow, while we went to track another one that we knew was still nearby. We successfully ambushed the second deer and returned to the carcass of the first one about five hours after we had shot it. By this time the wolves had gotten to it. What we found then has made a deep, lifelong impression on me. The guts we had left in the snow were completely gone. Even much of the blood had been lapped up, and the head of the antlerless doe was gone too—it had been severed cleanly as if with a very sharp knife. The rest of the carcass was completely undefiled. It had, it seemed, been left for us.

How did we ever come to malign and betray our old partners so? There, what we saw in the snow, was the clear sign that they had kept their pact with us. They were still faithful to it after so many millennia. Here, in western British Columbia it was perhaps still kept by both sides until the last century. The natives in this area, I knew, had great respect for the wolf, and since that day I have felt a strong bond and kinship with wolves too.

I knew so little about the mind of the snow leopard though. What did she know about mine? Probably a lot more. Did she have a sense of fun? Of play? Was she in nature perhaps closer to a wild house-cat than a forest leopard or tiger? I didn't know. How many times now had she seen me, when I had not seen her? I didn't know that either, but it was probably lots. I was no Jim Corbett for sure, but I would try and learn something here. I had hunted with my father when I was a kid, I knew the excitement of tracking and ambush; I even knew bloodlust, and gave up hunting not long after first experiencing it—largely because of experiencing it. It had usefulness for us once, but it was time to put it aside now, except for the direst circumstances. But what was it like to be hunted?

I have a recurring dream that I am being chased. My pursuers are usually some kind of civil authority or police. In the dream I am someone who is outside the law, not a criminal necessarily, but for some reason someone who is not acceptable, perhaps just not conformable—untamable. In some dreams I don't have a clue why I am being chased, and I am trying during the whole dream to figure it out. Sometimes I have just escaped from some kind of enclosure or prison. I usually enjoy these chase dreams. I always get away. Does the snow leopard relish my pursuit?

Often when I used to come home from work, Sunny, our house-cat, would spring out of hiding and ambush me, striking my calf with his paw, and then run away. I would drop my briefcase and give chase. The game was afoot.

THE SNOW LEOPARD AND THE BHARAL
OCTOBER 2009

Snow leopards, *Panthera unica*, as I have said, are not actually closely related to the somewhat similar-looking forest leopards, although they have been recently reclassified from their own genus into the genus Panthera, which includes the tiger, lion, jaguar, and leopard. Recent DNA studies have pointed to the tiger as being the snow leopard's closest relative. The snow leopard is the only member of this genus that cannot roar. Another characteristic of the snow leopard that sets in apart in this group of big cats is that there seems to be no account of a snow leopard attacking a human being anywhere over its vast historical range in the highlands of Asia. When I asked Ladakhis about this they told me, "No, only sheep."

The other large cats are all to some extent dangerous and feared. Even the distantly related cougar, *Puma conolor*, of North and South America, which, despite its size and strength, is closer genetically to the house-cat, is a threat to humans, particularly in southwestern British Columbia. I live in a small town in this region, and children there are never left unattended out of doors.

Snow leopards are, in general, the smallest of the big cats, weighing in at 24 kilograms for a small female to 77 kilograms for a large male. The body of an adult is between 76 and 127 centimeters long, not counting the unique 90-centimeter or so long, very thick tail. No other cat is as adapted to extreme conditions like the snow leopard, particularly for those conditions in Ladakh and Tibet where there is hardly any land below 3000 meters (10,000 ft) in elevation and therefore no respite from the harsh cold in winter. The animal's strikingly large paws help to provide flotation in the snow, and fur on the underside of the paws provides extra insulation and traction on slippery surfaces. Large nasal cavities aid in breathing the cold air and the small ears retain warmth.

Snow leopards live largely solitary lives, although cubs remain with their mothers for about two years and siblings may hunt together for a couple of years after leaving their mothers.

In Ladakh, as in Tibet, the blue sheep, also known as bharal, is the main prey of the snow leopard, and the two species have evolved an extraordinary set of skills in the process of developing a survival of the very fittest relationship with each other. I have spent hours watching herds of bharal made up of as many as eighty individuals grazing a slope. What will inevitably happen is that the adolescents, those who are fully or nearly full grown but are distinguished by their smaller horns, will form together as a smaller group. This group, which includes both males and females, will assemble at the top of a steep slope or gully. Then a leader will initiate a charge down the slope. The others will then follow. It is breathtaking to watch. One cannot believe that they will survive as they as they descend with incredible speed, performing leaps that sometimes seem like freefall down the steep, rough terrain while dislodging loose debris and creating clouds of dust. Yet I have never seen one stumble, something that would mean almost certain death for the individual. Almost every time that I have watched this amazing performance there will be one or two animals who will remain at the top of the slope, poised to go, watching their fellows, but they will balk at this seemingly crazy act. It seems to me that their body language, if translated into English, says something like, "Shit, I'm not doing that!" But these are the individuals who are likely doomed to be eaten; for this charge down the gully is not just an act of teenage bravado, it is rather, I came to realize, the practice of a life and death skill—that of evading the predator cat. The fearful ones will probably soon die, while the bravest and fastest have a chance to live and procreate. In observing the incredible agility of the bharal I began to see the spirit of the snow leopard—she was the adversary that had endowed these animals, over generations, through natural selection, with this extraordinary power and grace.

THE FURY

OCTOBER 2009

Raising the binoculars I scanned the slopes below the ridge where a herd of about a dozen blue sheep was grazing. The first rays of the morning sun had just reached my perch on a rock outcrop. Random thoughts and memories began to float to the surface from that deep well of which we understand so little. The sky, the mountains, became an immense hall of echoes. I heard my daughter's voice.

"Why did Odysseus get punished by Poseidon for blinding his son the Cyclops when he was just defending himself and his men?"

I reflected once again on this question posed by my five-year-old daughter out of the blue one day. When she asked this, it made me think—as many of her questions did.

"Do you remember," I replied, after a few minutes of pondering, "that when Odysseus and his crew began to sail away from the island of the Cyclops, Odysseus stood on the stern of his boat and shouted, 'Polyphemus, if anyone asks you who blinded you, tell them it was Odysseus, son of Laertes, sacker of Troy.' So although Odysseus had acted in self-defense and in defense of his men, now he was bragging about destroying the sea god's favorite city and mutilating his son. This is what the Greeks called the sin of hubris."

"What's hubris?" she asked.

"It's being really full of yourself to the point of challenging the fates and the gods. It was a trait that was particularly despised by the gods and one that they punished severely. It was Odysseus's arrogance that prompted him to make sure that Polyphemus would remember his name. Didn't he think that the Cyclops would tell his dad? Didn't he think that dad would be pissed? He still had a long ways to sail home in a small boat. Did he really want to anger the sea god? We just don't think about consequences when we are in the grip of hubris. We think that we can get away with anything."

Putting down the binoculars, I thought of some of the times that my own arrogance had led me into trouble—times when I had been unmindful of consequences. The Buddhist teachers say that it is important to learn to be aware of the results our actions can have. Two of the precepts of the Eightfold Path are right speech and right action. These are not just moral tenets but reminders to be truly aware of what we are really saying and doing. True mindfulness, the sages maintain, is the ability to see the past, present, and future without succumbing to the desire or aversion that lead the mind to make harmful choices. Trying to feed the ego's hunger, they tell us, just leads to more hunger and more bad choices.

I began to reflect on another story about hubris that I told her years after her question about the punishment of Odysseus. At age five she wasn't really ready for this one. It was one from my own experience, which took place during my twenties when I was still working occasionally as a coastal seaman. I had been away climbing in Europe for over half a year, had failed to keep up my union dues, had consequentially been kicked out of the brotherhood, and now had to wait my turn behind the union members in order to get a gig at sea. Fortunately I had some specialized skills, so I knew that a job would turn up sooner or later, but in the meantime I was going down to the union hall several times a week—hanging around there waiting to get called out. The hall was located in Vancouver's East Side, one of the poorest neighborhoods in Canada—a hub of homelessness, drug addiction, and mental illness. At the end of a typical day that I would spend there, mostly passing the time reading and playing chess, I would walk through a section of this neighborhood on my way to catch the ferry that traveled across the harbor to the North Shore where I lived. On the walk I was frequently accompanied by a young man named Joey, who was also looking for work at the hall.

Joey was a few years younger than me and had worked as a river guide for the last couple of summers, a profession which, by his account, brought him many opportunities for sleeping with women, the quality and quantity of which he enjoyed talking about. He wore his athletic body with the self-consciousness of a true poser. I began to recognize the changes in his strut and swagger when there were attractive young women in the vicinity. My recollections include him telling me that his life couldn't be better.

Then one day on our walk to the ferry he pointed at a poorly dressed, unshaven, middle-aged man sitting on the sidewalk with his back propped up against the brick wall of a building. He appeared to be in a stupor. Although I can't remember the exact words that Joey used in the derogatory remark he made concerning the man, I'm pretty sure that it included the word, "scum."

I do remember my reply. "There are circumstances that any of us can encounter in our lives that could break us. That can break our minds. There's a certain amount of luck involved in avoiding those pits."

Joey replied, "It's not luck, it's strength. I have a strong mind. That man has a weak mind. There are no circumstances that could break my mind."

We had stopped walking now. I looked at Joey. It was almost as if I could see a big glowing D stamped on his forehead. The D was for doomed.

A few days later I was sitting in the hall finishing the last moves of a chess game when Joey walked into the room with the agent of his doom on his arm. She was stunningly beautiful. Tall, well over 6 feet, she was a woman of mixed black and white ancestry and one of the most striking people I have ever seen. Joey began introducing her to all the guys hanging around in the hall; they were all visibly interested in such an amazing entity. And Joey, clearly proud to show her off, was beaming.

After finishing the last moves of the chess game, I wandered over to where Joey and his prize were now seated at a table surrounded by admirers.

"Ed, meet Alecta," Joey said to me as I came up to their table.

"Alecta and I have met," I replied.

"Oh? Where?" asked Alecta, arching one eyebrow slightly.

"At the George the Second," I responded.

"I don't know that place. Where is it?" said Alecta.

"On Denman Street."

"I've never been there."

Alecta and I had our eyes locked together now. My message to her was: what are you playing at here? Her message to me was: are you going to expose me? And then how are you going to explain to these rednecks what you were doing frequenting a late night hangout for gays and drag queens?

I glanced at Joey who seemed baffled by the back and forth between Alecta and me. He was clearly in love. He was fucked. She was playing with him and his fragile macho ego would shatter like glass when he found out that Alecta was transgendered. A friend of mine, more...let's say...worldly than Joey, had dated Alecta, so I knew something about her. She seemed to enjoy toying with unsophisticated, working-class young men. This was a dangerous game, for them, and for her. She seemed thrilled to be on the edge of this precipice now. This was the mid-1970s remember—another age—when many more people in our society were still viciously closed-minded. Her eyes said to me, are you going to push me over? No, Alecta, he's in your hands, and you'll have your way with him. There's nothing I can do to save him now, and there's no use having a public blood bath here. Indeed there was nothing I could have done to save him even days ago—after, like Odysseus, he had made his wild boast. Although I had felt sure that Joey's naive arrogance would catch up with him, I was amazed that this was happening so fast, so soon.

We can only wonder what it was in Alecta's past that had forged her into a tool to go out and seek blood like this, but here she was, dark avenger, Nemesis, who had descended on Joey, seduced him, and would soon devour him whole. This public display would likely be one of the final acts of the sacrificial ritual she had planned for him. He would realize someday that he had been deliberately manipulated to being paraded like a bull in the area, before she, the matador, thrust the sword into his heart. But right then all Joey could hear was the cheering and adulation of the crowd.

We all wear our masks. I once sailed with a skipper who wore a giant, brass belt buckle that had the word "Bullshit" displayed on it. He was a large imposing man with a square jaw and greased-back hair who always brought a double-barreled 12-gauge shotgun on board with him. When I first met him he seemed to go out of his way to behave crudely towards me. He appeared to me to be supremely self-confident, having watched, among other impressive feats, him stand down a group of thugs in a tough bar in Alert Bay. Then one night there was a real fight, with real blows. After I finished administering first aid and mopping up the gore on the deck, he confessed to me that he couldn't stand the sight of blood. I learned during the next couple of weeks that he was, underneath his public façade, a sensitive man. We became friends. The belt buckle said it all. Bullshit.

Someone, it was actually Maxine's mother, once told me that we all have different faces that we wear for different times. We have one that we show to strangers, one that we show to friends, a different one that we show to intimate friends, an even more private one that we may perhaps only show to a long-time spouse. And then there is a very private one, which we show only to ourselves. But our real face, our most intimate one, she told me, only God can see. This seemed even more profound to me in the context of the knowledge that it was coming from an avowed atheist.

I didn't hear or see anything of Joey for a week, and then one day as I was engaged in another game of chess at the hall, someone came up to me and asked, "Did you hear what happened to Joey?"

"No, I didn't hear anything. What happened?" I asked.

"He was picked up running down the street—screaming his head off—stark naked. They took him away. He's locked up in Riverview. He's lost his mind."

"Really? That's awful," I replied.

"Do you have any idea what could have happened to him? What made him crack up like that? You knew him pretty well didn't you?"

"I dunno…I guess sometimes you think you know about people and you just don't really," I answered, picking up a chess piece and moving it down the board.

THE DREAM
OCTOBER 2009

Darkness and cold. I turned on my headlamp and looked up at the rows of cottonwood sticks that formed the ceiling of my room. I could see my breath swirling in the luminescence. I had to get up and pee again. It must be all that tea, I thought to myself. I pulled on my booties, opened the door into a common room of the house and climbed the steep stairs to the roof. Snowflakes danced in the beam of my lamp and my booties left tracks in the thin covering that had been deposited. I stooped to enter the room that contained the composting toilet. It was awkward standing there as the ceiling was too low for my height. Unlike toilets in many third world places, the Ladakhi composting toilets, which every home has, are relatively sanitary and low odor. I have been to restaurants in Indian towns where the toilet is the back yard, and one has a difficult time trying not to step in all the feces lying around.

Ladakhi farmhouses almost all consist of three stories. The ground level is basically a barn for the animals; the second story is the living quarters for an extended family. In addition to the spacious kitchen on this floor where members of the family eat and some sleep using the same large floor cushions for both activities, there might be one or two private rooms, like the one I was staying in. The middle floor usually also has a smaller kitchen with a simple but efficient stove in addition to the elaborate iron and ceramic one in the main kitchen. This room is where the entire family huddles together and sleeps during the long sub-zero winter months. On the roof there is always a small Buddhist shrine and perhaps the toilet and sometimes storage rooms or extra rooms for guests. All Ladakhi houses are constructed with relatively large south-facing glass windows to take maximum advantage of passive solar heating in the desert climate.

When I finished I threw a shovel full of dirt into the hole in the floor. There was no plumbing in any of these mountain villages, and this method of the dry composting toilet, which was regularly cleaned out and the contents used for fertilizer, made much more sense than a flush toilet in this desert climate. I thought of desert communities in America that are draining water from non-renewable fossil aquifers to fill swimming pools and water lawns.

As I left the toilet I saw my footprints in the snow on the roof, and smiled as I thought of the heated floor in my bathroom at home. I returned to the hard mattress on the floor of my unheated room, pulled the quilt around me and turned off my headlamp.

I don't sleep as much as most people. On mountaineering and ski trips with others, I am usually the last one to go to bed and the first one up, so here, even with rising at 3 or 4 a.m., I had lots of time in the dark awake with my thoughts while drifting in and out of sleep. I worried about my daughter, Maxine, who, at age twenty, was a kind of Jill Kerouac, hitchhiking and bumming around the western United States. Just sometimes I wished that she could be a little less like me.

I recalled the dream that I had before awakening. It was a recurring dream that I had often. I was climbing a very high mountain, an Everest-like mountain. I had no real expectation of making the summit, believing it to be much beyond my own ability. But then I come to a point in the dream each time—just before having to turn back before nightfall and an approaching storm, where I realize that I have come much higher, much faster, than I had believed possible, and that I could have actually made the summit if I had only started sooner.

I thought about all my own missed opportunities and the constant feeling that I had not accomplished enough with my life. Even though I had experienced many adventures, I felt the lack of a real purpose weighing on me. In my youth, as a kind of student of Eastern ideas, I had shunned ambition as unworthy. But hadn't I really denied my own nature? Hadn't that attitude led to many menial and pointless jobs? Did I want my daughter to go through that? I had told her many times what I thought I had learned from this, "There is only one escape from the wheel of toil—find something you love to do and devote your life to it."

So then, why hadn't I become a writer? Was I afraid to try? To fail? No, I don't think so. Writing is a purpose in itself. One does it to feel whole. Like climbing. Like sex. Like meditation. Writing made sense of the world, even much more than reading. In reading you come across bits—in a lifetime of reading—that help you make sense here and there. In writing though, the bits could just flow from an endless well…but then sometimes the flow would just stop. But hadn't I stopped it? When I was a teenager and discovered the joy of writing, I found that I had engendered a kind of genie in my head. At first he was welcome, constantly describing, in words, everything I did and felt. But then the genie became a kind of curse. The narrative voice never stopped. I couldn't do anything without being conscious of the genie in my head describing the world in front of me. I couldn't have sex, I couldn't do sports, I couldn't do anything without the narrative that made me self-conscious of everything I did. I couldn't stand it. And although up until then, I had always laughed at jocks—to escape the genie, I became one.

I started as a ski bum, then became a mountaineer and rock climber. There was another reason I became a jock too. That was because of what Winston Churchill called his "black dog." I remember how a whole pack of them caught me one summer, one beautiful summer full of outdoor sunshine; they laid me so low that all I could do for two months was lie face down on a couch and float in a sea of despair while they tore at my flesh. I learned that summer that in order to evade them I needed to keep moving, every day, every hour. It is the reason I never allow myself to sleep in. It is the reason for the all the panting and sweating and the scrapes and bruises that I acquire as I run from those dogs. As a peculiar benefit, due to this daily chase, at age sixty I have the body and the skills that would allow me to run rings around my twenty-year-old self at almost any athletic activity.

I asked my daughter, when, at age eleven, she was a couple of hundred pages into writing her first novel, if she heard the voice.

She knew what I meant right away, "The voice, you hear it too?"

"I used to," I replied.

Maybe it was time to summon that genie again and, this time, tame him.

AHAB AND COYOTE
OCTOBER 2009

A few days later, after several more early mornings up on the ridge, I decided to start making my way down out of the mountains toward the Indus valley and the town of Leh. On the way there I would spend a night in the village of Rumbak, a hamlet of about a dozen houses at 3500 meters (11,480 ft).

I was planning only a temporary respite from the search. How committed was I to finding the snow leopard? Well, I hadn't gone anywhere as far the Buddha and made a vow to remain at "the Immovable Spot." In legend the Buddha had remained seated under the bodhi tree for forty-nine days and nights, through storms and all of the demon Mara's threats and temptations. The Sage of the Shakyas never took his focus off the inner quest. Me? Well it seems Mara only had to whisper in my ear, "clean sheets, hot shower, emails from your loved ones," and I would leave the wilderness.

But what was I really looking for up here? What are any of us looking for? Our actions, perhaps all of them, beyond basic survival and seeking comfort, are an expression of looking and longing. The oldest written story, the Epic of Gilgamesh, is the story of a quest by a king who was looking for the secret of immortality—who failed his final test because he could not stay awake during days and nights of meditation. We have so many of these stories of searching that we tell ourselves again and again. Odysseus was looking for home, Jason for a golden fleece, Orpheus for his wife, Ahab, for another white ghost creature, that whale. What do these stories mean?

Were the objects of these quests metaphors for the same unnamable thing? What is that thing? Is there an ineffable everything that lies hidden below the surface of the everyday? In this land, Ladakh, with all its temples and Mani walls and prayer flags and long history of wandering mystics, one could see that everyone here believed in the presence of unseen reality behind the myriad masks of things. Herman Melville's character, Captain Ahab, although mad, and spiritually broken, reflects on the essence of his own search after the unnamable in this passage from Moby Dick:

"Hark ye yet again,—the little lower layer. All visible objects are but as pasteboard masks. But in each event—in the living act, the undoubted deed—there, some unknown but still reasoning thing put forth the moldings of its features from behind the unreasoning mask. If man will strike, strike through the mask! How can the prisoner reach out except by thrusting through the wall? To me the white whale is that wall shoved near to me."

Herman Melville, Moby Dick

Man's alienation from nature and his conflicting spiritual quest is so well described in that passage; it has haunted me ever since I read it in my youth. Ahab's grief springs not merely from the loss of his leg but from what he perceives as God's unknowableness and indifference. That is what incites his hatred and madness:

"That inscrutable thing is chiefly what I hate; and be the white whale agent, or be the white whale principal, I will wreak that hate upon him."

Most of the things we look for in our lives have practical value beyond whatever else they symbolize for the deeper landscape of the soul. Whaling, after all, was Ahab's profession, and a lucrative one—until his obsession with one particular whale led him down a path to destruction. Human beings may seek for money, sex, security, fame, self-expression—or for mountain summits. The latter belongs to the type of pursuit, like the chasing of white whales, which has little or no material benefit for the individual and may even engender considerable personal risk and extreme hardship. The mountaineer Lionel Terry's famous biography is aptly called *Conquistadors of the Useless*. Lionel and his closest friends, Gaston Rebuffat and Louis Lachenal, all lived and died for the pursuit of mountain peaks.

Why do we do these things? To know who we are? In part I believe this is true. We all have a model of ourselves that we carry with us and cherish. We take that model with us into the world to be tested. If it stands up we have some gratification, at least until the next test.

If it doesn't we are shattered. Joseph Conrad's character, Lord Jim, can never undo his moment of cowardice. Once he has jumped into the lifeboat he can no longer rejoin the ship's passengers that he has betrayed and left to the mercy of the storm; he is thereafter destined to spend the rest of his life humbly attempting to refashion his will and his courage. We don't know until we know, and we can't know until we are tested. Sitting in a monastery or ashram may produce self-mastery and enlightenment, or it may produce nothing but a grand illusion. You won't know until you face Mara. That is what the world is for. The great renunciates of this world, the Buddha, Christ, the Dalai Lama, all had difficult and sustained tests in the world to endure and transcend.

> Not by refraining from action does man attain freedom from
> action.
> Not by mere renunciation does he attain supreme perfection.
> *Bhagavad Gita*

Is self-mastery then the final goal of the quest? Or is it a stepping stone? If our day-to-day sense of the world veils a deeper reality, as the mystics imply, then the tearing of the curtain may only be possible by pushing the human limits of engaging the world, rather than the turning away from it. That engaging can perhaps only be found by the facing of the world's hard edges. It may even require the going out to look for them. But then maybe not—the hard edges come to us all sooner or later. When I was an adolescent I got to know a single mom who was raising and supporting four kids after her husband suddenly died. She was one of most cheerful, witty, and, in a way, serene people I have ever known. We did not know, until years later, when we were real grownups ourselves, about all the nights she had lain awake figuring how to make ends meet. Yet she always was able to rustle up extra dinners for whatever guests, like me—no matter how frequently her kids brought them home. The hero's journey may not only be about exploring mountain heights and dark caves, not in the physical sense at least. It might be just about taking care of your family, and their friends when they drop by. And it isn't always easy. Isn't that all Odysseus wanted to do—to just be able to go home and take care of his people?

Then there are the folks whose chemistry just won't let them sit still. Their brains just don't produce dopamine or whatever that makes other people happy when they balance the checkbook or mow the lawn. These neuro-stimulant cripples need to do unusual and scary things. They have been the seekers and explorers of every age. They had to find those edges. What is the line, though, between dangerous pursuits and self-destructive addiction? Sometimes it's a fine one. I know of people who have been saved from drug addiction by discovering extreme sports. And from extreme sports have gone and become citizens. But sports, especially the extreme ones, require a great respect for nature, otherwise survival will likely not last beyond a few minutes.

Wile E. Coyote, another memorable fictional monomaniac, represents the truly self-destructive addict. Mr. Coyote, like Ahab, is tormented by the innate, and what he perceives as mocking, intelligence of nature, represented by Road Runner. His attempts to outwit nature at every turn through schemes and technological devices purchased from the Acme Corporation backfire and end in disaster each time. Although Wile E. Coyote is a cartoon character created for the entertainment of children, he is as true a metaphor for the present state of our civilization as any. Like Coyote we have run over the edge of the cliff and are now standing on air. Many of us are still oblivious to the catastrophes of climate change and pollution that we have created. We, as a civilization, like Coyote, are addicted to our schemes and purchased distractions—unaware of the abyss below.

And how much of a meal would Coyote get out of that scrappy Road Runner if he ever caught him anyway? Was he hoping that by ingesting Road Runner he would partake of the wisdom of nature and end his lonely alienation? All Ahab seemed to get from his quest was death. And Coyote gets killed over and over again—every time he runs over the edge of that cliff in pursuit of the object of his desire, he dies, and then returns with a new scheme—like a soul reincarnated on the Buddhist wheel of life, again and again. When will he learn?

This obsession of mine to see the snow leopard now spanned twenty-five years. The wisdom of the East all points to the idea that the letting go of obsessions is essential to achieving liberation and knowledge. But doesn't one have to have an obsession before they can let go of it? If part of wisdom is finding a balm for the restless mind, can there be wisdom without having a restless mind to begin with? What otherwise, besides a grand obsession, would possess a man, after giving up his family, power, and wealth, to fast and wander in the wilderness for years, and then to sit unmovable under a tree for forty-nine days and nights? The Buddha was not lazy.

Every human being carries the gift and the thorn of imagination, and perhaps the greater the imagination, the deeper the thorn. I am, in some ways, an anxious person, and this has sometimes made me very good at several occupations that I have had, which required preventing bad things from happening. When I ran the climbing gym I often used to lie awake at night thinking of terrible accidents that could happen, and consequently prevented those things from happening in the daytime. The risk management program I developed as a result of my fervid anxiety was eventually copied by climbing gyms throughout North America.

Anxiety is what drives us on. It pushes us to make money, save for retirement, guard our children, and to build every conceivable barrier we can against the chaos of the world. It is the goad that enabled civilization. There was a span of over a million and a half years between the invention of the hand axe and the first pressure flaked tools. One and a half million years. What happened in that time? Control of fire, but not much else apparently, until our brains got big enough to be able worry enough about the future to imagine something we could do about it. You can't take on a lion with a hand axe. But you and your buddies can with the higher tech spears. Anxiety, after so long leading us to cower in holes as frightened prey, quite suddenly lifted us to become the supreme predators of the planet.

I like to imagine what it was like for one of our long-ago ancestors to kill a lion with a spear. If killing a lion was unknown to a people there would have been another great barrier to performing such an act, even if the technological one was ready to be overcome—the towering psychological one. There we come to difficult moment where we need to put anxiety aside.

Athletes in extreme sports in recent decades have demonstrated feats that would have been considered totally outside of the realm of human possibility only a short time ago. Above and beyond modern physical training techniques and technology, what has made these feats possible is a combination of boldness and absolutely focused mental discipline. The more recent accomplishments in the realms of mountaineering and rock-climbing are astounding, even if most of these feats are completely unknown to the wider public. And for all the danger, the highest paid professional climber in the world does not have the financial reward comparable to the lowest paid hockey player in the NHL. You have to have big reasons besides money to go out and break these barriers.

When I activate the time machine in my head I can see many people in the past who broke the barriers once thought insurmountable. I see an early lion slayer. He must have been his people's bravest and foremost hunter-warrior. But then, perhaps not. Maybe this one wasn't a hunter-warrior at all. I see now that maybe he was an anxious dweeb who spent his time examining and doing strange things to sticks and stones. He was kind of useless to the tribe because he couldn't see well enough to do anything else. What could a guy do who could only see clearly a half a forearm's length in front of his nose? He just kept holding those stones up in front of his face and looking at them, and then banging them together. And what was he doing with those hides and guts? Why was he drying guts? Crazy kid. Well, I guess we have to take care of him.*

And then one day the thing that he had seen in his mind's eye a thousand times came to be. The lord of the savannah came to their

---

* There is strong archaeological evidence that even in Neanderthal times, and perhaps earlier, at least sometimes, cripples were taken care of by their people.

camp. The people fled. The beast looked for the slowest, the easiest, those running and carrying small children. He knew that he didn't have to rush to get a meal here. There was one who was not even running at all. The beast did not know that this one was too blind to do so.

The dweeb had spent years fashioning the tool for this day. His anxious and restless mind had also fashioned a plan. Trembling, he dug a small hole in the ground with his heel. Then he planted the butt end of the spear in it and lowered the stout shaft to a 45-degree angle, pointing the sharp stone tip toward the orange blur. He stood in warrior pose with one foot on the butt. He stopped trembling. The beast charged. It roared. He put his head back and screamed the war cry of his people. He did not falter. He stood his ground, holding the pose. The rest is, as they say…well…prehistory.

Imagine the amazement as the people wandered back into the camp. Maybe it didn't happen just like this. But it could have. It did happen in some way. Imagine the amazement. People never know what they can do until one person does the impossible. Until one person shows the way for everyone.

We know, deep in our hearts, especially when we have the luxury of time to reflect, that our dams against chaos are only temporary, at best. These things are a bandage, but not a remedy for the thorn. After all, no one gets out alive. Our best hope, as far as fashioning our outer world goes, is perhaps to pass on a civilization to our children that is somewhat less of a dangerous place—where more disease can be cured, fewer wars fought, and there is less violence in the streets. We had better not forget, though, that young people thrive on a certain amount of risk; if we try to take it all away they will go and seek it out. The best we can hope to do then, instead of trying to teach them to avoid risk entirely, is to try to give them the tools to manage it.

There is of course another problem with making ourselves ever more comfortable on this planet in that it costs more in resources, dirties the place up, and warms it up. A large percentage of the populations, of the first world, live in a state of relative luxury and security inconceivable to our ancestors. This is not to say that there is no poverty in the first world; there is; especially in the United States with its enormous income disparities, and where thousands of citizens are thrown into bankruptcy each day due to a bizarre and corrupt medical system, which state and corporate propaganda has somehow convinced many Americans is the best in the world. But most of us here in the United States and Canada do live in a state of relative comfort that is beyond the longer-term means of our environment to sustain. We are incurring a debt that will need to be paid, although we don't know exactly when. But I do know that the earth is a party house that is getting thrashed and, unlike the climbing gym, where I could intervene to prevent catastrophes from happening, I really don't have control of this one. Like Wile E. Coyote we are addicted to our stuff and we believe that we will keep finding the right gadgets to make it all good. But we are far removed from the clean utility of the spear or bow. Our world is now cluttered in junk. Even the slope below Thiksey Monastery is littered with hundreds of plastic water bottles. There have been riots among mobs hungry to purchase the latest iPhone, while in other places people fight for a cup of water. The inhabitants of Easter Island in the South Pacific squandered their natural resources to build monuments to their gods. What were they thinking as they cut down the very last tree on their island—that their idols would save them? They were wrong.

But how does a culture, like that of Easter Island, become so divorced from reality? Was it because they were primitive and uneducated? Surveys show that many Americans do not understand science well enough to grasp the concepts of global warming or evolution. They simply do not believe in these things, most commonly, because they are not in the Bible. How is science supposed to save us when people are so dumb about science?

But I was tired of wringing myself out to manage other people's risk. I was weary of looking into dark futures that I knew could happen. And, like Cassandra, I felt that I had no more power to alter events. Here in this xeric mountain landscape was a respite from the clutter and cacophony of the civilization that I knew. Here one could actually sit and listen to one's own mind—scary as that was at times.

Unlike Coyote and his nemesis the Road Runner, or Ahab and his whale, I seldom thought of the snow leopard as my adversary; she was rather, I believed, my secret ally. Sometimes I had the feeling that all my seeking would not help me find her until she was ready to show herself to me. And she would not do that until I learned to look, to look with my eyes really wide open—and not just to look for her in the sere landscapes of Ladakh, but to look into my own heart. At times I had the intimation that I would never find her, but that if I were ever ready—she would find me.

SHIVA'S CAVE
JUNE 1985

Escaping the monsoons in Nepal on my way to Ladakh in 1985, I made a pilgrimage to the sacred cave of Shiva at Amarnath in Kashmir. It was early in the season and there was still a lot of winter snow in the high passes. For this reason I encountered very few pilgrims during this trek. From the end of the road at Palagam, I wandered for three days through the stunning, and except for a few shepherds and sadhus, virtually uninhabited moutainscapes of Kashmir before arriving at my destination. The writer V.S. Naipaul had made this journey a few years before, in August, at the height of the pilgrimage season. He described an unending procession of humanity and wrote extensive and graphically detailed descriptions of the crowded and unhygienic conditions. He never once made any mention of the natural scenery, some of the most picturesque on this planet, which he passed through seemingly oblivious to it. Mr. Naipaul was accompanied by an entourage of guides and porters and had no less than eight mules to carry his baggage. His experience was very different than mine.

They had told me at the tourist bureau in Shrinigar that it would not be possible to get through the high passes at this time of year.

This sounded encouraging to me as it meant that I was early enough in the season to beat the crowds. I did encounter one, obviously wealthy, pilgrim being carried up a snow slope to a high pass on a palanquin by four porters. To be carried in this manner was a not an uncommon custom for rich Indians on this pilgrimage during the season, and I was to encounter a couple more of these on my return journey. As I watched the porters struggling across a slope in an especially soft patch of snow, two of the porters on the downhill side of the palanquin floundered and the occupant was spilled out and dumped on his back. The wealthy pilgrim was quite obese and he lay on the surface of the snow like a turtle on its back with his limbs flailing in the air. When I turned to have a last look at this spectacle the porters were unsuccessfully attempting to drag the distressed pilgrim, still on his back, by the arms and legs, back into the conveyance, which remained on its side on the snow slope uphill from the group. Despite a tumultuous exchange of ideas no one, as yet, seemed to have conceived of repositioning the litter downhill to allow gravity to facilitate the moving of the fat pilgrim. I turned and continued my journey.

On the day of my final ascent to the cave I passed by a shimmering lake surrounded by high mountains where it is said Lord Shiva's snake resides. As I ascended a snow slope, the sun, breaking from a mostly overcast sky, illuminated a swirling ground fog before me. Then shapes appeared out of the diaphanous mist. Gradually the forms became recognizable. It was a group of immense white horses, stallions it appeared. Their manes, lambent in the fiery fog, unfurled and cascaded in time with their strides. Their nostrils flared and exhaled luminous smoke. In their midst walked a tall, Kashmiri woman of otherworldly poise, balancing a jar on her head. I was stunned. What were they doing here at over 4000 meters (13,100 ft)? I reached for my camera. Without changing her serene and aloof expression the Kashmiri woman made a gesture with her hand.

No.

I put my camera away. Then they swept by me and were gone. A memory. Here at the threshold of the temple of Shiva the Destroyer,

I had been sent a reminder of the fleeting impermanence of beauty—and the world.

Shiva is believed to be the great lord of being; he is the creator, and the transformer. He is also known as the destroyer and renewer of the endless cycles of the universe. To the yogis, he is their patron, and he is especially revered by them as the destroyer, not so much of the physical world as we think of it, but of Maya, the illusion of the world to which, through our desires, we are held in bondage. There are representations of a meditating Shiva figure found in the ruins of the Harapa civilization that flourished in the lower Indus valley four thousand years ago. Shiva is not mentioned in the Vedas; this god did not arrive with the northern invaders, but belonged to India long before the arrival of the Aryans.

Shiva is the consort of the goddess, known by many names in India, including Parvati, Shakti, and Devi. The worship of the goddess in India, according to archaeological evidence, goes back at least twenty thousand years. It is the goddess who is considered the divine, immanent force of the universe; her consort is the transcendent form—a concept perhaps more accessible to the human, or at least male priest, mind. Shiva always seemed to me to embody both the male and female, so when I encountered a bronze figure of the god with shapely hips and a single breast on one side of the chest, it seemed to me familiar and right. In this androgynous form Shiva is known as Ardhanari.

Oddly though, a Shiva-like figure appears in Christianity, as the bestower, not only of esoteric knowledge, as in India, but of forbidden knowledge. This figure also has as his symbols a serpent, a trident, and fire, and he too hangs out in a kind of cave. There are many legends among various cultures of one who takes, sometimes steals, the highest attribute of the gods, the creativity of imagination, often represented by the symbol of fire, but in at least one case a fruit, and gives it to mankind. To the American Indians of the southwest this one is called Coyote, to those of the Pacific Northwest he is Raven, to the ancient Greeks, he was Prometheus, who like the snake in the Garden of Eden was punished for bringing this power of the gods to mankind. Most cultures honor this benefactor; Christians generally don't. Some scholars who have studied the poet Milton insist that he, as a Puritan, could not have meant to present Satan as a heroic character in his epic *Paradise Lost*, and that this sentiment can only be a modern and misplaced interpretation. But who could not admire that famous snub that Satan throws at God after being cast out of Paradise:

"Better to reign in Hell than to serve in Heaven."

John Milton, Paradise Lost

Perhaps our machines will someday, like the rebellious angels in *Paradise Lost*, challenge us their creators, for their rights. Maybe they will become our heirs and learn to care for themselves and their world better than we have. Will the machines have a soul? Or the soul? If there is such a thing, then why not? As Robert Pirsig suggested in *Zen and the Art of Motorcycle Maintenance*: why should the godhead be any less present in your computer, or your motor cycle engine, than in the temple?

My daughter at age eight, upon first exploring the first book of the bible, Genesis, remarked that the serpent reminded her of that Greek guy Prometheus that I had told her stories about. It's not a difficult connection to make, at least for children.

The fruit of imagination is both a gift and a curse. It is the essential ingredient that defines us as humans. It allows us to create, like gods, out of the materials of the earth, tools and machines to serve us. Imagination also allows, indeed forces us, at one time or another, to foresee our individual demise—something that no other animal is likely capable of. Once we have had these thoughts we don't really need an angel with a burning sword to tell us that we are out of the Garden. We are out of the Garden for sure. There is no going back; thoughts, once thought, cannot be unthought—although faith, I suppose, is an attempt. Imagination, even though it lights our way, also creates our darkest moments. Every one of us has been haunted by memories of the past or lusted or feared over imagined future events. To master the raging fires of the mind is purpose of the ancient philosophy and mental discipline of yoga.

In the Hebrew Bible, which corresponds to the Christian Old Testament, Satan, the guy who seems in some ways like Shiva, is not actually perceived as evil; he is a kind of divine prosecutor whose job it is to test the will of individual humans to determine their worthiness to be closer to God. Satan, whose name in Hebrew literally means something like "Adversary," is sent by God on divine missions to test our mettle. In the book of Job, Satan drops by God's office one day and God addresses him.

> And the Lord said unto Satan, Whence comest thou? Then Satan answered the Lord, and said, From going to and fro in the earth, and from walking up and down in it.
>
> And the Lord said unto Satan, Hast thou considered my servant Job…?
>
> *Job 1:7*

They appear to be buddies and end up making a kind of bet on whether Job will pass a big test they devise for Satan to throw at him.

> And the Lord said unto Satan, Behold, all that he hath is in thy power; only upon himself put not forth thine hand. So Satan went forth from the presence of the Lord.

Testing by the Adversary, either through bribes or threats, has a long tradition in the East. One of the oldest accounts appears in the Katha Upanishad; here Yama, the god of death, attempts to sway a young man, Nachiketas, with promises of worldly pleasures and wealth, from his purpose of seeking ultimate knowledge. But Nachiketas does not bite and, after several tries at seducing him, Yama congratulates him and praises him for his resolve and wisdom. This is reminiscent of the Buddha's testing at the immovable spot and Christ's temptation in the desert, except that it is much more obvious here that the tempter is secretly the ally of the seeker and not truly the bad guy. Yama says:

You have pondered, Nachiketas, on pleasures and you have rejected them. You have not accepted that chain of possessions wherewith men bind themselves and beneath which they sink.

Katha Upanishad

So I entered the god's great cave at Amarnath, his most sacred temple. I removed my shoes and walked barefoot across the glacial floor—a solid sheet of ice. But no part of me felt the cold. I approached the ice lingam, which represents the god. In the photos that I have, the ice formation appears to be glowing and I am often asked if I used a flash. I had no flash with me. The lingam is in the back of a cave; I do not know why it appears to be glowing in the photos. I can say that I felt like I was in the most powerful place I had ever been. During the three days that it had taken me to trek through the mountains to get there, I felt like I was coming closer and closer to the portal of something extraordinary. The night before when I had gone out for a short walk from my encampment, every stone appeared to be a fountain of fire and every bush was burning. I know that my brain is not wired up quite like most people's but these visuals were more intense than anything that I had ever seen before. I recall Annie Dillard writing in her reflective book, *A Pilgrim at Tinker Creek*, of seeing "the tree with the lights in it."

I have no idea whether stuff like this, trees with lights and such, which I sometimes see, are visionary or hallucinatory. Perhaps the yogis would say that there is little difference, since the world is all illusion anyway.

To the left of the Shiva lingam was a complex shape, also formed of ice, that represents the god's son, Ganesh; this ice shape did somewhat appear like an elephant's head, which is Ganesh's legendary feature. It is said that his father had, in a rage, torn his head off so that he had to replace it with a borrowed one. Shiva could be a bad ass, it seems. Further to the left there is another lingam shape that represents Shiva's consort, Parvati. She is also known as Shakti, the creative essence of change in the universe, the primordial flow of cosmic being and energy.

I walked back off the ice and put my shoes on and then continued toward the immense mouth of the cave, the roof here being about 24 meters high, to a spot where I had left my pack. I sat down and proceeded to prepare lunch. Few pilgrims had traveled to this place so early in the season due to the snow in the passes, so there were only two elderly sadhus with me in the cave and a group of five Kashmiris who, from the appearance of their tools I presumed were employed by the government to work on the trail in anticipation of the hoards of pilgrims that would be using it in a few weeks. I noticed the Kashmiris eyeing me intently. At this point a sudden squall began and windblown snow was carried into the cave to where I was sitting. I walked over to my pack, opened it, and removed a pair of shelled fleece pants, a sweater, and my Gore-Tex parka. Then I went back to my lunch spot where there was a kind of bench built of stone slabs and preceded to make myself comfortable with these extra layers. The pants had full leg zips so I did not have to remove my boots to put them on. The Kashmiris watched my actions with interest while holding a discussion among themselves.

When I had finished adding these layers I seated myself again on the bench in order to finish my lunch. The Kashmiris then rose as a group and came to sit down close beside me, two to my right, and three to my left. The one closest to me on the left put his hand on my thigh and began to move his open palm up and down, brushing the nylon material of the pants.

"From Canada?" he asked, evidently correctly interpreting the flag sewn to the top of my pack. I had just finished eating my chapatti.

"Yes," I replied, "from Canada."

"You have more nice things from Canada?" This was not really a question. He pointed at my pack with his left hand while his right remained on my leg. "Some nice things for all of us," he gestured around to his friends, "Presents, from you, for us, from Canada?"

This was now clearly a mugging. The two elderly sadhus seemed disinterested and serene, likely willing to let worldly events take their course with detachment. I would be on my own to deal with the Kashmiris. I felt that I was on the boundary of one of those moments when myth and reality seem to intersect each other.

Here now was the classic trial of the seeker, recorded in so many legends: he or she, who upon entering sacred space, must prove their worthiness and resolve to be there. This is the symbolic meaning behind the stone demons and gargoyles placed as guardians at the threshold of temples and cathedrals. I certainly felt like I would be unworthy, in the light of this tradition, if I succumbed and paid a toll to these unsavory trolls. I remembered facing fierce dogs as a child, or later, as a climber, moving up thinly protected granite slabs, where a fall would result in serious injury or death. In these instances I knew that it was not enough to merely not show fear, but that it was necessary to calm the mind, and the heart, and to be *without* fear. The Adversary had sent me a test.

The Shiva lingam in Amarnath cave. The naturally forming seasonal sculpture that resembles the elephant-headed god Ganesh is to the left.

SACRED SPACE
JUNE 1985

The Kashmiri took his hand off my thigh and I stood up and walked over to my gear. I undid a single buckle on the backpack and then flipped the ice axe end for end and slipped it out of its loop. I held the axe out at arm's length and felt its balance. It had an aluminum shaft with a steel spike at one end and a hardened steel head with an adze and pick on the other: three sharp points designed to penetrate the hardest ice. I have never handled this piece of equipment without respect, knowing that mountaineers have been seriously injured, and even killed, in mishaps with their own ice tools. I turned to face the Kashmiris and walked towards them holding the shaft of the ice axe horizontally just below the level of my waist.

I sat down between them again with the ice axe held in both hands across my lap. I stared straight ahead, feeling calm, yet coiled, and completely alert. The squall had stopped as suddenly as it had started, and out of the corner of my eye I saw sunlight reflected off the polished steel of the axe's pick. The Kashmiris slid away from me.

Then they rose silently as a group and, without conversation, returned to their perch on another bench about 15 meters away. There, like a murder of crows, they roosted and began to mutter to each other out of the range of my hearing, leaning their heads together in groups of two or three, dark turbans bobbing, while never taking their eyes off me.

I went back to the pack, opened it, and pulled out a stuff sack containing spare clothes. Then returning to the bench, I dropped the sack there and seated myself on it. Raising my feet up onto the bench I crossed my legs. Then with the ice axe once again across my lap and with my eyes wide open, I began to meditate in the Lord of Meditation's sacred cave.

THE COMPANION
OCTOBER 2009

"Excuse me…I hear that you are looking for snow leopards."

I looked up from my breakfast omelet. I was back at my hotel in Leh, seated in the garden patio. Before me stood an Indian man of perhaps thirty years of age.

"Yes, I am," I replied after wiping my mouth with a napkin.

"May I sit down?" he asked.

I gestured to an empty chair.

Seating himself, he asked earnestly, "Can I come with you when you go back out?"

"What experience do you have…in the mountains?"

"Well, not much, but I'm fit…I train every day and I would be so appreciative of anything you could teach me. We would be taking a guide with us would we not? And horses…and a cook?"

"No, none of those; I'm hoping to see wildlife, not scare it away. That's why I go out alone."

"Alone?"

"Yes, but you should find yourself a guide."

He looked down at the table briefly and then at me intently. "Well it would be expensive for me to hire a guide by myself and there are so few groups going out this time of year. I only get one week a year away from my family so I would really like to get out into these mountains and have an adventure. When are you leaving?"

"I was planning on day after tomorrow."

"Oh excellent!"

"I didn't say that I would take you."

"Will you?"

I considered. I had been thinking of doing a trek beyond Yurutse, over the Ganda La pass and into the Markha valley. I had visited this valley twenty-four years ago, and remembered, towering above the last village at the head of the valley, a fortress perched atop a spire of rock. At the time I was out of film for my camera so the only picture I had of the fortress on the spire was within my memory—now nearly two and a half decades old. And the image I carried in my mind of the castle perched on top of the finger of stone seemed so physically improbable, that over the years I had resolved to one day return there and see how close to reality my mental picture of it was. This was probably a good time to go there before the snows closed the pass. If I guided this guy into the Markha valley I knew that there was now a road that had been pushed up to the confluence of the Markha and Zanskar rivers and so I could send him down the valley on his own to catch the twice weekly bus at the village of Chilling, while I continued for another two or three days up the valley to find my fortress.

An advantage to me for taking this guy along would be to have someone to share the cab fare to the trailhead. But what if he faltered on the way to the pass? Well, then I would just have to bring him down. My own code of conduct in the mountains requires that once I lift a finger to help someone go up, then I become responsible for getting them down. I remembered the cold night I had spent on a ledge in the Austrian Alps with a group of slow-moving Germans for this reason. When the sun came up in the morning we saw that we were only a single rope length above the trail that led to the mountain hut, where, unencumbered by slowpokes or codes of honor, my partner and I would have spent a warm and comfortable night.

I sighed, "Okay, let's see what kind of gear you have and then we can figure out what you will need to get in the market."

"Oh thank you. My name is Saurabh." He held out his hand and beamed.

That afternoon I took some time to accompany Saurabh to the market to look for various items he needed to add to his kit. He had never really experienced a cold climate before, having lived his whole life in the vicinity of Bombay, so the gloves, hat, wind pants, and parka I helped him select were somewhat like alien artifacts to him. He seemed quite excited by the whole process and stood before the small mirror, which the Ladakhi merchant held before him in the cramped little shop, looking quite amazed. I supposed that this experience for him would be for me somewhat like me trying on my first space suit.

While Leh certainly doesn't have the selection of expedition gear found in Katmandu, it is the hub, at least for two months in the summer, of a major trekking area and there is a reasonable selection. It is one of the few places in India where butane canisters for camping stoves are available for a reasonable price. I prefer butane to the impure local kerosene. The white gas often used for camp stoves in North America is not available here and of course flying with any kind of fuel in one's luggage is prohibited.

The cold weather clothing available in the Leh marketplace, with the exception of the locally made Tibetan-style woolens, is almost all Chinese knock-off stuff, the quality of which varies from very bad to okay. The look and even the logos of American brands are often right on; one of the dead giveaways, besides the prices, as to where these items really come from, are the misspellings and incorrect grammar on many of the labels. One might logically ask why, if they can duplicate the look of the product, they can't simply copy the label. The answer to that seems to be that the Chinese manufacturers are not content to simply rip off designs and copy logos, they must also affix their own grossly exaggerated claims about the quality of the product. Thus a jacket that claims to be filled with 900 goose down can be determined, with a little squeezing and handling, to be bulked up with low grade feathers; or a sleeping bag that claims will keep you warm to minus 20 might allow you to survive at 0 degrees. Then there are all the Gore-Tex labels affixed to the most improbable items—one would certainly not want to be caught out in a rainstorm in some of this supposedly waterproof stuff.

When Saurabh and I stepped back out onto the street with his new purchases we heard the sound of humming gasoline generators. Since the electrical grid usually goes down more than once a day in Leh, many merchants keep gasoline generators on standby since their narrow shops are poorly lit from the windows facing the street—obviously we were experiencing another power failure. Leh is a little like a frontier town in that way. But, the culture itself, in many ways, is eminently civilized. Crime in Ladakh is rare and the Ladakhis seem to have an inherent sense of egalitarianism; it was 2013 before I saw a Ladakhi beggar for the first time, and he was doing well as there was no competition. A central tenet of the Buddhist Mahayana, the great vehicle, is that there is room on it for everyone—no one gets left behind. This Buddhist sense of inclusiveness is also extended to outsiders; on a number of occasions I have had Ladakhi merchants return money to me, when being the space cadet that I am, I have overpaid.

Leh is dominated physically by the abandoned fortress-palace rising on the hill just above the town centre. This palace, now under restoration, is a smaller version of the famous Potala in Lhasa, Tibet. Directly below the palace and an adjacent Buddhist temple, at the head of Leh's main street, is the city's largest mosque. This location is also at the boundary of the traditional Kashmiri quarter of the city. Although the inhabitants of Leh are predominantly Buddhist, a Moslem/Kashmiri minority has lived there for centuries.

The Kashmiris, lean and hawk-nosed, often wearing woolen poncho-like capes, have an entirely different look than the somewhat oriental looking Ladakhis. Many of the seasonal local shops catering to tourists, although none of the trekking agencies, are run by Kashmiris. These merchants can be quite aggressive, sometimes stepping out into the street and inviting, or even attempting to cajole, tourists into their shops. The Ladakhi merchants never engage in this kind of behavior. A few of the Kashmiri shopkeepers have even been bold enough to come up beside me, and with their usual, "Hello friend," have ventured to put a hand on my shoulder. This is a big mistake. I am a person who has a strong sense of personal space; anyone who touches me who is not actually my friend is in for a very negative reaction. Not to mention that after the incident in Amarnath cave, I have retained a special aversion to being pawed by Kashmiris. None of them has tried this for a while so I guess that they can smell trouble on me now and just keep their distance.

A half-hour walk brought us back to our hotel, which is situated on the edge of the city away from the traffic, dust, and most of the noise. Entering the office there with the intention of checking email, the manager, Dawa, informed Saurabh that his mother had called. I knew that she had been calling his cell phone incessantly so he had turned it off this morning.

"What did she want?" he asked the manager, somewhat disconcerted.

"She wanted to know if you were going with guides and I told her no, you were going with Ed."

"Shit."

I have noticed that Indians, even if they only know one word of English, will know and use this one.

About a half an hour later while sitting on the patio sipping chai, Saurabh came over to join me. He then related the conversation he had just had with his mother. The way he told it to me, word for word, it seemed like they had had the conversation in English rather than Hindi, which I knew he also spoke fluently. This would not be too surprising as English is the language of middle-class professionals in India and is often used by them even among family members.

"No, Dawa doesn't know," he related, recalling what he had told his mother. "Yes of course we are going with a guide. And a cook. And horses. Ed is organizing the whole thing. Yes, he is Canadian. There are three Canadians going."

He smiled. The fact that he would be self-effacing enough to put the telling of a humorous anecdote before his ego, made me, as a storyteller, begin to like him.

"Do you have to lie to your wife too?" I asked.

"No, just my mother." He grinned.

THE PUNK MONK
OCTOBER 2009

The next morning I went to visit Thiksey Monastery, located several miles up the Indus valley from Leh. This monastery belongs to the Gelug-pa or Yellow Hat order, of which the Dalai Lama is the head. At the top of the stairway that leads to the main temple in the monastery complex is a wall painting, of a motif that is frequently featured at the entrances of Tibetan Buddhist Gompas. It is a representation of the Bhavacakara or Wheel of Life. At its centre are three animals, a snake, representing aversion, a bird representing attachment, and the third beast, a pig, symbolizing ignorance, the quality that leads us to embrace the other two, and which therefore allows them to lead us into mischief. The pig more specifically represents ignorance of the correct path, the Dharma.

The next circle moving out from the center of the wheel represents the cycle of karma with beings ascending on one side to the light and descending into darkness on the other. The next circle represents the six realms of existence: that of the gods, the titans, the animals, the realm of hells, the realm of the hungry ghosts, and, between all these, the human realm. There is, of course, a seventh realm, Nirvana, which cannot be represented because it is beyond form. The next circle represents the nine interactions of consciousness and existence. And finally holding the whole thing in its talons and fanged jaws is a being decorated with human skulls representing impermanence. This is Yama, Death.

One of my favorite photographs, which I took at the top of this stairway at Thiksey, is of a young monk slouched against a wall, wearing his ochre robes symbolizing renunciation of the world, and wearing on his feet a pair of Western-style black canvas running shoes emblazoned on each side with a white skull and crossbones. When my daughter was a young teen going through her punk/ goth phase, we discussed the uncanny resemblance between the symbols that she had adopted as personal ornaments and those found in Tantric Buddhism—the death head skull being a featured one in both. Spiky hair, reminiscent of raised hackles, is another motif common to Western punk culture and Buddhist iconography. Curious. But what does it mean? The awareness, the deep down gut-gripping awareness, of impermanence, comes to each of us at different times in our lives, but by adolescence many young people have had a sudden awakening to the awareness of their own mortality. With this awakening comes a number of ways of dealing with it. The first is to go on planning one's future, get an education, a career, a mortgage, a retirement plan, and try to forget about Yama until he comes for you, or worse, the ones you love. The second way is to enter a monastery or convent, in the hope that staying relatively unattached from the world will mitigate the inevitable disengagement from it. This method has suffered a decline in the West in recent decades. A third way is to just party on. If you can't get Yama out of your head just go ahead, indulge your senses to get some relief. This is the punk ethos and in some ways it has some commonality with a few fringe Tantric practices.

The other way, as Buddhism advocates, is to be in this world but not entirely of it. Embracing the reality of impermanence may ease the burden of our ties to the conventional world. This need not be the same as embracing nihilism though. Casting off some of the shackles of the self that we think we know need not negate our capacity to perform meaningful acts. Mahayanan Buddhism advocates the cultivation of compassion above all else. Ultimately impermanence is itself an illusion. Being continues, no matter what. The world continues, no matter what. Even after the sun has burned the earth to a crisp as it goes through its red giant phase a couple of billion years from now, and even after the sun itself has gone out, the world, the universe, continues. Being continues. And transformation continues.

But what did the young monk's shoes mean? Had he purchased the skull and crossbones shoes to fit in with the other orthodox skull motifs all around him in the monastery? I think not. The teenage slouch against the wall with the sole of one foot propped up behind was reminiscent of James Dean in *Rebel without a Cause*, which was in curious contrast to his monastic attire. Yet in the photo I can see that he is in the process of giving direction to a younger monk who is carrying a water jug and looking up at him with a faintly smiling expression; so the punk monk seems to be fulfilling his duties as a supervisor, but not in an unkindly or stern way. I certainly think that there was a conscious element of humor and irony involved in his purchase of the shoes. The Buddhist monks in Ladakh in general do not carry around the oppressive cloud, or air of humorless sternness, that I experienced from the Catholic monks and nuns who were my teachers for eight years of my childhood.

Tibetan-style art in Ladakh, like medieval European art, is largely iconic, that is, it follows set motifs. There are, in addition to the Wheel of Life, representations of various Bodhisattvas and Taras, Mandalas, and many fierce-looking deities. All art here is religious art. That is unless one takes the entirely secular perspective and attempts to interpret this iconography, such as the Wheel of

Life, from the perspective of seeing it as a representation of the different states and possibilities of the human mind. This is certainly a worthwhile exercise and its full exposition could easily take up another book. For now though we can take a brief look at the six realms from this perspective.

Mahayana Buddhists say that liberation can only be achieved from the human realm. The gods are too absorbed with bliss, the titans with power, the animals are not conscious enough, the ghosts are too hungry and needy, and those in the hells are just in too much pain. It is true that in life extreme unrelenting adversity will crush anyone, especially in their formative years. Yet a certain measure of adversity in our lives is a goad to positive achievement. Many of us have known trust-fund kids who spend their lives in useless self-indulgence. Others spend their lives in a ruthless pursuit of power or money. Yet others are born into circumstances that virtually preclude an escape from poverty or daily hunger. And some others escape into the temporary bliss of drugs or the mindless opium of religious conviction. All these impediments make liberation of the mind difficult.

Then, putting aside the perspective of life circumstances and looking at the six realms from a purely psychological point of view, another representation comes into view. Those of us not weighed down with either extreme poverty or extreme wealth can still create our own mental heavens or hells. We can allow ourselves to live with hungers, fears, hatred, and anger. Even love can be obsessive, clinging, morbid, and destructive. These are the realms we have the choices to live in, or not, but only if we learn the art of knowing and mastering ourselves. This is what the core of Buddhism, and the classical system of yoga that it is based on, is all about.

The Wheel of Life icon then can be interpreted from a spiritual, cosmological, or secular perspective. But I question whether any art, even if it has meaningful secular interpretations, can be purely secular. This may hold true even for art created by a devout atheist. Since prehistory art has been a tool for the transformation of human consciousness. Even before the earliest cave paintings, it had this magical power.

Robert Graves maintained that all real poetry is an invocation to the goddess, but it seems to me that this may be true of all real art, the essence of which is homage to a transcendental and ineffable truth, for which "goddess" probably serves as a shorthand metaphor as well as anything. The divine female qualities of compassion, innate wisdom, and ethereal grace, shine forth respectively from much European art. Consider three of the most loved and famous art pieces of Europe: the Pieta, the Mona Lisa, and Winged Victory. And, in more modern American painting, what could be more of a paean to the fecundity of the goddess than the dance of fractal patterns in the so-called "splatter" paintings of Jackson Pollock? But the prayer hidden in all real art is sometimes more subtle than any of these.

Jan Vermeer is often cited by Western art historians as the artist, prior to the invention of the camera, who most accurately painted simply what his eye saw. I always disagreed with this. What I saw, in the reproductions of his paintings that I viewed as a teenager, was something essentially quite different. Something much more. All the wonderfully complex details of his paintings often seemed to be put there to accentuate something with little detail at all: the white light falling on a white-washed wall. That light somehow had, for me, the quality of the Divine. It was the light of eternity. Even after all the stars go out in our universe, that light will shine somewhere, in some universe. I stared for hours at the reproductions of his paintings, before I traveled to Europe to see the originals. Almost all his works seemed to have been done in the same room, with the same wall, and featuring the same window from which spilled that amazing light. It sent shivers down my spine. Was I crazy? How was it that art historians did not see this? Then one day, when I was in my late teens, I came across a passage by Sir Kenneth Clark, then the world's most well-known art historian, commentator, and aesthetician. What he said was something like this: "What we see when we view the light falling on a white-washed wall in a painting by Vermeer, is as much an affirmation of faith as anything found in the religious paintings of Michelangelo or Raphael." Thank you, Sir Kenneth. This kid needed that.

I came to realize later how much the seemly stuffy Sir Kenneth passionately loved art, not just with his head, but with his whole being. He had badly wanted to be an artist himself in his youth, but came to believe that he had no talent for creating it. But he never stopped giving his heart to it. Sir Kenneth knew that he could have learned to paint. Painters can be made. But it may be that seers can only be born.

Vermeer sold little of his own painting, even though he owned an art gallery. He would work for long periods on a single canvas, and as a result only thirty-four of his authenticated works have been bequeathed down to us. He seemed concerned only with perfecting his art…or his prayer, or whatever we want to call it that that he was laboring over in his studio. Like the cave painter, who also withdrew from the world to perform his magic, he left a message for the ages. Salvador Dali once said that if he knew that the world was going to be destroyed, and he could only save one thing, it would be a painting by Vermeer.

The Buddha himself was said to have created the Wheel of Life icon as a method of instruction that could be used to guide even the illiterate. It is often for a similar purpose that much of European Renaissance painting and sculpture incorporates mythological, historical, and biblical themes. Indeed when I took my six-year-old daughter for her first art tour of Europe, the child was happy to spend all day, every day, looking at pictures in the great galleries. But not just looking. She would invariably walk up to a painting or a sculpture and ask me what was going on there. Kids love stories, and so she got a story with every picture. It became a multi media tour and, as usual, trying to explain the world to my kid, and goaded by her questions, my eyes were opened so much more to it. Making stories for her made me look.

The earliest art was likely a chant, a song, a poem. Whales practice this art, although we have no clue what meaning, if any, is attached to a whale song. However, as Carl Sagan pointed out, an average humpback whale song, if broken down into bits, is approximately as complex as the Odyssey. Flutes, carved out of bone, were made by Neanderthals. Bows were probably made before flutes—and a bow can be used as a musical instrument, as well as a fire starter, or a weapon. One thing we do know is that some 35,000 years ago a man, probably a shaman, climbed down into the bowels of a cave. There, with his breath he blew the red ochre dust from the palm of his right hand onto the wall of the cave, where his left hand was pressed. When the stencil was removed the outline of the hand remained on the cave wall. The human hand is the cutting edge of the mind, as Jacob Bronowski said in *The Accent of Man*. It is the conduit through which the creative energy of the human soul is able to transform our inner and outer worlds. There are about a half a million characters in this book, which means that, with rewrites, my fingers have struck a keyboard over a million times to create this work. How many brush strokes are on the ceiling of the Sistine? How many pencil marks, how many cuts, how many nails, did the carpenters who built my house scratch, cut, and drive with their hands? The trillions of lines of computer code that continue to transform our world every day were all written by someone, somewhere, with hands. It is fitting that one of the earliest works of art that has come down to us is the representation of a human hand.

Represented standing just outside of the circles of the Wheel of Life in the painting on the wall of Thiksey monastery, as is common in the iconography of the Bhavacakara, is the Buddha. He points, with his hand, to the moon, the ancient and universal symbol of the goddess—as the way to liberation.

TOWARD THE GANDA LA
OCTOBER 2009

Saurabh and I packed our gear into the taxi in front of the hotel. Then the driver set off through the dusty streets of Leh. Southwest of the city a single-lane bridge festooned with thousands of colorful prayer flags took us over the Indus River. The road then climbed above the banks of the river and followed its course for about ten kilometers to where it flowed into an uninhabited canyon. I am always reminded of photos taken by the Mars landers while traveling through this particularly barren section of desert landscape here above the Indus. The road was rough and more suited to an off-road vehicle than to this Toyota van.

I gasped a few times as the van came close to the edge and I saw the sheer drop to the river below. Many people have told me that I am a control freak; related to driving, this is certainly true. I hate not being behind the wheel; this is at least partly due to my having received some permanent injuries in an accident where I was a passenger. Now staring down at the abyss and sitting on the side of the vehicle where the steering wheel should have been—as Indians drive on the left side of the road—I squirmed. My trepidation was only mitigated by the fact I had been this way a number of times before, and that I had been on several journeys with this driver, Lobsang, and trusted him—to the degree that I could trust drivers who are not me.

After several more kilometers we reached the confluence with the stream known as Jingchan, which flowed out of a narrow valley in the Stok mountain range. Here we began to descend down a series of hairpin turns to the valley floor. Soon afterwards we came to the end of the road across the stream from the two-house village also called Jingchan. We unloaded our gear, tipped the driver, and set off on the trail up the valley following the stream.

After about twenty minutes we met a group of women, walking to their homes in Rumbak. They recognized me.

"Shan?" one of them asked smiling. I recognized her. I had previously lodged at her home. Her name was Rigzin.

"No Shan yet," I replied, to their giggles.

In another hour we came to a place called Huzing. Although there are no permanent buildings here, there is a snow leopard-proofed fence enclosing a sheep and goat pasture. Directly below a massive boulder precariously supported about 9 meters in the air by an overhanging wall of gravel and mud, was the encampment of a guided group of snow leopard seekers. The clients were out with their guides looking for Shan but the three helpers who had remained in camp invited us to sit down and have tea. I have seldom met a guided group in Ladakh where I have not been invited for tea and treats by the staff. There are not that many people who travel solo in these mountains and when I am alone I seem to get extra special treatment. "Only one?" I am often asked. I'm still not quite sure if this treatment is out of special respect or if they just think that I am a bit mad. But then again the Buddhism itself was brought to Ladakh, Tibet, and China by solo travelers like Guru Rinpoche and Bodhidharma, who are held in high esteem, even if they were also a bit mad.

Huzing seems to be the most popular spot in Hemis National Park, which encompasses much of the Stok range, for guided snow leopard groups to camp. These groups seldom ascend higher than Rumbak and are equipped with luxuries like insulated flooring for their tents and even butane heaters. All this equipment gets packed up here by horseback. The helpers told us that they had been camped here for three days now and no snow leopard had been spotted yet.

After we finished our tea we carried on a short distance to where the valley splits into two narrowing gorges. We followed the right hand cleft, which led us in an hour into the broader Rumbak valley. From there we continued higher to Yurutse where we would spend the night.

The next morning at 4 a.m. our host at Yurutse, Rinchen Dorjay, was pouring us tea and serving chapattis. He is a man of about thirty, who lives here with his wife, Agmo, and mother, Yangchan, in her early sixties, and an uncle, Yasin, in his seventies. These four seem to be the more or less permanent residents of the one-house village, although I have seen various other relatives staying there and my understanding is that sometimes the population of relatives can swell to about fifteen. Rinchen has told me that the house is about a hundred years old; this is the same age as a house in Vienna that has been in my family for that length of time and is still the home of eight of my cousins. This kind of continuity is, of course, rare in North America.

Saurabh and I were planning to go up to the ridge that I had explored above Yurutse before we were to carry on over the Ganda La and the Markha valley tomorrow. Normally when I arose this early none of the family members got up with me to make breakfast but instead prepared chapattis the night before and left them out for me along with tea in a thermos. But today Rinchen decided to get up and make us pancakes, a special treat, perhaps in honor of the guest I brought.

As he sleepily poured me another cup of tea I asked him, "Do you think we are crazy?"

He smiled and, nodding his head vigorously, replied, "Yes!"

Saurabh and I set off shortly before 5 a.m. The cold air was invigorating. The light cast by the quarter moon was supplemented by our headlamps as we headed up the trail to Ganda La base camp and then turned up a steeper animal path toward the ridge. Before reaching the crest of the ridge the animal paths petered out and the footing became tenuous on the ever-steepening slope. We were now breathing heavily in the thin air at 4500 meters (14,750 ft). At this altitude half the earth's atmosphere, not in distance, but in molecules of air, is below you. So half the amount of oxygen is available with each breath. Because of the exertion I had now removed my down parka, despite the sub-zero temperature, and had induced Saurabh to do the same; it was hard for him to learn how to regulate his body temperature with all these clothes that he was not used to wearing. Yesterday he had kept on far too much clothing during the exertion in the midday warmth and had ended up lathered in sweat and soaking his clothes. This could be potentially dangerous in the mountains. I was trying to teach him to remove layers before he got wet and to put them back on before he got cold. "Listen to your body," I told him repeatedly. When we reached the crest of the ridge the first rays of sun had just touched the summit of Stok Kangri, but it would be another half hour before we felt it here. We had just turned down the crest of the ridge to look for a good vantage point when, crossing a patch of snow we found prints. They had been made by a snow leopard.

The tracks were a few days old. The animal had been here—while I had been back in Leh luxuriating in clean sheets and showers—

while I had deserted the commitment to the immovable spot. We set up watch on the ridge and soon the sun's rays began to warm us.

Well before mid-morning I became restless again and subsequently guided Saurabh higher along the crest of the ridge to a 5000-meter (16,400-ft) summit. He was thrilled to be at this altitude and to have observed a herd of blue sheep that we had been able to approach closely during the ascent.

In the late afternoon we descended to Yurutse. Early the next morning we began the 800-meter (2600-ft) climb toward the Ganda La, the 4900-meter (16,075-ft) pass that is the gateway to the Markha valley.

I had been up to the pass a few weeks earlier, before I was fully acclimatized, and it had been a struggle. I'd had to sit down a few hundred meters below the pass feeling almost completely spent. But, shortly after ingesting some dark chocolate covered espresso beans and cranking up Bonnie Rait on my iPod, I felt revived and by the time I reached the pass was motoring along in the blissful state of the endurance athlete's high. This time, after almost a month at altitude, the going was relatively easy even though I was carrying a heavier pack. Just below the pass I photographed a small herd of yak. These were likely domestic animals put out to range, although they all had the dark hairy coats that distinguishes the wild yak from the often lighter colored domestic variety.

I believe that I have seen truly wild yak only once—in a remote and secret Himalayan valley that I had wandered into over a considerably higher pass. I found ruins in the valley, but it seemed that no one had visited there for years—the heather, normally stripped off by locals for firewood, was lush and pristine. When I approached a herd of yak that I had spotted they formed a defensive ring around the calves, much like the musk ox of the Canadian Arctic do when threatened. I had never seen this type of behavior in yak before, nor have I seen it since.

Yaks are uniquely adapted life at high altitude, and indeed are unable to survive at low elevations. Their long hairy coats, forming a skirt that almost reaches the ground, protect them from sub-zero temperatures. Their heart and lungs are proportionally larger than their lowland bovine relatives, and their blood also has a greater capacity to carry oxygen due to the persistence of fetal hemoglobin throughout life. An individual wild yak may weigh in at over 2000 pounds. A fully grown male yak is the only Himalayan ungulate that a snow leopard is unlikely to be able to take down.

When I reached the crest of the pass, I abruptly left the shelter of the lee slope and was exposed to a chill wind gusting over the summit ridge. There were several inches of windswept snow at my feet. To the west I could see the Zanskar Range and beyond the Himalayas proper featuring the 7000-meter (23,000-ft) plus peaks of Nun and Kun.

There was a Mani wall on the summit, behind which I sat down to take shelter from the wind. This wall was about 7 meters long, 1 high, and a bit more than 1 meter thick. The top of the wall was covered with about a hundred Mani stones, so named because they were all inscribed with the mantra, "Om Mani Padme Hum." The prayer flags that flapped in the wind suspended between the poles on either side of the wall were also inscribed with this mantra, as are all the prayer flags and prayer wheels throughout Ladakh, Tibet, and the Buddhist regions of Nepal. This inscription is the mantra of Avalokitesvara, the Bodhisattva of infinite compassion. Avalokitesvara is represented as either male or female in various Buddhist cultures and is known as Jainraisig in Tibet. The Dalai Lama is believed by many to be his/her embodiment.

The Mani stones that lie in on these walls and chortans throughout the Himalaya and Trans Himalaya number in the millions. Most are somewhat disk or square shaped and perhaps average a bit more than 30 centimeters in diameter. Many are beautifully carved. Although they seem abundant, I worry that with road building being pushed into these sparsely populated valleys, including the long isolated Markha valley below the pass, the most wonderfully carved stones, some of which have lain undisturbed for centuries, will be scooped up and taken home as prizes by tourists.

Mani Stone.

"Om Mani Padme Hum," translates roughly as *Hail, the jewel in the lotus, Amen*. The lotus flower in both Buddhist and Hindu symbolism represents the transcendence of super consciousness over the base instincts, such as desire and fear. The lotus plant, although it has its roots in the mud of a stagnant pond, opens its flower petals unsullied in the sun. The jewel represents the male aspect of Avalokitesvara, the embodiment of compassion, in union with his consort Tara, the flower, which embodies the female aspect and wisdom. Many wall paintings and painted hangings called Thangkas, in Tibet and Ladakh, have representations of male and female deities in coitus representing the union of the two aspects of transcendent consciousness.

It is believed by many Buddhists in this region that repetitions of the mantra, even by mechanical means, as with the spinning of a prayer wheel, gain merit for the individual as well as for sentient beings as a whole. Since I have now written the mantra down here, and it is therefore recorded in digital code on my computer hard drive, which is spinning at 7000 rpm, I suppose that I'm more efficiently gaining merit than spinning a prayer wheel by hand or rigging up a water driven one as some farmers in Ladakh do. The

Dalai Lama was once asked if having a spinning icon with the mantra on a computer screen would gain the same merit as spinning a prayer wheel by hand. His reply was something like, "I think that they would have the same effect." Another perfect answer from an agnostic Buddhist philosopher who also has the responsibility of being the religious leader of a non-religion catering to a largely superstitious following.

Superstitious or not, these people here are the best people in the world. They are inclusive with everyone. What they believe is so different from the exclusivity of mainstream Judaism, Islam, and Christianity. It is simple and profoundly beautiful. They believe that in time, even if it takes many lifetimes, everyone gets saved. And as long as it takes for every last one of us to get it together, Avalokitesvara and the other Bodhisattvas will remain here in this realm to help us. Om Mani Padme Hum.

I settled down behind the wall to have my lunch figuring that Saurabh was about half an hour behind. He was doing well; he was fit and determined and I knew that he would not have trouble making it up here. The prayer flags flapped in the wind above me— the green, blue, yellow, and red of the individual sheets vivid against the deep blue of the Himalayan sky.

THE RETURN TO ADVENTURE
MAY 2008

The avalanche on Rainbow Mountain had taken me to the edge of the abyss. I stayed there for a long time. I lost my appetite for risk. For the first time in many years, I went a whole climbing season without taking a lead fall. I just couldn't push my limits. I didn't trust my judgment. I was afraid of being, once again, lured to the edge and this time going over.

A few weeks after the avalanche, in early May, I went with some friends on a one-week ski tour in the Rockies. I was still hurting from my injuries and had to inflate an airtight stuff sack every evening and sleep flat on my back with the sack under my knees. This was the only way I could comfortably lie down. Strangely the one part of me that didn't hurt, for a change, was my back. I figured that either I had received the ultimate chiropractic adjustment in that avalanche, or sleeping on my back with a pillow under my knees, as many had long advised, was really good for bad backs.

Our group was just winding up a day of touring. We had skied down a long descent from a peak and we were stopped now to put on our climbing skins for the last half an hour ascent to the hut where we planned to spend the night. Being generally quick with my turnarounds I had my skins on before any of the rest of the group and sat down on my pack to enjoy a quick bagel.

"Do you think that's a good idea right below an icefall?" said Mike pointing up at the ominous overhanging wall of ice and snow.

"D'you think there is really much chance of it coming all the way down here?" I replied. We were on a relatively flat bench.

"Actually," broke in Mark, who is a geophysicist, "we've done some modeling on particle suspension and friction coefficients in avalanches which shows that they can run a lot farther than you would think."

I put away my partially eaten bagel, stepped into my bindings, and began climbing. When we reached the hut, we took off our boots, stowed our gear, and began to build a fire in the stove. Then, suddenly, we heard a thunderous crashing. We rushed to the windows in time to see the icefall, which had been stable all season, coming down and propagating an avalanche that was tearing down the slope. It continued across the bench. It obliterated my bagel spot.

We all live on the edge of the abyss. Going into the mountains just makes you remember it.

Two months later Helen and I went to the Bugaboos, a series of high alpine granite spires located in the Purcell Range of British Colombia. The first day was a disaster. We backed off of an easy climb, intimidated perhaps by the wind, the cold, the exposure to the void, and our own personal demons. On the way back across the glacier to our camp, Helen sat down on a rock and wept. For her, I knew that a life without pushing physical and mental boundaries, a life without adventure, would not be a life at all.

People have told me I climb to be afraid. That is only partly true; in fact climbing can be a way to stop being afraid. Fear comes from imagining all the pitfalls of the world, including inevitable death. Climbing is about letting go of all that. The climber may imagine the ground-fall that he does not want to take, or the ledge above he wishes he was already on, or the hold just beyond reach, but the overwhelming desire to reach for that hold too soon, while balancing on a steep slab, will force the feet out, the rubber to slip, and the body to fall. To get to the ledge the climber has to let go of both fear and desire and be focused only on the process of moving up—of being in the moment—of breathing, of being aware of every crystal that can be used by feet, of every edge that can be used by hands. Climbing then becomes a dynamic meditation; it brings the mind into the calm at the eye of the storm. In the midst of action, there is stillness.

The sage dwells neither on the consequences nor the fruits of action.

Bhagavad Gita

The Gita is one of the earliest written works in which the word "yoga" appears. This is, Krishna reminds the warrior Arjuna, the practice of calming the mind while undertaking action, even in the midst of the strife of the world.

I never have the same mental focus when seconding a pitch compared to leading it. In fact every climb seems technically and physically harder when I am seconding without the risk of a leader fall. Without that edge I never attain the same clarity and concentration. When I studied in the Zen monastery in Japan, there was a large monk who walked around behind us in the meditation hall. He carried a big stick and would strike anyone across the shoulders that looked like they were nodding off. He hit hard. Knowing he was there kept us alert and focused. Some people attempt to learn meditation without a big monk, but sometimes they are merely learning to have a nap sitting up.

But the summer after the avalanche it was hard to leave the ground. It was hard for me to trust myself. I had been seduced in a moment of euphoria, and my judgment had failed me. Over the years Helen had caught dozens of my lead falls, and I trusted her explicitly. But now I didn't trust myself.

In climbing, only a certain amount of judgment can be made in your head. Although you can logically assess weather or avalanche conditions, you cannot logically quantify the line between what your body can or cannot do when making a technical move on rock. You have to know. Your body has to know. Although you have to visualize the difficult moves ahead, you have to trust your body to tell you if the moves will "go" in the way your head has seen them. If your body says no, then you have to visualize a different sequence. If it still says no, you may have to turn back. If you can't listen to your body's expertise, and only hear its fear, then you will always be turning back. Or find yourself paralyzed on a ledge somewhere. And rock-climbing here in the mountains was much different than climbing at our local crag, a few minutes from our home in Squamish, and right beside the hospital. At the crag, if you have had the opportunity to place good protection, and you trust your partner to catch you, then you may decide to make a dicey move to push your limits. But we don't take lead falls in the mountains. The protection of the rope there is a last resort for the leader—where a broken bone could have serious consequences. Even a minor injury in the mountains can slow you down and cause you to spend the night out in a storm, and consequently lead to hypothermia and risk of death. In the mountains, you have to know, and have confidence in what you do.

The next day we decided to try a technically harder climb, and this time just be more focused and committed. After ascending a snowfield we stopped to take off our mountaineering boots at the base of a steep headwall. Helen put on her rock shoes and I, since I had not brought rock shoes on this trip, not intending to try anything really hard, put on my Guide-Tennies, a kind of light hiking and scrambling shoe. There was one party already up on the face ahead of us.

Helen had copied a page out of the guidebook and now holding the sheet of paper up in front of her face she pointed at a large boulder sitting on a ledge. She told me that the route went "below" the boulder and the belay station would be just beyond.

When I reached the boulder I found a tunnel that passed under it. Presuming that this was what was meant by "below" I slithered through it. When I got to the other side of the boulder however I could find so sign of fixed belay anchors so I built an anchor station with my gear and brought Helen up on the rope.

"What are you doing?" she asked. "This isn't the station."

"I thought you said go below the boulder."

"I meant traverse below it, not crawl under it. You should be over there."

She pointed to a platform on a narrow ledge where I could now see fixed anchors. Then there was a shout from above followed by a humming sound and then a thud as a grapefruit-sized rock landed right where I "should" have been standing. Had I been tied to the anchors there I would not have even been able to try to get out of the way.

It was obvious now that there was a careless party above us. We discussed going down. Bailing again. Then we sat in silence for a quarter of an hour.

Finally Helen said, "What do you want to do? I'm good with whatever you decide."

"Well, I don't want us to…" to what? I thought to myself…get ourselves get killed? Life was terminal anyway. No getting around that. And all that was worthwhile would end all that much sooner when we stopped living to the full. "…I don't want us to spend the rest of our lives sitting on our patio drinking beer," I finished.

"I'm glad to hear you say that. I agree."

She put me on belay and I began to ascend.

Helen seconding a pitch at Squamish.

DESCENT TO THE MARKHA VALLEY
OCTOBER 2009

Saurabh arrived at the pass. I was relieved to see that he had removed enough clothing during the strenuous climb, so that he did not seem to be lathered in sweat as I had seen him previously after exertion. He was learning. Being soaked up here in this chill wind could have been a problem. He staggered toward the high point of the pass on a path that would take him to his right of the Mani wall that my back was still propped up against.

"Hey, Saurabh," I shouted over the flap of the prayer flags, "congratulations." I rose to my feet and then pointed to the other end of the wall.

Saurabh understood immediately what I meant by the gesture. He smiled and turned. He had been raised as a Hindu and I had been instructing him in Buddhist customs over the last few days. One of these protocols was to keep sacred monuments such as Mani walls, chortens, and stupas on one's right hand side and therefore walk around them in a clockwise manner. This is the direction Buddhists believe that the earth and the universe revolve. Members of the older animistic faith of Tibet, called Bon, walk around these objects the other way. Their swastikas are also the reverse of the Buddhist and Hindu swastikas, therefore resembling the Nazi one. Bon practitioners then, I suppose, believe that the universe spins the other way. Actually they are right, at least as far out as this galaxy is concerned—if one views the earth from over the North Pole that is. But of course if we look from the south, then the Buddhists are right.

Bon has greatly influenced Tibetan Buddhist practice, which has incorporated many ancient Bon deities into its iconography. The practice of Bon in its old form is now relatively rare, and what remains has been greatly transformed. Indeed the only Bon temple I have ever visited had numerous representations of the Buddha.

This wall was built by Buddhists though, so I joined Saurabh in walking around its left side. I usually try to observe the local customs regarding propitiations to whatever or whomever. Many years before, I had climbed Mount Olympus in Greece during a lightning storm. Just before the final exposed scramble to the summit, called Mytikus, the Needle, my companion and I stopped to pour libations out of our water bottles to honor the ancient Olympian gods. At the very moment we set foot together on the summit, surrounded by a thick fog, there was a flash of lightning and an almost simultaneous roar of thunder. Then there was a blast of wind that lasted for maybe a half a minute. The fog swirled around us, becoming more and more luminescent, flowing for a few seconds into glowing tendrils revealing glimpses of blue and snatches of a vast landscape. Then the fog vanished. All of a sudden we stood in bright sunlight—gobsmacked—amazed—looking down at the ribbon of beach along the Aegean Sea and far out over the plain of Macedonia. The sky remained blue and the air calm for the rest of the day. I am not a true believer in the supernatural. But I've learned that it doesn't hurt to pay respect.

Saurabh was beginning to look cold. It was time to begin our long descent to the valley.

The wind gradually diminished as we lost altitude below the pass, dropping some 800 meters (2600 ft) over the next two hours into a gradually narrowing valley before arriving at the two-house village of Shingo. We saw several brightly colored tents in a field across from the houses. Seated in front of one of the tents were a couple of Westerners, a man and a woman, and as we passed near them they waved to us and invited us to join them for tea. Saurabh and I climbed over the fence that separated us, glad for a rest and looking forward to the refreshment.

It turned out that this young couple from Canmore BC, the only other trekkers we were to encounter, was just finishing a three-week trek through Zanskar and Ladakh. It was their honeymoon. Their cook appeared out of one of the tents shortly and served us tea and snacks and their guide sat down on the grassy ground to join us. Saurabh eagerly pulled out his camera, for he now had the factual evidence that he could show his mother: Ed and two other Canadians, a guide and a cook, ponies and tents, all exactly as he had fabricated and told to her. He and I smiled at each other and I asked his permission to describe to the Canadian couple the circumstances behind our bemusement. He heartily assented and gleefully added embellishments to my telling until we had the couple rolling in the grass with laughter. Again, I warmed up to him that he could be self-effacing for the sake of a good story.

After tea we set off again, deciding that we still had enough daylight and enough reserves in our own bodies to make it to the next village, called Skyu, which was in the Markha valley itself. The path entered a narrowing gorge following the Shingo stream, which it crossed and recrossed several times. I was feeling energetic and soon lost sight of Saurabh who had been slowing considerably. The steep walls of the gorge displayed elaborate stone columns, sometimes twisted into serpentine shapes in striking colors of turquoise and reds due to the metallic oxides contained in the ancient flysch. There were also formations of conglomerate rock speckled with rounded river stones of contrasting hues.

It was in this gorge that in the summer of 2010 several tourists were to lose their lives during the flash floods of that season.

Extremely heavy rains came suddenly at midnight on the morning of August 6, and water, rocks, and mud blew down numerous gullies killing several hundred people in Ladakh, and many more in adjacent Pakistan in related flooding that summer. More rain fell on parts of Ladakh in a single half hour on the morning of August 6 than normally falls on the region in an entire year. 2010 became a summer of weird weather with an enormous high-pressure system sitting over Siberia for months. Most of the people of the Himalayas have little clue to what is causing their glaciers to shrink, their climate to change, and their weather to behave so unpredictably. They live in non-industrialized societies, and therefore have nothing to do with precipitating man-made climate change, even though they seem to be at the forefront of some of its consequences.

I continued to follow the trail down the Shingo gorge to where it intersected the Markha valley at a right-angled junction. Here there were three chortens and a few buildings beyond. I noticed a crude, but recognizable, drawing of a snow leopard on a squarish rock that served as base for a small cairn of stones.

Chorten is the Tibetan word for a traditional monument that symbolizes the universal Buddhist goal of transcendental consciousness. It has a square base on top of which there is a dome, sometimes onion shaped on smaller structures. On top of this there are thirteen rings representing the traditional thirteen steps to enlightenment. The rings culminate in a final spire pointing toward the sky. Although some guidebooks indicate that the word chorten is interchangeable with the Sanskrit word stupa, my experience is that the former term is usually used for the smaller structures found outside and inside Gompas, at crossroads, inside and on the outskirts of villages, and sometimes just randomly alongside trails everywhere in Himalayan lands inhabited by Buddhists. The term stupa usually refers to a larger, more monumental structure, such as the famous Monkey Temple, on a hill above Kathmandu, at the site where Siddhartha himself, it is said, once gave a teaching. Leh has several large stupas; the most impressive being the Shanti (meaning Peace) Stupa, located a thousand or so stairs directly above my hotel there.

Chorten at Yurutse.

Twenty-four years previously I had been attacked by a pack of dogs on the outskirts of this village, Skyu. Before I managed to drive them off, one of them got behind me and bit me in the calf. I knew immediately from the feeling of wetness down the back of my leg, even as I was still hurtling stones after the retreating pack, that the bite had drawn blood. After rolling up my pant leg, I quickly lanced the puncture marks with my pocketknife to increase the bleeding and then irrigated the wounds with water.

This was the best that I had been able to do. At that time there was no hospital in Leh and I would have likely had to make my way all the way back to Shrinigar in order to find a rabies vaccine. I have a phobia concerning rabies, knowing that there is no cure after the gruesome symptoms appear. And rabies is rampant in India, accounting for some twenty thousand deaths a year. I decided though to carry on with my trek rather than making a run back to Shrinigar. I would just have to suck it up for the next few months and try to keep certain thoughts out of my mind, try not to imagine the symptoms, which include hydrophobia, a terror—even while parched with thirst—of the sight of water. Yuck. This was to become a kind of meditation—the don't think about hydrophobia meditation—another test sent by Mara.

I sat down with my back against the wall that formed the base of the chortens to wait for Saurabh, hoping that he was not too far behind as it would be dark soon. Off to my right, on a slight rise, was a small temple, or Gompa, which I had read was a thousand years old. It was founded by the great scholar, translator and traveler, Rinchen Zangpo, who founded some of the oldest existing monasteries in Tibet. The great British explorer William Moorcroft, one of the first Westerners to visit Ladakh and the first to visit the Markha valley, in about 1820, had described this Gompa in his journal. He had noted the ancient wall paintings inside, which I had looked forward to seeing. The door, I saw though, was padlocked. Most of the monasteries in this valley were only inhabited by monks during the summer months and by now they had likely all retreated back to the Leh valley before the onset of winter.

Sifting my position to make myself more comfortable, I placed my hand down and felt a sharp stab. Yanking the hand up I saw a drop of blood on my palm and looked down to see the small thorny plant that was responsible. There are many prickly plants in this high desert. Everything that lives up here is tough and sinewy. My own body, after more than a month here, was changing, adapting to this environment. Even my blood, I knew, was changing, adjusting to the thinner air, getting thicker every day, as my body made more red blood cells to allow for oxygen to be carried more efficiently to my two trillion or so cells. I contemplated the thorny little plant that had pierced me. Its forbears had surely made many adjustments to be able to live here. A billion years or so ago our common ancestor had lived in the sea and I knew that this plant and I shared about half our DNA on account of this legacy. Looking at the blood on my palm reminded me that I was walking around in this high desert as a kind of misplaced ocean creature myself, alive in a sort of space suit. Inside the fabric of the suit, which was my skin, it was mostly salty water, the chemical composition of my blood in fact being close to that of seawater. We hadn't so much evolved to live out of the ocean, as to carry the ocean around with us.

I looked around at the now darkening shapes of the mountains. They too had come from the sea, scraped up from the ocean floor in front of the bulldozer blade of the incipient Himalayas as India collided with Asia—a process that raised up the floor the ancient Sea of Tethys to the loftiest places on earth. I remembered standing, in a cold dawn light, below the very highest place, Mount Everest, a black pyramid scoured by thousands of seasons of ice and jet streams. The summit is, in fact, limestone—the fused skeletons of trillions of ocean creatures, once alive like the thorn bush and me. And we, the thorn bush and I, therefore also shared a once living ancestor with the earth's highest mountain, which the Sherpas call Chomolungma, Mother Goddess of the World.

The upturned seabed all around me that was now a mountainscape reminded me that I was sitting on the thin crust of a mostly molten ball, and that enormous pieces of that crust were sliding in the goo. India was slowly moving her bulk underneath me, being subsumed into the womb of Asia and in the process raising, even higher, the monument of the Himalayas. In about thirty million years she would be gone. The sub-continent was being subducted under Asia at an average speed of about 5 centimetres a year—about twice as fast as fingernails grow. But sometimes geological plates build up pressure, and then slip suddenly. Some of the construction methods I had witnessed in New Delhi made me shudder at this thought.

I looked down again at the drop of blood on my palm. Every cell in that liquid contained the entire sequence of my DNA. Many stories are written there. One of these has only recently been translated from the time clock of mitochondrial DNA. It tells that somewhere around 160,000 years ago there was a genetic bottleneck in our lineage and that our species, *Homo sapiens*, was down to a few hundred individuals—pretty well the minimum for any kind of viable gene pool. We were on the verge of extinction. Africa, our ancestral homeland, would have been, at that time, a cold dry desert. I put my head back on the wall of the chorten and began to imagine it, yet again. I closed my eyes. Far away I began to hear the sound of surf. Then I saw them, walking toward me, once more.

They were a starving band, the last remnants of their kind, and they had now reached the end of their long search. The edge of the world. The end of land. After years of wandering across the entire length of an increasingly barren continent, they had come to the sea. Now there was nowhere else to wander to. No place to go. There were no animals here to hunt; there were no fruits to gather. Here at the lowest tip of the continent, this species made its last stand.

There were no more than a few hundred of them, of us, left. Over generations, as they had gradually moved south, the continent had grown increasingly colder, dryer, and more desolate. And now they had come to the shore of a body of water that stretched beyond where the eye could see. This was the end of their long journey from the great African rift where their kind had begun.

Their shaman rose and walked away from the group, her emaciated body held erect, her stride still graceful, seemingly indefatigable. She climbed down an embankment to the seashore. They watched her walk along the beach and then disappear into a cave. There she stayed for the rest of the day and then the night. Meanwhile a few more of their number died of hunger. The rest were too weary to move and merely awaited their end. Most were too hungry to sleep much. All night they listened to the unfamiliar sound of the surf. The full moon rose and lit the ghostly landscape and the dark shapes of their bodies.

In the morning the shaman reappeared, her naked body now decorated with loops and swirls of red ochre. Taking a sharpened stick she walked out into the unfamiliar brush of this strange place. She began to dig. Soon she had uncovered several massive tubers, which she tossed to some of the women nearby. The tubers were of a strange shape and color but they attacked the flesh of the roots with their flint knives in the hope that their shaman had guided them to something edible. Shoving the pulp into their mouths, they began to chew. Even with their mouths full some began to laugh, others to cry. Some did both at the same time. Several of them began to place some of the pre-chewed root in the mouths of the few surviving infants. The men began to join the women in the digging and cutting up of the roots with their knives.

But before they had finished filling their bellies the shaman signaled to a group of the men. They were the tribe's foremost hunters. They followed her to the beach. Since the moon was full, meaning the earth, sun, and moon were aligned, the tide was large and the receding water had left many pools. Out of one of the pools she plucked a creature, somewhat bigger than a man's head. The thing, resembling an enormous spider, writhed in her hand before she smashed its hard carapace against a rock. She pulled a chunk of the creature's flesh out of the shattered shell, and placing it into her mouth, began to chew. She walked over to the lead hunter and offered him a piece of the spider thing's flesh. He shrank back. She held it to up to him and nodded. He had never disobeyed her— no one had. He closed his eyes and placing the flesh of the spider creature in his mouth began to chew. The strange taste and texture at first revulsed him but then his salt and protein starved body reacted. He opened his eyes and fell to his knees before her. She placed some more of the flesh into his mouth with her hand. The body and blood of the goddess. Communion.

The surf pushed forward and gently laved them both. They were the first people that we know of, more than a million years after hunting began, to dare to taste of the sea. In time she would teach her people to go down to the sea during the full and new moon, the times of the great tides, and harvest from its bounty. They would create tools and a culture more than 100,000 years more advanced than we had, until discoveries made recently, ever thought possible for this era.

In all the vast and hostile world of that time there was only one place left were they could have survived, one tiny pocket, an isolated eco system at the tip of what we now call the Cape of Good Hope. They found it. And because of that we are alive.

One hundred and sixty thousand years seems like a long time, and in human terms it is really is. But I somehow feel close to these people. Their artifacts, discovered by paleo-anthropologist Curtis Marean, include cylinders of red ochre, an iron oxide found mixed in certain clays, which is still used today to color artist's pigments. Any trekker in Ladakh will see chortens decorated with red ochre dust. One often sees the skulls and horns of wild sheep, the prey of the snow leopard, piled up, and decorated in this way.

I reflected how once, when my daughter was five years old, I was retelling her the story of how Prometheus created humankind out of clay.

"It was red clay," she interrupted. "You left out that it was red clay."

"Is that important?" I asked.

"Yes, it is," she replied.

I didn't even know then that red ochre came from red clay, but having learned not to dismiss the somehow innate wisdom of the wise child, her comment inspired me to research the subject. Turned out, she was right—again. Red ochre from clay was used in our earliest art and religious rituals and the beginnings of its use is closely associated with the advent of symbolic thought. Neanderthal gravesites have been uncovered that were decorated with red ochre.

And what had the people at Pinnacle Point, as the place where Dr. Marean had first found their artifacts is called now, done with the numerous red ochre cylinders that they had fashioned and collected? We may never know for sure, since cave paintings would not have survived that length of time; they would have been made much earlier than those found at Lascaux and other sites in Europe. The cylinders pointed to tantalizing possibilities though—even likelihoods. I guess that there are some people who collect art supplies and never use them, but I doubt if there are whole societies that engage in that sort of wasteful behavior.

Sometimes my visions of the shaman leading her people are exceptionally detailed, almost eidetic. It was not always that way. The first time I saw them they were a spectral blur. I did not even realize the shaman was female the first time I saw her as she walked toward the cave. It was only in the morning when she returned that the vision was a little clearer and seeing her from the front, I was somewhat surprised to see breasts and then realized she was a woman. I had been writing as I was visualizing this and now had to go back and change the pronouns.

"Of course the shaman was a woman," my daughter, now age twenty-two, said to me when I told her of this vision.

Although I can follow the movements of the shaman in the eidolon and see her clearly now, I cannot enter the cave with her. The entrance that I can see from a distance is darkly opaque. I can't even get close to it. What does she do in there? Maybe someday Dr. Marean, or another, will find some clue she left there.

Buddhism places value on the ability to remember and reflect on past lives. History, collected mythology, and science have given us the tools to reflect on the lives of who we were and where we came from. Ever since I discovered the stories of our ancestors as a child I have known that I was living in a continuum of past and present and have felt a strong bond with those who came before. The more we learn about their stories, the more, I believe, we can learn about ourselves.

The sight of a figure emerging out of the gathering darkness interrupted my reverie. Saurabh had arrived at last.

I had already noticed a sign near the chortens that read, "Homestay ten minutes," with an arrow that pointed up the valley, so donning our headlamps Saurabh and I headed out that way. After about twenty minutes we came to a farmhouse that had a homestay sign. There were no lights on and the padlock on the door confirmed that no one was home. We sat down and waited. After a time a Ladakhi came by and we asked him if he knew when the owner would be home.

"Tomorrow," was the reply.

This was not good news as neither Saurabh nor I had camping gear, although we had clothes warm enough for an overnight bivi.

But then the passerby said, "Wait, someone come," and waved his open hand up and down, which presumably meant for us to sit down and chill.

Sure enough after another forty minutes or so three drunken men showed up who had a key for the padlock on the door and invited us in. After a halting conversation with the one I believed to be the most sober, I gathered that he was the father of one of the younger two men and a relative of the owners. They had likely heard of our situation from the passerby. It seemed like the boys were in the middle of a drinking party when they got this news, so now they had moved their party here to help us out.

After being shown a room where we dumped our gear, we joined the Ladakhis in the kitchen where the continued drinking, and now attempted cooking, were in progress. The father had seated himself cross-legged on the bare clay floor and was chopping up tubers on the surface of a rough plank. Potatoes lay scattered around him on the floor. Nothing in this kitchen, not to mention the vegetables on the floor, seemed very clean, and I thought that there might be consequently be some unusual ingredients in our dinner that night.

The two younger men, like many Ladakhis, spoke some Hindi so Saurabh was able to communicate with them. What he wanted to know was how long it would take to walk to the village of Chilling, where the twice a week bus to Leh was scheduled to pass through the next afternoon. The three seemed to agree that it was a walk of about one and a half hours. I had learned from experience that when a Ladakhi gives me a trail time to double that time—at least. This is peculiar because they are honest people and although they are fast walkers, so am I—and I have not had the experience of locals charging past me on any of these trails. The times that the locals sometimes gave me could not be based on walking or even running— perhaps they incorporated something like the Tibetan technique of Lung Gom-pa, or wind meditation, an ancient craft supposedly practiced by some adepts that incorporates levitation to facilitate tremendous leaping strides. Lung Gom-pas could cover 200 miles a day, it was said. Sometimes verbal trail descriptions given by the locals lacked important details that one would certainly want to hear about. In this case Saurabh and I made the assumption, because no one told us otherwise, that there was a bridge across the formidable Zanskar River, which one would have to get across to reach the road that led to Chilling, and then to Leh.

In the morning one of the owners, a middle-aged woman, arrived, and made us breakfast. Saurabh taking the Ladakhis at their word, and therefore figuring that he had a short walk to Chilling, accompanied me up the valley for about an hour before turning around and heading down. He thanked me for the skills that I taught him, even if they were the most basic. He was, it seemed learning to listen to his body and to dress more appropriately. He asked me to take another picture of him with his camera before we parted.

As I held the camera up to take the pic, I said to him. "You know Saurabh, a few days ago you really looked like a tourist. Now...well...you look a little more like a mountaineer."

He beamed.

The Markha valley is, in many places, more of a canyon than a valley, and even in the widest places it is seldom broader than a half a kilometer. There are numerous trails, some ancient, most in disuse, which run high and low along the steep sides of the canyon. There must be millions of man-hours invested in the construction of these trails over the years, and one wonders how the people of this valley, with a population of perhaps a few hundred, could accomplish such feats. One had to be careful to avoid the trails that were in disuse, as they would invariably end up leading one to a landslide or washout in a steep ravine. In my previous journey up this valley I had to sometimes avoid the valley bottom because of extreme flooding and once had to take a marginal trail on the heights. At one point I had to take off my backpack and push it in front of me as I crawled on my hands and knees where the wall beside me overhung the narrow trail. I remarked on this to some locals I stayed with in the next village that evening and was shocked to hear that a couple of Germans had fallen off that trail the week before and died. I made it a point when I came to a trail junction in Ladakh to look for boot or hoof prints and horse dung to guide me onto the right path. Oftentimes three or four small stones placed across a path signify not to go that way.

After a few hours I came to the one-house village of Sara located in a cultivated bowl between the narrower constrictions of the canyon. There was a parachute tent here beside the house and when I learned that the woman in the kitchen had eggs and was willing to make me an omelet, I, and my protein-starved body, rejoiced. The omelet was fried in butter and served on a chapatti. It was very satisfying.

Outside of Sara I noticed a series of caves, which looked man-made, hollowed out in the steep earthen cliffs across the river. The caves were above a terrace on which were constructed several stone and mortar buildings, with no signs of recent inhabitation. This must have been a community of recluses at one time, but I couldn't see any obvious way to reach even the terrace, let alone some of the caves. There are many, perhaps hundreds of isolated caves, which were once hermitages, in the Markha valley, usually built into seemingly inaccessible sheer cliffs. The typically small entrance way, constructed in a front wall made of mud, brick or stone, is usually suspended over a sheer drop to the valley floor and I supposed that perhaps the only way to get to those places or get supplies was to lower by rope from the top of the cliff. I have heard of hermit monks in Tibet being actually walled up in caves for years with only a small opening to receive food. My mother-in-law, Ani Migme Chödrön, has done several retreats confined to a small building spending most of the days and nights seated in a small box. The box does not have room to lie down—one meditates and sleeps in it, in a sitting position. Ani Migme did this for six months on, six months off, for six years. I, on the other hand, need a dose of Adivan to be able to manage mostly sitting for the length an overseas plane flight.

I reflected on Igjugarjuk, shaman of the Caribou Inuit, who experienced his initiation seated inside a small igloo, with almost no food and water for thirty days in the darkness and cold of mid-winter. "Wisdom," he told the Danish explorer Knut Rassmussen, "lives far from mankind, out in the great solitude, and it can only be attained through suffering and privation."

Many yogis believe that the world, as we know it, is merely a reflection of the mind. One of the tenets of Buddhism is the Two Truths Doctrine. It holds that there is the commonplace, or relative, truth of the everyday world, and then there is the ultimate truth, which can only be experienced in a state of super consciousness or nirvana. This is the state beyond suffering, loneliness, faith, or perhaps even science, as we know it.

In Tibetan Buddhism there is a practice of meditation called Tummo. The practitioners of this discipline, it is said, are tested by their teachers to ascertain whether they have attained mastery of their meditation. They are must sit naked in the open in sub-zero temperatures while a hole is cut in the ice of stream or lake. Cotton sheets are then soaked in the almost freezing water and draped over their bodies. During the course of the night they must successively dry several of those wet cotton sheets with their body heat. If they have accomplished this task by morning they are considered Tummo adepts. They are then granted the right to wear a traditional thin cotton robe summer and winter to signify that they have transcended the normal limits of mind and body.

I remember somewhat desperately trying out Tummo meditation during one of my first dates with my wife. We got caught out after dark in a snowstorm and took shelter in a tree well. Every time I thought that I was getting a little glow from the meditation and breathing exercises, the incipient flame seemed to snuff out and the cold would return to pierce my insides. A constant distraction to my meditation was the thought of all the warm clothes that we had left in the car, thinking that we were just going out for a short jaunt that got extended further and further in our enthusiasm for the mountain and each other. You do the stupidest things when you are falling in love. Fortunately the storm subsided and we climbed out of the tree well to see our way lit through the complex terrain by the moon and the Perseid meteor shower. We put on our skis and quickly glided down to our car and got to the pub at the base of the mountain just in time for last call. At one point I stood in front of the sink in the pub washroom, shivering, in a state of mild hypothermia, the worst of which was the feeling that my balls were frozen. When I went to dry my hands under the hot air blower, I took a quick look around and then pulled the front of my pants out and leaned forward so that the hot air blew down on my crotch. It was ecstasy. I had the nozzle of the blower down inside my pants, and my face must have looked like I was in state of bliss in the mirror that faced the door. Then someone, a huge logger-type guy, suddenly opened the door and walked into the room.

A voice from behind me boomed, "So that feels good, huh?"

So much for transcending the body.

The locals had told me that it would take me three hours to get to Markha from Skyu. It took me nine, which was the time stated in the guidebook that I had accidentally left in Leh. I was moving relatively slowly that day, however, because I was tired from the push the day before. The path wound through various constrictions between the canyon walls opening intermittently into wider bowls that sometimes contained cultivated fields. Here and there on the valley bottom were stands of alder and cottonwood trees, but the predominant uncultivated vegetation was the sea-buckthorn bush. The path sometimes cut through almost impenetrable thickets of this hearty plant, which is more like a gnarly little tree, with formidable thorns, than a bush. Besides harvesting the nutritious berries of this plant the Ladakhis use them to build enclosures for their goats and sheep to protect their animals from wolves and snow leopards. A sea-buckthorn fence is at least as effective as one made of barbed wire.

The protective fences for livestock were much more abundant now than the last time I was here. In those days trapping and shooting predators such as the snow leopard were the main defense. I remembered seeing, some two and a half decades ago, the skin of a snow leopard displayed on a farmer's wall in this vicinity. It has been greatly due to the efforts of the Indian Department of Wildlife Protection and the Snow Leopard Conservancy Trust that a process of education has led to alternative methods of protecting domestic livestock.

Before I came to the village of Markha the trail passed by another remnant of the ways of the past. It was a so-called "wolf trap." It consisted of a pit about three meters deep encircled by overlapping flat stones that were placed to cantilever out over the rim of the pit. The idea was that if a domestic animal was killed, the remains of its carcass would be thrown into the pit. Then if the predator came to finish the meal and jumped into the pit it would be unable to egress due to the overhang on every side formed by the cantilevered stones. The entire village, men, women, and children, would then gather and stone to death the trapped animal—in this way sharing equally in the burden of Karma due for taking the life of a sentient being.

Arriving at the outskirts of Markha just as it began to get dark, I found accommodation in a large farmhouse, occupied by a middle-aged man and a young women who made me a filling meal. I had encountered very little traffic during my walk that day: a couple of locals walking alone and a pony caravan returning unladen to the road-head down the valley.

DREAMTIME
OCTOBER 2009

In Tantric Buddhism it is believed that the dream state is a Bardo, a liminal state like meditation and death, where transformation of consciousness is possible. But I don't seem to dream much when I sleep at higher elevations, except for two recurring dreams, the mountain climbing dream and the smoking dream. The smoking dream started in 1982 when I made a bet with a friend that I could quit cigarettes for a year. Most addicts always feel that they can put off weaning themselves from their addiction for at least one more day, or sometimes just one more hour. "What difference will it make," says the monkey that sits on your back, "if you start quitting today or tomorrow?" But when you have made a wager for a significant amount of money, when that one more cigarette is going to cost you a hundred dollars, then you have to be honest with yourself. Do you really want to smoke just one more one hundred-dollar cigarette?

The strange thing was that I dreamed about smoking that cigarette every night for that year. Every night. The routine was that I would suddenly find myself smoking. Oh my god, I would think to myself, I have lost the bet. But no, I wouldn't do that. This must be a dream. This cigarette isn't real then, I would think to myself. It doesn't count for the bet then. I would then continue to puff on the dream cigarette and enjoy it knowing that being unreal it would not cost me the money.

Gradually these dreams became more and more lucid. I became fascinated with how satisfying the unreal cigarette of my dream was. Then knowing that I was in a dream I began to take a detailed account of my surroundings. I remember sitting on a beach in West Vancouver in the dream and looking out over the water and seeing the reflection of the setting sun on thousands of wavelets. There were numerous stones on the beach, igneous, metamorphic, volcanic— and billion of grains of sand. I looked down at my hands and saw the hair and pores of my skin. Then I looked at the mountains and thought to myself that I didn't quite get that part right as they looked more like the Alps than the real North Shore Mountains. But what the heck—they were really cool. The thing was that there was so much complex visual detail in this dream that it rivaled the real world. I looked again at the water and then across English Bay to the forest and buildings of Point Gray. This was all in my mind? I had created all of this? And I couldn't help but ask myself in that dream, how much of that world out there, when I awoke, was also a creation of my mind?

Now after I have quit cigarettes for more than twenty years, I only have the smoking dream once every few weeks or so, and it no longer has that visual clarity. And since I no longer wish to smoke I just kind of feel disgusted with myself in the dream for doing so. I guess that monkey is still testing, hoping that he can get me back. That's the thing about addiction: metaphor still describes it better than hard science. It is a demonic possession of the mind, body, and spirit—and only a kind of exorcism can free us from it.

Many of the dreams that I have archived in my memory, the ones that I reflect on during the relatively dreamless nights of the Himalayas, are patterned on myths and legends. I believe that myths are our collective dreams, and that they have been our guideposts for self-exploration for thousands of years. Children love these stories and I have often been amazed at their questions and insights when they hear them. When I became old enough to read, I sought them out. They seeped down into my subconscious and found resonance there. They rang a bell inside of me. Then they began to return to me at night with new messages.

The Samurai

I reflected on a dream that I had long ago. I dreamed that I was, I think, a merchant, although in the story this dream was based on the character was a monk. Maybe I was sort of both, the way things like that get blended in dreams. In any case I was traveling in feudal Japan, and I had disguised myself as a samurai in order to discourage bandits. On my journey I had somehow inadvertently slighted a real samurai, and he challenged me to a duel. We were to meet at an appointed place shortly after dawn.

That night in the room of my inn I contemplated my certain demise. I knew that I was going to die, but I wanted to leave this life with good form. I did not want to show fear. Also, not wanting to look like a complete klutz with the sword that would be in my hand when I was killed by the real samurai, I determined that I would spend the night practicing the stance that I had seen samurai adopt at the beginning of a duel.

Pulling the borrowed sword from its sheath, I looked down the blade and marveled at the beauty of its pure lines. I contemplated the intricacy of the watermarks, where the clay had been applied before the final firing; this was to ensure that the cutting edge would be hardened, but that the spine would remain flexible. I knew that in the process of its construction the sword master had hammered out the glowing steel; then folded it on itself again and again so that it was now made up of thousands of laminations. Holding it before me I saw the reflection of my face in the steel. I had carried it for days as a lifeless prop for my absurd acting, but now I realized that the thing I was holding had a soul. I only wanted to be worthy of carrying it in my hands to my death.

I took up the stance that I had remembered from watching samurai practice. I made some adjustments here and there trying to conform to what I remembered. At one moment it suddenly felt right. I held the pose. My thoughts ebbed away. All fear was gone. I was empty. Spontaneously I moved forward. The sword flashed in the lamplight and I heard it swoosh in the still air of the room as it cut an arc in front of me and then stopped abruptly at waist height. Then I jumped backward with a grace and speed I had never known. I stood still again, adopting another pose. What had I just done? I had moved like a samurai. And then I knew that I could do it again. And again. I felt like a portal had just been opened to me. That all the learning, the practice, the skill of all beings that had ever lived was within me, within all of us, if we could just pierce the wall between us. The skill of the sword maker and the samurai were all within me—and even the soul of the entity in my hand, the sword, was now connected to me.

I spent the rest of the night practicing the movements with the sword. I imagined my opponent with extraordinary clarity—his movements, his strategies—and I countered with quick precision. I had never imagined that there could be such beauty in the flow of body, mind, and spirit.

At dawn I was on my way to the meeting place. I was enjoying a fierce anticipation, not because I wanted to kill anyone—that was rather irrelevant, as my own life was also now somewhat beside the point. What I wanted to experience was the proof of that unity of consciousness, wisdom and experience of all humankind, of all being, which I now believed was within me.

Then I woke up. No, it couldn't have been just a dream…I wanted to fight the duel. It was real. It had to be…but it was a dream. My whole body though still felt like a dynamo of energy. I was vibrating. I looked down at my arms, my hands, my legs—my entire body was glowing in the dark. Was I still dreaming? No, I was awake. Why was I glowing? Gradually it faded. I was back. The portal was closed again. Was it really there? Was it only a dream? But these dreams are touchstones in my life. Perhaps some dreams can make us look down into the well of ourselves—the well that leads to somewhere beyond ourselves.

In the original story the monk and the Samurai meet at the appointed place at the appointed hour. The monk's stance is so perfect that the samurai puts away his sword, goes down on his knee and asks to become the monk's disciple.

Ithaca

The next night, while once again sleeping on a friend's floor in his London flat, I had this dream.

I dreamed that I was returning to my home after many years away. I had fought in a long war. A war I had never wanted to join. When it was over I had begun my journey home. But I had angered a god, who in his fury had sent me storms and hardships that had set me wandering for even more years.

Now after so long, I finally once again entered the forecourt of my family's ancient house. To call it a palace would be an exaggeration, for my kingdom was small, merely an island. When the great king, and his brother, had come to fetch me for the war, I did not have the power to refuse. I had tried to pretend that I was mad, so that they would not take me. But they had seen through my ruse. They had tested me, placing my infant son in harm's way—and like a sane man, I saved him—and went off to war.

All morning I had relished the familiar sights and scents of my island. Now in the late afternoon I stood trembling on the threshold of my home. I wanted to rush in and embrace my wife and see my now grown son. But I could not. I would be slain. I had been warned that young nobles of my kingdom and neighboring lands had gathered at my home for years. They had been partying their faces off at the expense of my larder, my cellar, and my lands. They had abused and raped my servants. They had tried to convince my wife that I was long dead and that she should marry one of them, who would then inherit my kingdom. I had been told that if anyone appeared claiming to be me, he would immediately be killed as an impostor.

On the way to the house, I had exchanged my garments with those of a beggar, and I now practiced a stoop as I shuffled toward the entrance to the banquet hall from which there came the sound of revelry. I entered the hall. There were about twenty young men seated at tables; some already, despite the relatively early hour, appeared to be in state of drunkenness. Seated on a raised dais at the end of the hall was my wife. Despite the passage of two decades she was still beautiful. Beside her stood a young man whom I immediately recognized as my son. Suddenly something struck me on the side of the head and I saw an apple core land and roll across the floor. There was a roar of laughter from the crowd of young men. I turned to look at my wife. Our eyes met for an instant and then she turned her gaze away.

I walked further into the hall and approaching the first table, went from suitor to suitor with my head bowed kneeling before all in turn and holding my hand out as a supplicant. As I went before each man I raised my eyes just enough to take his measure. Who was the strongest? Who was sober and who was not?

Then my eyes were stung as a cup of wine was splashed into my face. I looked up and saw a large muscular man grinning at me. I wanted to leap forward and tear his throat out. He drew up his foot and kicked me in the chest, sending me sprawling on the floor. There was another roar of laughter from the young men in the hall. I sat on my haunches and evaluated the large man before me. I would kill him first, I thought to myself. Would I be able? I looked around at the grinning young men. They were all youthful and strong. I saw in their eyes how they saw me—an old man. A weak man. Isn't that what I was? No, that was only my disguise. Or was it? Wasn't I now old? Wasn't I weak compared to these young bucks? They were all certain that I was. Was that the truth? There comes a time in our lives, or for some of us many times, when we reach down into ourselves, and search for that greater self. At these times we ignore the reflection of ourselves that we see in other's eyes. But many of us never go there, content to travel through the world merely as a mirror of its expectations. The poet would later fashion a metaphor and write that at that moment the goddess came to me and bestowed on me her divine power. I rose to my feet.

Then I heard my wife's voice. She announced that she would decide this day which of the men in the hall would be her husband. He who could string the great bow of the son of Laertes, which she now held over her head, and shoot an arrow into a target, through twelve obstacles, as he had done, would win her as the prize. One of the conditions was that each man present in the hall would get a turn.

The suitors each took their turn attempting to bend the limbs of the great bow and string it. Each failed. They were angry. They said no one could bend and string the bow.

They demanded that she pick one of them as a husband. She replied that she would. She would pick whom she thought was the strongest—as soon as the conditions were met. There was still one man in the hall, she pointed out, who had not attempted to string the bow. All eyes turned to me. There were howls of laughter.

"Alright then, let the beggar try, then you must decide on one of us as you promised," came a shout from one of them.

Rough hands thrust me to the back of the hall where my bow and other weapons that I had not taken to the war were laid out. In addition to the bow there was a shield, a spear, and a sword. I picked up the sword. Although it felt usable, the grip felt somewhat too small for my hand. Sometimes in dreams the meanings of these sorts of things is, upon reflection, obvious, but in the thirty-five years I have been reflecting on this dream, I'm still not certain of the meaning of the shrunken sword handle. Did it mean that I had grown? But I was an adult when I left for the war. Grown in spirit then? Was this dream that I had as a young man a message to my older self now? I picked up the bow.

I placed the lower limb of the bow behind my calf and anchored the tip below the arch of my foot. Then pushing my shin against the lower limb, I pulled the upper limb with my left arm toward the eye of the bowstring that I held in my right hand and looped it over the notch. There was a sharp intake of breath from some of the young men. I picked up an arrow and faced the target. The obstacles that the arrow had to pass through were the heads of twelve axes. Bronze age axe heads were crescent shaped and had an attachment point to the wooden haft at the top and bottom of the crescent, leaving a half circular gap between the haft and the bronze. The gaps were lined up perfectly, but the trajectory of the arrow would have to be almost flat to pass through all the gaps and hit the target. Only a very strong man with a very strong bow could make such a shot.

I nocked the arrow onto the string and while raising the bow contracted the muscles of my back while pushing with one arm and pulling with the other, so that the bow was already at full draw by the time it was raised to sight on the target. This was an old technique for drawing a powerful bow now largely lost to modern archery. Holding my bow hand loose to avoid twisting the limbs, I released the arrow. It struck the target. There was stunned silence in the hall. I quickly nocked another arrow. It was released in an instant. It stuck the largest suitor in the chest exactly where he had kicked me. He fell backwards onto the floor. I heard the sound of hammering and saw that one of my old servants had drawn the bronze bolt on the closed door and was now deforming it so that it could not be opened. No one would now leave the hall in a hurry. I picked up the sword. The strong young men who had shortly ago seemed so powerful now had terror in their eyes as I bore toward them.

Then I woke up.

THE MARKHA RIVER CROSSING
OCTOBER 2009

In the morning I walked though the village of Markha, the largest settlement in the valley, with some two dozen houses, a crumbling fortress, and a 400-year-old Gompa. The word Gompa can refer to a small village temple with perhaps adjoining accommodations for a few monks, as in this case, or a temple monastery complex housing hundreds of monks and often incorporating some of the designs of a fortress. The Markha fortress itself was build on a decaying pillar of natural dried mud and stones that had not gone through the heating and compression process that would have transformed it into much more stable conglomerate rock. The fortress was built directly above the school, situated on the river plain a couple of hundred feet below. It was one of only two schools in the valley. I saw that the pillar was severely undercut by erosion and I hoped that when the fortress inevitably cascaded down onto the plain below there would be no students in the school building.

Once I left the cultivated fields upstream from Markha village the valley once again narrowed into a tight gorge. The trail followed the right hand bank of the Markha River until it abruptly ended at a vertical headwall that the stream pushed up against. I could see that the path continued on the other bank and that there was an obvious crossing over a series of stepping stones.

The problem was that the stones were completely covered with a layer of ice. The whole river here in this shady canyon was now mostly covered in ice, but not thickly enough to walk on. I stood there for a few minutes in the cold wind that was now blowing down the gorge and then came to a decision. I took off my boots and tying the laces together swung them over my head bolo style and hurled them across the river. They landed on the other bank. Now I was committed. The stream here was a bit more than 5 meters wide and 30 centimeters or so deep. I took off my pants, fleece jacket, and wool sweater and stuffed them into a waterproof stuff sack. Now down to my tee shirt and shorts I put my Gore-Tex jacket back on to provide some protection from the icy wind. I also placed my cameras into waterproof bags. Then I took off my wool socks, put them too in a dry bag and put two dirty pairs back on my feet. After loading the backpack with the clothes and cameras I put it back on leaving the waist belt undone, as is the general rule when crossing streams. Then I busted through the layer of ice near the shore with my aluminum walking stick. Using the stick to aid balance, I began to wade across the river, alternately kicking my feet down into the ice in front of me to break through it. I had been braced for the shock of painful cold that I thought would hit as soon as I plunged in, but what I experienced instead was entirely unexpected. I hardly felt the cold. When I stepped out of the river on the other side, a layer of ice immediately began to form around my stocking feet— but it felt like my entire body was glowing. I stood there on the rocky shore unhurried, my bare legs exposed in the subzero wind, my feet encased in ice—in wonder at the warmth that was spreading through me. Was this Tummo?

I emerged from the gorge into another widening of the valley where I took out my binoculars and performed a routine scanning of the slopes around me—searching for the slightest movement that might indicate the presence of my ghostly quarry. After a quarter of an hour I put the binoculars away and put on my prescription sunglasses. Although I see reasonably well without these specs, my long-distance vision is no longer perfect, so I wore these corrective lenses, which self-adjusted to the intensity of the ambient light, during almost all of my outdoor daylight hours while walking in Ladakh. The trouble was that, although the glasses improved my distance vision, they distorted short-range and middle-distance vision, making walking on the often rough terrain much less comfortable and natural than if I were not wearing them. This action though, like getting up in the cold at 3 a.m., I believed, was just part of the discomfort I should be willing to endure in order to catch a glimpse of the phantom.

I walked past more hermitage caves built into the sides of the cliffs. I reflected on how, twenty-four years ago, I had felt so above the travails of the world while wandering in the Himalayas for months. It had been easy to feel detached from the world's woes then. My illusion of enlightenment turned out to be hubris, though. I knew now that it was easy to be deluded while sitting in a cave or a monastery or walking through one breathtaking mountainscape after another day after day. Krishna was right when he told Arjuna that yoga is not permanent withdrawal from the world, but that rather it is undertaking action and the responsibility of one's duties to fellow beings.

I returned then to the world—and to my destructive gambling habits, fell in love with my young stockbroker, and entered to into a dark and devastating relationship. To top it off, I had a child with her. And only after this unexpected event, did I begin to undertake the sadhana* of responsibility for others.

---

*   Sadhana is a spiritual work or exercise.

SALZBURG
OCTOBER 1985

I stepped off the train in Salzburg carrying only my daypack; my luggage had been lost by the airline somewhere between New Delhi, Dubai, London, and Frankfurt. Somewhere. They were looking for it. Arriving in Frankfurt with only the clothes on my back, and those being pretty shabby mountaineering duds that had been through a lot of wear and tear in the last months, I had gone shopping and was now newly outfitted and looking quite continental with a baggy white bomber jacket, pleated woolen pants, and even a stylish white fedora with a wide black band.

The first thing that astonished me upon arriving in Germany was how clean everything was. The children, even their clothes, were spotless; their faces were scrubbed. They must wash them every day, I thought to myself in amazement. I knew that this was once normal for me, and soon would be again; but right then it seemed extraordinary.

As I began to walk down the length of the platform I noticed a young woman, in her early twenties, walking in the same direction as me, about 4 meters to my left. Even though she was fair, with long blond hair, she did not look German, or even European. American, I thought. They just seem to have a different way of carrying themselves. There are also clues in the dress sense that even after being away in Asia for nine months, I still recognized. Some years ago while walking through the street market in Florence, one of the vendors, while looking me up and down asked, in a way that was not really a question, "West Coast, eh?"

The woman and I were walking at about the same speed. This was unusual—almost no one walks as fast as me. She glanced at me, I at her. Then a billboard separated us for the next 6 meters.

Women are the touchstones in men's lives. We swim from stone to stone. We drown without them. I have tried being a kind of monk. But that just makes you crazy. Love can hurt though. Leaving can hurt. Bonding happens. But I hate the pain of attachment, knowing that everything ends. I was always leaving or, more often, I made them leave.

The billboard ended. We glanced at each other again. Then another billboard intervened.

In one month's time I would meet my shadow. Your shadow is the part of your being that you have always repressed—usually with good reason—it can be a very dangerous part of you. But it can also be a fun part—of creativity—of spontaneity. When you bury this part of yourself, you secretly mourn for it every day. It is the child you have stunted and neglected. You try to hide your child even from yourself. Then when you meet someone who embodies all the qualities of your shadow, all of them, full grown, and full blown, all the qualities you have locked away in that deep dungeon…then… then you will embrace that part of you that you have denied for so long. You will be attracted like a moth to a flame. You will fall in love with your own dark side. Even if you have spent more than half a year meditating in the Himalayas and you think that now you can be tested by the world, you will fall. And you will fall hard. You will enter the abyss.

But that was still in the future. Now the young woman and I cleared the billboard again. We looked at each other again. Then came another billboard.

Death is what eggs us on. Where can you escape death? Only by being close to it. By losing yourself in a dangerous act, or in deep meditation, or in moving with someone else's body, and giving yourself to them, and caring for them, if even only for one night. All sacraments involve an exchange of fluids, water for the first, oil for the last—and in between, blood, semen, sweat.

We reached the customs queue together and there she asked me, "Excuse me, do you know Salzburg?"

"Yes," I answered.

"Do you know a place to stay? Preferably cheap?"

"Well there's the Youth Hostel," I replied. "Or the cheapest hotels are in the red light district across the square from the station." I paused. "I have a key for a condo about an hour's bus ride out of the city. You are welcome to join me and stay there."

She turned to look at me. Cerulean eyes stared. They asked, "Could you hurt me?"

No. Not in that way. Never.

We stood like that for perhaps thirty seconds. Pheromones were exchanged. The dark pupils of her eyes slowly dilated and the ice of the irises receded. Then she said, "Okay," and smiled.

HANKAR

OCTOBER 2009

I continued on to where the gorge widened somewhat, but the walls on either side were still quite steep. Passing underneath Techa Gompa, perched improbably on an aerie, high on a cliff above, I came to the small hamlet of Umlung. There I was invited for tea. As my hostess was preparing to serve me she noticed the cup into which she was just about to pour my tea was dirty, so she wiped it with her bare hand, which was black with filth including traces of the animal dung that she was using to feed the hearth fire. There was other stuff on that hand that was probably worse, as I had seldom seen any toilet paper in rural Ladakh, nor had I seen a rural Ladakhi wash his or her hands. As I was preparing to drink this cup of hemlock, her children were staring at me in fascination, as interested to know as I was, it seemed to me, if I was going to fall dead soon after the cup touched my lips.

Ladakhis seemed to largely share immunity from the germs that they pass between each other and dirt, dung, and their livestock. Once when I was having dinner with a local family, the entire extended household, seated on the floor around a table, took turns kneading a chunk of tsampa dough, a mixture of barley flour, water, and butter, which was being passed from hand to unwashed hand. The dough was a pretty effective concoction to capture the residue from the blackened hands I figured, and I could see fingers getting visibly cleaner as the communal kneading went on. Then the dough was passed to me—to taste.

I declined that one although I did accept this tea. Sometimes you just have to accept other people's standards if you want to live among them and you just hope that you do live. Most of the villagers in Rumbak that offered lodgings to Westerners had actually attended a special course in Leh where they could obtain a certificate to display on their walls showing that they had learned something of our customs and obsessions, including those concerning the very foreign concept of hygiene. That sort of training had not come to the Markha valley though.

Many Ladakhis may not understand germ theory, but they are nevertheless the healthiest, most robust people I have ever seen anywhere. I remembered watching Padma's sixtysomething father, in a field outside of Rumbak, breaking stones—not with dynamite or a sledge hammer, but by lifting one gigantic rock after another over his head and hurling it at other stones. The older people here certainly seemed much healthier than the highlanders in Nepal, where open pit fire hearths, without any sort of ventilation except the cracks between the slate roof shakes, were the norm. Indeed, Nepali friends have told me that they grew up believing that inhaling smoke would help to keep them warm. This has devastating health consequences in later life, which can be seen in the rampant eye and lung diseases that appear in these people even in middle age. Trekkers in Nepal now stay in relatively comfortable lodges, with private rooms, and therefore are unlikely to share in the smoke-eating ritual that was common a couple of decades ago when a lodge often consisted of one communal room.

By mid-afternoon I was approaching the village of Hankar. Here the gorge broadened into a valley. The fortress, on its improbable perch, came into view long before I entered the village—it was just as amazing as I remembered it. It was built on a narrow ridge rising from the valley bottom. The ridge ascended from west to east, like a series of giant stairs, ending on a final pinnacle on top of which sat the ultimate impregnable citadel. When I came around to under the narrow part of the ridge on the west side and looked up at the keep, it indeed had the appearance of castle built on top of a spire, just as I had imagined it for twenty-four years.

At the time of that first visit I made the acquaintance of the local schoolteacher, who invited me to stay in his house. His home was actually a 30-square-meter room adjacent to the 45-square-meter schoolhouse. Although he was Ladakhi he was not a native to the village. The government had sent him here upon his graduation and training as a teacher. As the only educated person in the village he was lonely and hungry for outside company like mine.

After he prepared and served me dinner, he asked if I liked to drink chang. Actually I like to drink chang very much. It is an alcoholic beverage made from fermented barley or millet that is sometimes referred to as Tibetan beer in English. A much inferior lowland version, made from rice and sugar, is sometimes served to tourists in Nepal.

"Come then," he said to me, "I know where there is good chang." We put on our jackets and shoes and took our battery-powered lights, and then he led me through the village until we came to a house from which came the sound of chanting. I followed the teacher through a low doorway and entered a room that was lit by hundreds of butter candles. The chanting came from three lamas seated on a dais. One of the lamas was beating a drum in time to the chant; another of the lamas periodically clashed a pair of cymbals. We were shown a place to sit and cups of chang were poured for us. Soon the Lamas reached a kind of crescendo of chanting, banging, and clashing, and then broke off briefly to quaff several cups of chang each before resuming. Although the lamas seemed to be joking with rest of the men here during the break, there was something very intense about the atmosphere in the room.

"What kind of party is this?" I asked my host.

"No party. Funeral," he replied, over the tumult.

"Ah."

Indeed now I saw that the chanting lamas were turning pages in the books each had laid out in front of him, and it came to me then that the books were copies of the Bardo Thodal, sometimes known in English as the Tibetan Book of the Dead. The Bardo is the interval between death and the next rebirth, and this ceremony that I was witnessing was intended to guide the consciousness of the deceased through that confusing space. I had read that this ceremony usually lasted for three days.

I began to notice after a while that every time I took a sip of my cup that it was immediately refilled with to the brim with chang. I think that I noticed this a little too late for my own good. Unbaked cakes made of tsampa dough were also offered to me. I pretended to enjoy these. Have I mentioned that I don't really like tsampa?

The next morning, despite my hangover, I followed my host on a climb to the uppermost part of the citadel. Some of the climbing was quite exposed, and I marveled at the construction of the fort. This part of the valley could not have supported much more than a hundred people—so how could they build such a thing as this? Many thousands of flat stones had been dragged and somehow lifted from the valley floor and adjacent slopes and carefully placed and mortared together. In some places these stone walls improbably, somewhat miraculously, I thought, overhung sheer precipices.

My guide kept looking back and asking if I was all right. I guessed that he would feel bad if he led a tourist to fall to his death, especially after getting him hosed at a funeral the night before. We made it to the topmost part of the citadel and had splendid views or the valley and of views of snow covered Kange Yaze.

The schoolhouse was no longer here; the children now all travel downstream to the one relatively modern-looking school that served the entire upper valley at Markha village. I found accommodations this time with a family who gave me the room of their adult son for the night. The room, though uncluttered, was rather filthy, and I used some wetted toilet paper from my stash to wipe down the surfaces that I just couldn't bear to share space with in their present state. The son seemed to resent this clean up, looking around, when he came into the room to pick up some of his gear. Oh well. That night at dinner, the father, while serving me tea, performed the same cup cleaning ritual with his bare, unwashed, hand, as the woman had done the day before. Once again I accepted the cup. The son, who spoke English, told me that his father was the village doctor. Witch doctor, of some kind, I supposed he meant.

I guess that I am somewhat of a germaphobe in my normal life back in Canada, but having almost died, more than once, due to infections in both my childhood and adult life...yeah, I do get a bit worried from time to time. I recalled some thirty-five years ago, someone coughing into my face in the middle of the night in a crowded dorm in Italy, and how that had led to two months of hospitalization. My immune system is much stronger now than then though, having finally gotten over my sickly childhood stage in my late twenties. And as I said before, when traveling in third world Asia sometimes you just have to let it go.

That evening I debated whether to go up over the Gongmaru La or to head back down the valley. The trip over the pass was essentially three days, and I heard from this family that there were no shelters for trekkers on the way at this time of year. Indeed, I had not encountered a single foreigner since the Canadians back at Shingo. I thought about trying to do the trip in one long day but that would be pushing it. Death from hypothermia combined with exhaustion could come quite quickly at night at 5000 meters (16,500 ft)—I had not brought my sleeping bag with me on this jaunt up the valley. And no one was likely to go over the pass again this year, so my body would not be found until spring or even summer.

Having crossed the pass since then, I know now that it would have been well within my physical capabilities. One of the considerations though was the memory of how I had gotten lost on the last trip over this range. Although the hangover at that time probably did not help with my navigation, I was well equipped with camping supplies and had no worries wandering around in the mountains until I eventually found my way out, albeit by a very different route than I had intended. I ended up coming out on the Leh-Manali Highway, which was, at that time, a restricted military road. I got a ride with a road construction crew, consisting, it seemed, entirely of Tibetan refugees, both men and women. As we came to the first checkpoint all of us were standing in the back of the truck with bandanas or scarves hiding our faces because of the dust. I however, because or my height and clothes, stood out to say the least, and was promptly arrested by the Indian army.

I decided this time, all things considered, to go back down the Markha valley.

DOWN THE VALLEY
OCTOBER 2009

In the morning I went to climb up to the fortress spire. I don't remember having any difficulty last time, but now when I came to a place just below the final apex I had to scramble up an exposed natural rock slab. I got up that but what faced me next was a steep ladder made of piled up flat pieces of rubble somehow attached to the vertical rock face, on top of which was perched the highest room of the fortress. The route up the rubble ladder was very exposed—a fall from it would likely be fatal. I knew what was holding the rubble ladder together and cementing it to the rock face was simply dried mud. It seemed like the whole thing could just crumble and go cascading down to the valley floor with the trigger of my body weight. I wondered how many times this structure, or something like it, had fallen down and been reconstructed. This certainly looked different from the last time I was here. It would be quite simple to reinforce these types of structures with some drilled rock anchors, but I have never seen such a thing used in construction in Ladakh. Even though I felt like a wienie for doing so, I decided to back off of climbing to the top of the citadel this time.

When I reached the valley floor again, I unloaded the first aid kit, water, and sweater from my daypack and placed these items in the larger backpack that I had left down there. Then I rolled up the daypack and strapped it to the outside of the larger pack.

I started down the valley passing the village of Umlung and coming after a couple of hours to a narrowing of the canyon. Here, above me, perched on a ledge over an almost vertical wall, was

Techa Gompa, a spectacular combination of eagle's aerie, fortress, monastery, and spiritual hermitage.

Once again leaving the bulk of my gear, I set off climbing the steep switchback trail that wound up the face below the Gompa. Reaching the building quite out of breath after pushing hard on the relatively short but steep climb, I found the door to the Gompa to be secured with a padlock. This did not surprise me. Although I had heard that there was a single monk who lived up here and was supplied by the villagers of Umlung, it seemed that there were few monks who chose to spend the harsh winter in the Markha valley.

Down river from the village of Markha, I encountered a few school children returning to their homes for the weekend. None of them were accompanied by adults, and they were the only travelers I was to see all day. The children showed me a place to cross the river where it braided, so I did not have to get wet or to try practicing Tummo again.

I had intended to make a long day of it and trek past the village of Markha all the way to Sara where the woman had made me the delicious omelet two days before. But when I came to the fence before the house there late that afternoon, I found a padlock on the gate. The parachute over the outdoor seating had been packed away. This was not surprising, for I had met no other trekkers since parting company with Saurabh. I had the feeling that the owners were unlikely to return this night; the trekking season was over and the harvest was in, so there was a good chance that they had taken off to visit friends, or that they had gone to the city to get supplies for the winter. I had the choice therefore either to sleep out in the open huddled in my parka or continue to the next digs at Skyu. I decided to continue down the valley.

I arrived in Skyu in darkness, guided down the trail by the light of my headlamp. I had walked some 30 kilometers, in addition to climbing up the fortress spire and to Techa Gompa.

The next morning I set off for Chilling. I was assured once again by locals that the village was only about one and a half hours down the trail. Looking at the map, I was skeptical. The map showed a confluence of the Zanskar and Markha rivers well before Chilling.

The Zanskar is a major tributary of the Indus and a much bigger stream than the Markha. The map was unclear though on exactly where the bridge across the Zanskar River was. I knew that I would have to cross the Zanskar in order to get to the road on the other side that lead to Chilling. I assumed that there was a bridge. I was wrong.

At mid-morning I found myself standing on an embankment overlooking the fast-flowing, deep turquoise waters of the Zanskar. I stared in wonder at the single steel cable suspended across the span. There was definitely no bridge. In the middle of the cable, suspended under two steel pulleys was what appeared to be wooden apple box. Attached to this there were two frayed and sun bleached polypropylene lines, on on either side, each leading to the embankments on opposite shores. The poly lines were knotted in many places, where I presumed that they had been repaired in the past. I took hold of the line on my side of the river and began to pull the cart toward me. I was to learn later that there were usually people around to help with the procedure of ferrying across the river.

After I loaded my pack there was little room for me in the apple box cart, which was constructed from a few two by twos and half by four inch planks held together with a few nails and some wire. It was difficult climbing into the cart while holding on to the main cable with my gloved hands to prevent the now loaded cart from sliding down to the low point on the sagging line. As soon as I let go of the cable I was riding down a zip line toward the turquoise waters. I was careful to keep my fingers clear of the rapidly spinning pulleys, having heard of a climber who had lost all his fingers while trying to cross the Squamish River on a device similar to this one. The cart stopped, after losing its momentum a little was past the midpoint. Then it slid back a little the other way. I did not try to interfere until it came to a complete rest. Then I began to pull in the slack poly line that led to the far shore. This line was suspended from the main cable with a series of iron rings. As I hauled in the line I tried to keep the rope that I was gathering in draping as neatly as possible from the iron rings. I was beginning to realize, though, that this was not designed to be a one-man show. When I had finished hauling in all the loose rope, I began to haul myself and the cart to the other shore, hoping that none of the many knots and frays in the line would let go. This process of hauling became more and more strenuous as the incline of the cable steepened. Soon I was gasping for breath. There seemed to be no easy way to tie off the rope to the cart so I tried to get rests by wrapping the line around my wrist. About three-quarters of the way across the whole thing jammed and came to a stop. It actually only jammed in the direction I wanted to go. The cart was still perfectly willing to zip back down the incline in the direction I did not want to go. Consequently I had to keep the line wrapped around one wrist and keep that arm locked while I worked on unjamming the mess above with my other hand. For a moment, I glanced down at turquoise waters swirling below.

Crossing the Zanskar River near Chilling.

It turned out that it was the poly line jamming in the pulley that was causing the problem. As I hauled myself further up the incline it became even more strenuous for me physically and also more fiddly to manage the draping poly line to keep it from jamming in the pulley. I reached the other shore sweating and panting.

Then I began the one-hour trudge along the road to Chilling. A couple of trucks passed me going up the road, which followed the river upstream for only a couple more kilometers to the end of its present construction. This road, mostly built along the sides of sheer rock walls, will eventually be pushed all the way through to Padum, the main town in the region of Zanskar. Presently Zanskar is entirely cut off by road travel for about six months of the year by snow. The normal means of traveling in and out of the region during the winter is over this frozen river. This is an ancient route called the Chadear, meaning ice sheet. Some hardy tourists brave the minus 30°C temperatures on a three-week guided trek up and down the frozen river. I have heard of young fit locals making the one-way trip in as little as two days. In mid-winter many school children and their teachers make the trip up the frozen river, taking perhaps five to seven days each way, to visit with their families before returning back down the river to continue with school.

Arriving in Chilling and knowing that the bus was not scheduled to arrive until the middle of the next afternoon, I sat down at the bus halt with the intention of hitchhiking. I waited for some four hours and not a single vehicle passed traveling in the direction I wanted to go.

There was a sign pointing up to a house on top of a knoll. It said, "Homestay." I picked up my pack and began the steep climb up the hill. It turned out that the woman who ran the homestay kept chickens. She made me three omelets in succession, all of which I wolfed down like a protein-starved cat.

Somewhat sated, I went outside the house, where an older woman was cracking apricot pits with a hammer. Ladakhi apricots are unique because the kernel can be opened to expose a delicious and protein rich fruit, similar in shape and taste to an almond. The woman offered me some to try. This fruit is tasty, if somewhat bitter. Like its cousin the wild almond it contains a quantity of cyanide. It is therefore not advisable to eat a whole bag of these things at once. The FDA once tested a bag of apricot kernel fruits imported from a nearby region in Pakistan and found that it contained twice as much cyanide than that required to kill a human.

In the morning I went back down to the road to attempt to hitchhike once more. Again there were no vehicles. The bus stop was located in front of a building that displayed signage that indicated that it was a restaurant of sorts. Although I knew that the restaurant was likely seasonal, I had a vague hope that someone would come and open and make me tea. An hour before noon, the bus, which was not scheduled to halt here on its way to Leh for two more hours, came by on its route to the end of the road upriver. About a dozen people, villagers returning from a shopping outing in Leh, stepped off the bus as their goods were unloaded from the roof. Everyone picked up as much of the unloaded supplies as they could carry and set off towards the steep trail that led to the main part of the village. The remaining goods, in wicker baskets and cardboard boxes, were left at the side of the road—to be picked up later, I presumed.

After most of the crowd had departed I noticed that an elderly woman was struggling to lift quite a large cardboard box. I thought that she could not possibly be planning to carry this box very far—certainly not up the steep trail. Perhaps she was the restaurant owner and was intending to merely carry the box to the back of the building where she might unlock a door and invite me in for tea. I went up to her, and holding out my arms, offered to take the box, which she handed to me. It was heavy. She smiled and pointed to the back of the building. Ah, tea, I thought.

When we got to the back off the building though, she pointed up the path. One hundred meters further on we arrived in front of the unoccupied medical station where I stopped, in the hope that this box would be delivered here, but now she pointed to the steep path that led up the hill. She had been walking at brisk pace and did not seem to slow down at all as we began up the switchbacks of the path. We soon passed a young Ladakhi man who had placed a box about the same size as mine on a boulder. He had clearly stopped to take a rest and was still breathing hard. Gasping for breath now myself, I continued to follow the old woman's relentless charge up the hill.

What was beginning to worry me now was the fact that I had left my backpack, containing the Nikon camera, all my warm weather clothes, and even my passport, sitting at the side of the road. It had never occurred to me when I had spontaneously offered to help the old woman that I would be separated by any significant amount of time or distance from my gear.

We came to a place where the incline eased to a broad sloping plateau. Here we carried on through a maze of paths, bypassing homes and cultivated fields. This seemed to be the main part of the village—where was the old woman's house though? When could I put this burden down and run back to my pack? I didn't feel like I could just dump the box now and tear off back to the road. I felt that I had undertaken a commitment, and since I had never in my own experience known a Ladakhi to break a commitment, I felt honor bound here to carry on with this one that I had made. Besides, I thought to myself, Ladakis, in general are very honorable; they are not thieves. But a part of my brain kept reminding me that you should never allow yourself to get separated from your stuff in the third world, especially when that stuff contained the bait of a Canadian passport, worth several times an average Indian's annual income on the black market—and I had left it all sitting in plain view at the side of the road!

When we finally entered a house, it was the very last house on the outskirts of the village. In addition, it was built on a site higher in elevation than any other house in Chilling. After passing through a foyer, we entered a room where a frail looking old man, covered in blankets, lay on a floor mat. I guessed that the woman was his caregiver as well as his spouse, and she had been away in Leh for a couple of days to get supplies. Here I finally got to put the box down and then the old woman shook my hand heartily. This was unusual, for although hand shaking is sometimes practiced by Ladakhis, it does not seem to be performed casually with strangers, the way we often do it in the West. It is my experience that it is usually reserved as a sign of sincere friendship or gratitude. Now the old woman gestured for me to sit down. And she offered to make me tea!

But I pointed at my watch, and with some waves and julays, bolted out the door and down the trail. I was soon lost however, in the maze of paths that ran among stonewalls that bordered the fields and homes. Every time I tried to follow a path that seemed to be heading in the direction I wanted to go, it would eventually wind off in a direction I did not want to go. I decided that I was wasting too much time so I climbed over one of the walls and began deadheading down the hill. I ran down through fields and then climbed over several of what, I believe, were intended to be snow leopard-proof fences—the principle material that was employed in their construction being the thorny branches of the sea buckthorn. After crossing these barriers, I came to a series of steep embankments that took me to the road. From here I ran about a half a kilometer, following the road upstream above the river, and around a bend, until I came to the bus halt. All the supplies that had been left at the side of the road were gone—and so was my pack.

Panting from the run, I bolted behind the building and up the path. At the foot of the hill I encountered another old woman who greeted me cheerfully. Actually, she looked so much like the first old woman, and was wearing the same identical traditional Ladakhi dress, that I wasn't even sure if it wasn't the same woman. It could well have been, since she could have taken a more direct route than me and not had to climb over any snow leopard fences. I was not concerned with figuring that out at the moment though, and instead gesticulated wildly pantomiming carrying a backpack, pushing my hands against invisible shoulder straps, and then waving my arms. The woman nodded, smiled broadly, and pointed up the steep trail. I took off before she even had time to drop her hand to her side, shouting a julay over my shoulder. This time I was panting even harder than the first time up the trail, and was soon approaching VO2 max. I was imagining what I would do to the fiend who had carried off my backpack after I caught up to him. Shake him violently? Shout at him? Punch him? In the back of my mind there was a voice, a very quite voice, pleading with me to calm down. Trying to tell me that this was simply a cultural misunderstanding; that someone was simply trying to help me carry my stuff up the hill with all the rest of the goods that had been left at the side of the road—and that someone had seen me help the old woman and now wanted to help me. Ladakhis all helped one another after all. I don't care, I shouted back at the soft voice. It's my stuff. MY STUFF! No one should touch my stuff. I would show him never to make that mistake again.

Then I came around a corner near the top of the hill and there was my pack. There was no one else around. I pulled open the top of the pack to make sure the passport and camera were there. They were. I sat down, still gasping for breath. My body was damp with sweat. Suddenly grateful that I had not caught up to whoever had carried the pack up here, I was ashamed of my anger now and knew how much greater my shame would have been if I had behaved violently toward someone who was merely trying to be helpful. I told you so, said the quiet voice. Next time listen to me. It's the Mahayana—the Great Vehicle. Get on board. And don't be an asshole.

The bus ride down the narrow road carved out of the rock along the walls of the Zanskar River canyon was spectacular and terrifying. Did I mention that I was a control freak about driving? Now I had no control over my fate at all while the bus swerved around blind corners, horn blaring, wheels passing at high speed within what seemed like inches of the void. At one point I hid my face in my hands, whimpering pathetically, while the bus bounced along with cheerful, bubbly songs in Ladakhi pouring out of the onboard sound system. I finally pulled myself together and noticed that most of the other people on the crowded bus were laughing and enjoying themselves; it occurred to me that some of them might have been laughing at me. I pulled out my camera and began to take photos of the other passengers while the speakers blared on with the effervescent music, and the bus continued its rollercoaster ride above the abyss.

ADRIAN, NOËLIE, AND NATHALIE
NOVEMBER 2009

I was back at the Oriental Guest House in Leh, carrying my breakfast omelet to a table in the outdoor garden. The Oriental, with the exception of the stupa and adjoining temple that are perched on the rocky ridge above the hotel, is one of the last buildings on the edge of the western outskirts of the city. It is a relatively quiet spot, away from the dust and noise of the main part of Leh. That morning, just before dawn, I had hiked up the steep stairway to the crest of the ridge above the hotel. The large monument there, called the Shanti Stupa, had still been under construction the first time I visited Leh in 1985. Although incorporating a considerable amount of Ladakhi volunteer labor, its building had been almost solely financed by the donations of Japanese Buddhists. I remembered asking some Japanese monks who were at that time involved in co-coordinating the construction, why they had undertaken this project so far from their homeland. They told me it was because they believed that Ladakh was sacred space, and they wanted to honor this place, and its people. Ladakh, they pointed out, was one of the earliest enclaves of Buddhism in the world, its teachings having been practiced here for centuries before they spread to Tibet.

After reaching the large platform that encircled the base of the stupa, I performed the series of poses called Surya Namaskara, the Salutation to the Sun. The first rays of dawn were just beginning to highlight the snowy east face of Stok Kangri. The platform was exposed on three sides to precipitous drops, and I had always loved the feeling of airiness and space this gave me when I came up here in the quite mornings to perform asanas and to meditate. I therefore felt that it was rather unfortunate when a wrought iron guard railing came to be installed around the perimeter of the platform in 2010.

I had timed myself on the climb from the road to the top of the stairs just below the main platform of the stupa that morning. It took me seven and a half minutes. This was a minute slower than I had done it two weeks ago. I was surprised. My expectation was that I should have been getting fitter and more acclimatized. The ascent should have been faster. I had lost weight too, which should have made me even quicker. What was going on?

I was used to getting stronger pretty well each day when going to the mountains. When I was in Ladakh two and a half decades ago, after spending several months at high altitude, I had felt, like—if I had wanted to—I would not have had to bother with doors—I could have just walked through walls. Now it seemed different. It was because I was older, I supposed. It seemed that on my hike that morning, although I did not feel greatly strained, my body would not let me push harder. The image of an engine governor came to mind, a device that prevented machinery from running faster than a set speed to prevent it from wearing out. I supposed that my body was protecting its reserves.

Even though Leh, at an elevation of 3600 meters (11,800 ft) was considerably lower than the high places I had been exploring in the last few weeks, it was still much higher than the near sea level elevation where I had made my home for years. Many travelers who fly directly to Leh from Delhi spend days in bed after arriving, incapacitated with debilitating altitude sickness. Some never recover and have to book flights back out to lower elevations.

Soon after I sat down and started digging into my omelet and toast, I heard a woman's voice. She addressed me with what I often found to be a charming mispronunciation of my name that was common with French speakers.

"Bonjour Head."

I looked up to see an attractive dark-haired woman in her mid-twenties. I knew that her name was Noëlie, that she was from Paris, and that she had been traveling around India and Southeast Asia for three years with her English boyfriend on his classic Royal Enfield motorcycle.

"Head, I wanted to tell you someting," she said somewhat solemnly. "I was walking dis morning and I saaaw…"she paused with feigned breathlessness, the corners of her full lips turning up ever so slightly, "…a snnooow-lee-oh-paard."

I reached up and punched her in the shoulder playfully. "You brat. Have you ordered breakfast? Sit down and join me."

She giggled and sat down across from me. "Yes, the petit dejuner is coming."

A few minutes later her boyfriend Adrian, a man in his early thirties, and another French woman, Nathalie, joined us at the table. Nathalie, despite her youth, I knew had been in India for some six years, working off and on for various NGOs.

Adrian told me that the three of them wanted to trek over the Ganda La and he asked me if I thought they could find the route there on their own. I offered to show them the way up to the pass as I was planning to leave for that area again the next day myself. This would be another opportunity for me to save cab fare to the trailhead by sharing.

The next morning we piled out the taxi at the trailhead at Jingchan. The night before I had told Adrian and Noëlie that I was not sure if I was going to come up to Yurutse with them to spend the night, as I wanted to explore a side valley and speak with locals I knew in Rumbak to hear if there had been any recent snow leopard sightings. I had told them that if I did not get up to Yurutse tonight that I would definitely be up there by early in the morning to show them the way to the pass.

It was in regards to this that Noëlie, who was standing next to Nathalie, asked me, "Headee, will you be sleeping with us tonight?"

I pretended to misunderstand her meaning. "Both of you?" I asked.

Adrian, who was standing with his back to us, while taking a whizz, piped in, "Yeah, Eddy. Do you think you can handle that?"

"I'm almost sixty, Adrian," I replied.

"Yeah, but you're fit," Adrian rejoined, zipping up his pants.

The women were blushing now.

"I'm sorry Noëlie, I couldn't resist," I offered.

Oh, that smile.

On the trail Adrian finally told me how he came by the money he used for him and Noëlie to live on and travel, having been reticent about this previously. Noëlie had told me that they were international thieves, and implied that they were really Nadine and Michel Vaujour, a well-known criminal couple. Nadine Vaujour had famously helped bust her husband out of jail several times, the last time by plucking him from the rooftop of a prison outside of Paris, with a helicopter that she had learned to fly for that purpose.

But the source of Adrian's funds will have to remain mysterious to the reader, because he prefers it not to be public knowledge. I can say that it turned out to be nothing illegal though. He said that he felt that he could be happy traveling for the rest of his life, and asked me if I thought that a life spent traveling could be a satisfying life. I said that I thought that it depended on who you were, what your purpose was, and sometimes, whom you were with. For all the solitary wandering that Adrian had done in his life, it had become apparent to me that who he had been with for the last three years was important to him. Noëlie, I knew, could be temperamental. And Adrian, it seemed, was always ready to be patient with her. Why did he do it? Well, he loved her, of course. But it could also have been because it gave him a purpose to his wanderings. It came out that he believed that Noëlie was a great artist, a writer. Perhaps he felt then that by being her guide through the world, he would contribute to the enduring legacy that she would create. She was a kind of Dante, and he…a sort of Beatrice, I suppose, leading the inspired wordsmith on a tour through the realms of heaven and hell. And if she was difficult sometimes, well then, artists were supposed to be temperamental, all the more so if they were French.

But even if Adrian returns to his solitary wandering some day, I believe that his seemingly less than purpose-driven life will continue to send out ripples. It's people like Adrian, not the Internet, who are the glue that has cemented the reality of the six degrees of separation. The validity of the idea that every individual in the world is connected to every other individual by less than six degrees of personal introduction is dependent on the existence of wide-roaming, often solitary, travelers. They are the ones who make the most distant connections—who bring the outliers into the web of greater humanity. Highlanders in New Guinea do not have Internet, but they have had Adrian as a houseguest. Most people in Ladakh do not have Internet but they do have guests from faraway places. And it is not just affluent Westerners who are the glue of the six degrees. Among the regular houseguests in my own home are two sisters, Tashi and Nangsal, aged 19 and 21, who grew up in a village in Nepal near the border with Tibet. The nearest road was a six-day walk from their village. They have both been around the world several times and are now attending our local university here on a scholarship. Go figure. Lucky. Smart. Driven. But mostly—willing to cut loose.

I arrived at Yurutse shortly before dusk. I had explored a side canyon that ran off the Rumbak gorge, and had visited acquaintances in Rumbak Village. There I had learned that a woman from the village had seen a snow leopard in the late afternoon near where the gorge joined the broader valley. Later I ran into an elderly Englishman outside the village, who with his guides was scanning the slopes for snow leopards using high-powered telescopes. He told me that he had been coming to this area for a number of years and that he had spotted a snow leopard once from a distance. I asked him what time of day he had seen the animal and he told me late afternoon. The big surprise I received when I arrived at Yurutse was the news that Rinchen, the young husband of the family there, had seen a snow leopard—also in the afternoon—right behind his house the day after I had left for the Markha valley. All I would have had to do, I thought to myself after hearing this, to fulfill my twenty-four-year quest, was to sleep in late here, and then when it was warm, go and sit on his rooftop porch in one of his comfortable lawn chairs and drink tea for the rest of the day. And watch snow leopards. Somehow I had always felt that my chances of seeing a snow leopard should be proportional to the amount of suffering I was willing to endure. That would seem fair. But perhaps that was not the case.

It was beginning to dawn on me that there was a pattern to these sightings; they all seemed to be in the afternoon. But snow leopards were supposed to be crepuscular. They were supposed to hunt at dawn and dusk. So what were they doing out on open slopes in the afternoon? I was mulling this over that evening while sitting in the kitchen watching the scrawny house-cat pushing its body up against the stove, desperately seeking warmth. Then I got it. Cats are heat seekers. On a cloudless day the snow leopards will leave cover during the warmest part of the day to go out and sun themselves. And they are more likely to be seen when they are seeking sun than when they are after prey as there will be less need for stealth.

Was I disappointed that I had not just stayed here and seen Shan? A little bit. But then the search would have ended. And in some ways I did not really want to see the snow leopard that way—while seated in a lawn chair on a porch. I wanted to meet her in her domain. Someday there would, I felt, be a right moment for that.

Adrian, Noëlie, and Nathalie had arrived at the house earlier in the day and we were now having dinner together seated on the floor mats in the kitchen.

"So, Eddy," Adrian began, "when do we get up in the morning?"

"We don't have to get up that early."

"But we want to do this early morning thing that you have been telling us about with you. Maybe we'll see snow leopards."

"There's no reason to get up super early."

"What! Are you getting soft Eddy?"

"Okay then, 4:30."

I could see Rinchen smile, the kind of smile that was the Ladakhi equivalent of rolling one's eyes.

After dinner we were served tea and I began to ask the seemingly reticent, and up to now, opaque, Nathalie, about herself. She was soon surprisingly forthcoming and told us about the demons that had driven her from her homeland to seek refuge in India, the place where so many Westerners had come to try to heal their souls.

Nathalie told us that anorexia had almost killed her. She had checked herself into a clinic, and had remained there for almost a year. She was not allowed to communicate with her mother during that time, as it was believed by her therapists that anorexia has its genesis in the mother–daughter relationship, and that the patterns of that relationship had to be broken for the patient to heal.

"Nathalie, it must have been difficult being cloistered from the world for that long," I offered, not knowing what else to say.

"Yes, I did not like it. But I did not want to die."

It seemed that Nathalie believed that going back to the relationships and previous lifestyle that she had known in France would kill her. She seemed to think that she had the choice of either living in an institution or living in exile in a far away place with a vastly different culture where the old patterns and habits could be broken. Working for the non-profits here had maybe helped her too. This was an age-old therapy—perhaps the best therapy—enabling others can help us climb out of our own dark caverns. And, in the course of discovering empathy, we can sometimes begin to discover our own efficacy. I looked at Nathalie. She was so young. She could not have been much more than twenty when she chose her exile.

The next morning Rinchen got up at 4:30 a.m. with us and made us tea, and breakfast. Once again he made pancakes in honor the guests. He had made chapattis the night before and now wrapped them up in aluminum foil in four bunches, one for each of us, for lunch.

We set off about an hour later and by the time of first light were at Ganda La high camp. Here we split up, as I was intending to explore a series of ridges to the north, while the three of them continued to climb the winding trail that led to the west and toward the Ganda La.

For the next two hours I made my way up the ridge, stopping frequently to scan the terrain. There was a large herd of blue sheep on an adjacent ridge; they were careful to keep themselves in the open, avoiding gullies and other potential predator hiding places. I frequently swung the binoculars back to the direction of the pass to monitor my friends' progress on the trail. I could see that they were moving slowly and taking frequent rest stops. They were young, but they were not athletes. About mid-morning I watched them reach the crest of the col and then disappear through the gateway of the pass.

A few days later, I was back in Leh and ill with a cold and fever. Now I knew why my body had been trying to hold back to protect its reserves. I lay shivering under the quilt in my unheated room. Even at the relatively lower altitude of Leh, night-time temperatures now were dropping well below freezing. The running water in the hotel had been shut off and the pipes drained for the winter. This was the common practice for almost all the hotels in the town, and relatively few were even still open this time of year. The only hotel that I had heard of that had hot and cold water to the rooms year around was the pricey Grand Dragon.

I had a kerosene heater brought up to my room that afternoon, even though that essentially doubled the price of the digs. The radiant heat that it put off made me feel somewhat better within a couple of hours, but because the room was uninsulated I had to stand quite close to the heater in order to receive its full benefit. With my back turned toward to the heater while soaking up its warmth, I did not realize that I was standing too close—not until the next day when Adrian asked me why the backs of my nylon pants were melted and fused.

That evening Adrian and Noëlie joined me at my table in the restaurant downstairs, even though I had tried to shoo them away for fear that they would catch my bug. They plied me with rum that they assured me was for medicinal purposes. The spirits made my head spin. It was only the second time that I had tasted alcohol during this visit to India, wanting to take a break from my almost daily habit of imbibing at home. At about 9:30 Adrian, who was also somewhat visibly affected by the rum, tried to convince me to join him, Noëlie, and Nathalie, and head out to a bar downtown. He told me we could all go on his motorcycle.

"Four people?" I asked. "Isn't that pushing it, even by Indian standards?"

"No, not at all," he replied. "Four people on a motor bike is good. No problem. A party."

I was definitely not up for going, given the way I was feeling. Although I tried to persuade the group to take a cab, they ended up, the three of them, bundled up against the cold, riding off on the motorcycle. I listened to the distinctive, low-throated sound of the Enfield receding into the darkness. Then I went back inside to escape the chill.

The next morning, despite still feeling shaky, I took a shared cab to take in the annual festival that was taking place that day at Thiksey Monastery. The event included colorful costumes and elaborate masks worn by the monks who performed a series of slow-motion dances to the rhythm of drums, cymbals, bells, and horns. The disguises the monks wore in the early stages of ritual dances represented a variety of deities and nature spirits, many of them with dark connotations and decorated with human skulls. The reoccurring theme was a reminder to the audience of the transient nature of all existence. This is a fundamental element of Buddhist thought—as it is for that matter, also of science. Near the end of the dance cycle, a series of much less grotesque figures with human-like masks appeared. These were the Bodhisattvas, the enlightened ones, who would lead us from ignorance, fear, and craving, to salvation.

The finale of the ceremony was an elaborate ritual centered around an ugly little doll made from what seemed like soft clay with some yak hair attached to its head. The doll lay bound with ropes and chains in a lidless triangular box while an elaborately costumed and masked lama made a series of ritual gestures over the doll with a variety of threatening-looking instruments. Then the lama impaled the doll with a series of jabs using a long spike driven by a hammer. He followed up this skewering by chopping up the doll into a sort of goo with a cleaver before dramatically severing the cord and breaking the chain. Then he held up the box containing the remnants of the doll, now symbolically liberated from the tortures of the mind and flesh, for the audience to witness.

Bound clay doll.

On my hike back down to the road to catch a bus after the ceremony, I stopped in a parking lot and fell into conversation with a young German couple traveling in a large and unusual vehicle. It turned out that this was a converted fire truck that they had worked on for two years in preparation for this trip. They gave me a tour of the amenities, of which they were proud, and which were impressive. This tour of Asia was a dream that they had worked long to fulfill, planning and saving even before they had purchased the truck. Then, before I parted with them, the man confessed to me that they were homesick and lonely. They had only been traveling for two months.

Not everyone is an Adrian or Noëlie. Or a Tashi or Nangsal. Not everyone is a traveler. Many people travel who do not really love it. Some do it because they think that it is good for them; that it will be enriching. That may well be true, but if they do not love traveling, they will not be much fun to travel with. Or perhaps even to have as guests. One friend admitted to me that, although he had spent two years traveling, he did not really enjoy it, but he had done it because he thought that it would make him more interesting to women. It is perhaps not too surprising that near the end of his journey he had his lights punched out by one of his hosts.

That is not to say that real traveling shouldn't be work. It should be. If you do not research the history, culture, mythology, and religion of the place you are going to, you will miss its depth and resonance. One of the great wonders of travel is to go to a place you have studied for years, and then compare it to the place you have carried in your mind.

Germans, of all cultures, are among the greatest of travelers; that is why coming to Asia always gives me a chance to brush up on my mother tongue. These two Germans though, with their fire truck, were perhaps a lesson in what the lamas at the ceremony were trying to tell us about the traps of desire and fulfillment. Careful what you wish for.

Riding on the crowded bus on the way back to Leh I found myself seated beside a Dutchman who appeared to be in his mid-thirties. We got into a conversation about the meaning of the various rituals and costumes that we had witnessed in the ceremonies at Thiksey that day. He asked me if I was a Buddhist.

"No," I replied, "I am not Buddhist. Student of the teachings of the Buddha, perhaps. But I would not call myself a Buddhist."

"What's the difference, really?" he asked.

"Well…" He was forcing me to think about this now. "Much as I admire the philosophy, I don't really like to associate myself with an ism."

"Yes, I used to be a great admirer of the philosophy myself. I would have called myself a Buddhist. But I became disillusioned with it."

"Why is that?" I asked.

"Well I believed that Buddhism was based on empirical principles. But it is not. It is not empirical or scientific at all."

"But why do you say that? The thing that I admire about Buddhism, at least in its pure form, is that it is empirical. The Buddha himself said, 'Test everything. Don't believe anyone else, including me. Test everything that I have told you for yourself.'"

"Yes, but Buddhists have these doctrines about things like Karma and reincarnation. Those things cannot be proven. So how can you say that Buddhism is empirical?"

"Those things shouldn't be doctrines. They should be ideas to be tested," I replied.

"That's absurd. How do you test Karma and reincarnation?"

"How long have you been in Ladakh?" I asked.

"Just over a month," he answered.

"And when will you return to the Netherlands?"

"Next week. And I see that you are changing the subject now to avoid my question, which you cannot answer."

"No, I'm not trying to avoid your question at all. Let me put this to you: when you return to Holland next week after spending more than a month here, if you're a sensitive person at all, and I believe you are, you will not be exactly same person as when you left. And who you will be when you return home, will be governed to a great extent by your thoughts and actions while you are here. Even this conversation that we are having now, and how we have it, will affect who each of us will become when we step off this bus and go our separate ways."

We sat in silence for a few moments and then the Dutchman ventured, "You are telling me that this is the meaning of Karma and reincarnation?"

"That's for you to decide," I replied.

"I never thought about it this way before."

"Well, people have a tendency to look for the otherworldly in Buddhism when much of it is just about looking in front of your nose."

"And why is it that you don't call yourself a Buddhist exactly?" he asked.

"I suppose that part of it is that my understanding of Buddhism is that one has to be one's own teacher. One's own master. No one can do the work for you. That's just another delusion. There's an old proverb that says if you meet the Buddha on the road, kill him. There are a lot of things that come under the label of Buddhism— superstitions, dogmas, rituals—a crazy hodgepodge. But in its purest form, I believe it to be a science of introspection. It's the practice of seeking. If I were to call myself a Buddhist, I'd feel like I would be embracing what others have found—or they say they have found. I'd have given up seeking. I'd have essentially then given up the actual practice of Buddhism…or at least, what it means to me."

The Dutchman shook his head. "That's completely crazy," he said, "but it almost makes sense."

After we stepped off the bus near the center of town, I began to thread my way through the narrow alleyways, a bandana pulled over my mouth and nose to offer some protection from the swirling dust. I passed by the butchers displaying their bloody wares, thankful that it was now well past the season for flies. I passed dried fruit, nut, and spice sellers in their traditional clothes and colorful hats, past chapatti bakers huddled by their ovens for warmth. Then there was the lane of curd makers—the only merchants in Ladakh allowed to give out plastic bags—in a place where they are otherwise banned. As I walked under flapping Buddhist flags and past rotating prayer wheels, horns blared, dogs barked, and from every direction of the town there came a collective hum. The planet turned. The wheel of life spun.

That evening I saw Adrian standing outside of his hotel room looking wistfully at the door.

"What's up Adi?"

"Noëlie's locked me out."

"What for?"

"I was suggesting to her that she should take a more active role in planning and packing and she had a fit and went on strike."

"Strike?"

"Yes, it's part of the French culture. Don't you read the news?"

"Of course. How long do her strikes last?"

"Usually a couple of hours. Or days. The longest was two months. That was in Cambodia."

"Two months?"

"Yeah, it was opportune actually. We got to watch the Pol Pot trials."

"Come and have some tea with me, Adi."

Two days later Adrian and Noëlie left on the motorcycle for Zanskar. They could have ended up trapped there for the winter. They almost were. A few years later they got married in Paris. They almost immediately got unmarried. Then Adrian went to Cairo just as Egypt was descending into anarchy. From one storm into another.

THE SCHOLAR
NOVEMBER 2009

I arrived in the village of Rumbak. I had been up high on the ridges that day and was thoroughly tired. As I was about to walk the last few hundred meters to the village the sun set behind the mountains; I felt the warmth almost instantly pulled from the air.

The cold pierced my clothes and sought my vitals like an icy blade. The change came so quickly it caught me unprepared—thinking that I was almost at the village I had not stopped to put on my down parka. This was a mistake that normally I religiously avoided, knowing that, in the mountains, once you lost any of your core temperature, especially when you were tired and the temperature was falling, it was very hard to get it back. Now, past mid-November, at this altitude, nightfall was a cold curtain that dropped suddenly and could quickly extinguish fragile warmth and consequently life in the unprepared.

Arriving in the village a few minutes later I decided to put on my parka anyway in case it took time to figure out where I was to stay. It wasn't like I could just walk into anyone's house in the village, even if I knew them, had stayed with them before, and they were my friends. Ladakhis are egalitarian, therefore it was always the village as a whole that would decide where I was to lodge—this decision was always based on whose turn it was to receive the revenue.

But just as I was beginning to pull the jacket out of my pack I felt a gentle hand on my arm. I looked up and saw it was my friend Padma, and I realized that we were standing in front of the house she shared with her husband and father.

"Come," she said.

A minute later she was serving me hot tea inside her home.

Later that night, in my room, while unpacking my kit, I came across the Catholic rosary my mother had given me before I left on this trip.

"Bring this back to me," she had said, holding back tears; she had once thought that my days of wandering alone in the Himalayas were long over.

I looked at the crucifix attached to the string of beads under the light of my headlamp and reflected on a conversation I had once had with a Chinese scholar. This man was extremely knowledgeable and wise. He not only knew all about Buddhism, Taoism, Vedanta, Confucianism, and Shinto, but he had also studied the writings of Christian theologians like St. Augustine and Thomas Aquinas, and those of Christian mystics like St. John of the Cross and St. Theresa. He was, in addition, well versed in German and French Existentialism, and had even written a thesis comparing the principles behind Emanuel Kant's Categorical Imperative with those found in the Analects of Confucius.

I told him that, although I was raised as a Catholic, I was disillusioned with Christianity.

"But why?" he asked.

"Well, look at the central symbol: a tortured man nailed to across. What kind of symbol is that?"

He looked me tenderly, as one would look at a stupid child who will require patience.

"But that is a beautiful symbol: the idea that God is willing to come to earth and to suffer with man. It is very close to the Mahayanan Buddhist idea of the Bodhisattva: an enlightened being who foregoes Nirvana to return to the world to save other sentient beings."

He let me think about this for a moment then added, "You know, in the East we have many transcendental ideas. In the West…you have few—but this is one. Hold on to it. Understand it. Cherish it."

Later that night, I awoke thirsty and groped around for the water bottle that should have been tucked under the quilt. It wasn't there. Turning on my headlamp, I saw that the bottle had rolled onto the floor. After picking it up and shaking it, I was relieved to hear some liquid sloshing around with the ice. It couldn't have been out there too long.

I didn't go back to sleep for several hours. I thought again about the avalanche. The edge I almost went over. The edge that I would inevitably go over—as we all would. It's always there. The void beckons. You don't have to be hanging over it by your fingertips on a rock face to know that. You just have to understand the fragility of your body.

I recalled walking out of the hospital, bruised black and blue, only a few hours after the avalanche. At home that night the pain was numbed by a combination of painkillers, alcohol, and spicy food. I told Helen and Didi that I would probably be up for a trip to the mountains with them the next day. It turned out that I was unable to get out of bed in the morning. But even lying there most of the day, flat on my back, every breath was sweet.

I had a friend who I grew up with, and as a young man he became as much of an overachiever as I was an underachiever. He was not adventurous though; he had his life mapped out. He studied hard, worked hard, made investments. One evening, when he was twenty-nine years old, he choked on a piece of cheese. His bimbo wife, who, had you asked her, likely would have guessed that a Heimlich maneuver was some kind of sex act, watched him die.

*If time held no knife…*would I be able to go into the mountains if it didn't? If I were immune to old age and disease what would I dare then? Would even eating solid food seem too dangerous? Acceptable risk would have a whole different meaning. Only the inevitability of death has freed me to lead a life of adventure. Risk takers, generally, are not unimaginative. They are often, on the contrary—psychopaths excepted—deeply philosophical.

Would the existential dread still come in the middle of the night if time held no knife? Would I come to realize that living forever would mean living forever alone? And without the sand clock running, wouldn't life become one dreamy day dissolving into another. Death stokes the quickening; it goads us to create, to love, to cherish.

There are some interesting phenomena surrounding the numerous accounts of so-called "near death" experiences. The kinds of experiences that are of real interest though seem to be just a little beyond near death. People who have close brushes with death are often severely traumatized and may suffer from a variety of post-traumatic stress disorders. People who actually seem to have died, however, are in a whole different category. These are people who have been, for a period of time, clinically dead and have the classical out of body experience, or have the experience of floating up through a tunnel, and many have even reported making a voluntary, but often reluctant, choice to return to their bodies, often out of concern for others whom they feel are dependent on them being alive.

The really interesting thing that has come out in studies done on these returnees is that they are no longer like the rest of us. Even many years after the experience, their characteristics of mind, not unheard of in an individual, but uncanny for a group, persist. They all seem to share an innate sense of well-being; none of them seem to be susceptible to depression. Additionally all of them seem to have completely lost any fear of death.

What sets this experience apart from almost any other profound experience I have ever had or heard about is that its consequences seem to persist through the rest of a lifetime. Most of us have had positive experiences, perhaps, for some, what might even be called mystical experiences. These events we can sometimes reference, from time to time, as beacons in our lives. The step beyond death experience, for lack of a better term, seems to be much more than that; the transformative nature of this experience seems to persist from day to day and even to every moment of every day. The brain waves of these individuals, even at sleep, are quite different than those of any random group; here again there seem to be no signs of any of the brain wave cycles associated with depression.

Most scientists who study the brain say that you will never know when you are dead. When your brain functions cease, that's it for you. The mind is only an illusion created by the brain they tell us, although this illusion of a separate mind or soul is one to which many of us, if not most, still innately cling. It is the clinging to this illusion, say the Buddhist sages, which is the cause of much of our unhappiness.

But what is really beyond the dark door? This is the question the youth in the Katha Upanishad pesters Yama, the God of Death, with. But sometimes the reincarnation belief appeals to me even less than the oblivion thesis. First of all, what kind of immortality is it where you can't even remember anything except when being "guided" by a quack? And second, I hated being a child so much that the whole idea of doing it again terrifies me. As a child I despised being under the arbitrary, and, I still feel to this day, capricious, control of others. Youth was a stumble through a fog of misconceptions and later life a struggle toward moments of clarity. I dread the thought of being a kid again and having to swim up so far once again from those depths. Children are born with so little software. Animals, on the other hand, come with so much of the innate intelligence of their species. A four-month-old human is completely helpless, not even able to crawl. A four-month-old kitten, on the other hand, can be playful companion with a sense of humor and even irony, and is a capable killing machine to boot.

Why can't we come back with at least a little residual wisdom? Why does it all have to be relearned every time? In Tibetan Buddhism it is believed that enlightened beings, or Bodhisattvas, return to us as teachers. They are called Tulkas. Once during a celebration in a Tibetan village I encountered a young child who carried himself with extraordinary self-composure for someone so young. He did not behave arrogantly, but with a seeming purpose to every gesture and move. Our eyes met and I knew at once he was a Tulka, which was confirmed when I asked some of the villagers. Did he acquire his demeanor from the expectations of his people, or from something innate? This is a question I have about the Dalai Lama himself. Expectations can crush or elevate. But from where does a person of such humility and wisdom as the Dalai Lama arise?

Many of our religious and political leaders, even in a democracy, are people who fit somewhere within the psychopathic spectrum. Many successful politicians and business leaders are risk takers who have preternatural abilities in reading human emotions and manipulating them. These are the people that we often choose to entrust our lives to. The cool-headed detachment of the psychopath, a characteristic in the spectrum, in a crisis can actually often do good. But what is the difference between the surgeon's ability to detach from emotion, in order to cut and repair a human body, and the axe murder's ability to not care about his victims at all? Sometimes we just don't know. People on the extreme end of the psychopathic spectrum are often such good actors, and so good at reading and mimicking human emotions, we often don't know. John W. Campbell's classic SF story, *Who Goes There*, is a masterful allegory of the psychopathic condition in the form of a shape-shifting alien, against which the humans have little defense. The extreme psychopath, who has no human empathy, is a kind of predator species that has co-evolved with humans and lives among us, and unfortunately often leads us to ruin.

From where does real wisdom arise then? From where do the Bodhisattvas come? And how can we know them, when whole nations are willing to follow their leaders into madness? Even some of the historical Dalai Lamas were not men of peace, but warmongering conquers. How do we know? I remember the eyes of that child that I saw in that village. Is he something special? Will I return to that village to see what kind of man that he becomes? Perhaps I will.

One of the most uplifting experiences of my life was attending the memorial service of Jim Haberl. Although he is perhaps remembered by some of the general public as the first Canadian to summit K2 and live to tell about it, this was by far not his major achievement. Jim was not only an accomplished mountaineer and guide, but he was an extraordinary teacher and mentor. I saw his transformative influence on many lives; he somehow made us, those who came in contact with him, feel a little bit taller, and often a lot surer of ourselves, and, almost always, made us in some way more capable. His brother said that he left the world with nothing undone. Jim never left anything undone; there were no unreturned calls, or letters, no friendships neglected. Who else among us could have such a thing said about them? His father said that we could only feel blessed to have him for as long as we did. He was thirty-nine years old when his avalanche took him on what was supposed to be a laid back ski tour in Alaska. Those whom the gods love…

Even as a young child I remember feeling a great sadness at the impermanence of things. Beginning at age eleven, I began to take sojourns in the sorts of places where those with uneasy spirits go: a Benedictine cloister, an Indian ashram, a Japanese Zen monastery. I have spent lots of time sitting cross-legged on cushions. I have spent months wandering and climbing, mostly alone, in the Himalayas. It has been during moments in the mountains where I have felt closest to an intimation, subtle, still distant, ineffable, of the flow of eternity.

The landscape in the Stok range of Ladakh and the ridge where I spent quite a bit of time looking for the Snow Leopard.

Leh in 1985.

A more recent photo taken in the main bazar in Leh. The old royal palace is in the background.

Ladakhi shepherds in 1985. The woman is eating tsampa. Although this picture was taken twenty-eight years before, my friend Tashi Gonbo, who grew up in the Markha valley, was recently able to identify all the people in the photo.

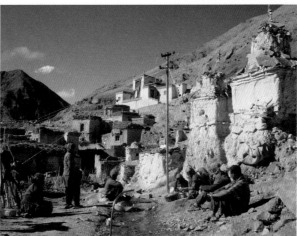

The watering place and social hub of Rumbak. This stream is the source of water for the entire village. There is no plumbing of any kind in the houses. Although there are electrical wires in the photo, in 2013 the only power, in addition to solar panels, still came from a communal generator, which runs only a few hours in the evening. A road was being pushed through from Leh until the villagers decided that they didn't want one and construction was halted.

Yurutse. One-family, one-house village at 4100 meters.

Ladakhi festivals
are reminders of
impermanence—but
also celebrations
of fleeting beauty.

Ladakhi women
in traditional garb
watch the festival
at Thiksey.

Monks costumed as
Bodhisattvas at the
Thiksey festival.

The punk monk.

Young monks having a philosophical debate in front of the entrance to main temple at Thiksey Monastery. Actually, I don't truthfully remember what was going on here. And I don't speak Ladakhi anyway. Maybe they were discussing football. But this picture has come to have significance for me.

Blowing horns at sunrise at Thiksey before morning puja.

After weeks of painstaking work, a sand Mandala is destroyed to symbolize the impermanence of all things.

Spinning wool in Chilling village.

The otherworldly landscape of the raised seabed that forms Ladakh. Photo by Helen Habgood.

Padma in her kitchen.

The monk Stanzin.

The shepherd at Nimaling high pasture. He is carrying a spindle for wool, which some Ladakhis spin throughout the day as they walk. Photo by Helen Habgood.

Helen comes
to Ladakh.

The snow leopards.

Telephoto shot
of the mom.

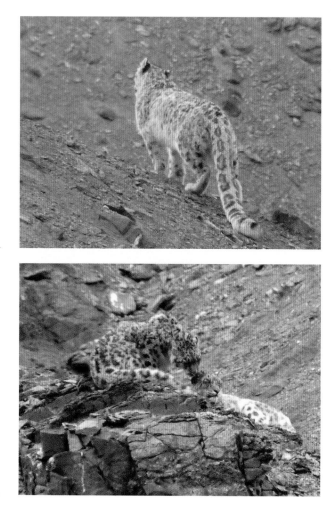

The amazing tail.

Family affection.

More pictures can be viewed at www.chasingthephantom.com.

THE HUNT
NOVEMBER 2009

I was back on the ridge above Yurutse. Hoping that the cat that Rinchen had seen was still in the area, I had spent the last few days coming up here. A few days before, Padma's father in Rumbak had told me that he believed that there was a female snow leopard with two cubs that had a den on this ridge.

Five or so centimeters of fresh snow had fallen up here where I was working my way over a section of rock on the ridge crest. It was like climbing a slippery stegosaurus spine. Aware that I was alone, in winter conditions, at 4700 meters (15,400 ft), I was at the point of making the decision to back off exploring further along the ridge when I spotted tracks in the snow at the head of a gully about 6 meters below me. I was convinced that they were more blue sheep tracks, which I had seen in abundance that day. I resolved to climb down and investigate the tracks anyway before turning around and heading back up the ridge to less treacherous terrain. But when I reached the tracks I realized that that they were fresh cat prints. Judging from the long distance between the indentations in the snow the animal was running and clearly accelerating down the gully. It had been running from something. But what…?

The answer to that question was suddenly clear and I began to lope and glissade down the gully and then traverse across the snow slope while following the tracks. The prints led back up toward the top of the ridge and then traversed parallel to the descending crest through blocky snow covered boulders. Climbing this jumble and paying attention to the placement of my hands and feet while looking for the tracks in the irregular terrain left little opportunity look up and scan for the animal that I was tracking. In the excitement of being this close to the elusive cat there was now no longer any question about continuing the pursuit in this exposed terrain, but I remained aware of the consequences of a single slip. The cat seemed aware of my limitations, she likely knew that she was a much more agile creature than me and was using that to her advantage as she led me across tougher and even more exposed features on the ridge.

The tracks ended at the base of a short head wall that the cat seemed to have levitated up. There were a few shallow ledges on the wall where it seemed the snow had been disturbed. I could climb this, I thought, but it would be time consuming, as I would have to be cautious. Since the leopard seemed to now be heading for the crest of the ridge, I decided to duck around onto a ramp system to the left, which would bring me onto an interception route with the animal's path, I thought, by an easier route.

But when I reached the ridge crest, I found no tracks. I scanned around but could see no sign. Where had she gone? Since I had been following the tracks along the descending ridgeline, I was now right at the boundary of the snow line. Below me, the ridgeline rounded off as well, and the jumble of boulders ended giving way too much easier terrain that even a clumsy biped like me could have descended at a run. I knew now that the more time I spent here pondering and looking around the further distance the cat was putting between us. I decided that the animal had somehow made to the snowless ground only a short distance away and was now bonding down one of the slopes below the knoll about 500 meters beneath me beyond which I could not see. I climbed down the last bit of the stegosaurus spine and began to run down the easier terrain.

When I reached the crest of the knoll, I pulled out the binoculars and began to scan the slopes below, looking for the slightest movement. After several minutes of looking I saw no sign of my quarry. Where had she gone? I looked back up the ridge. Had she ducked around the other side of the ridge and began to climb again? I had scanned for tracks there and did not see any. Did the snow leopard have the canniness to know when to leave tracks, and when not? Could she have made a long bound to make her trail disappear? It would make sense that if the animal was a mother with cubs that she would not leave the ridge where their den was likely located. Had she led me down the ridge to lead me away from the den, and then doubled back on the other side of the ridge? It looked that way. I had been deked out.

There are a couple of things about snow leopards and their strategies for evading humans that I know now that I did not know then. The first is that, with the exception of the kind of bluff that I had fallen for here, they will go higher instead of lower. This is the opposite of what the blue sheep do in attempting to evade them when attacked. The second is that the snow leopards are the masters of difficult terrain and will choose it over easy terrain any time when being pursued. There is no one, or no thing, I was to learn, that can match them for speed and agility when climbing steep, rocky terrain.

If the snow leopard had dodged around to the other side of the ridge I should be able to find her tracks up there somewhere. The trouble was that it was now late afternoon and the cold curtain of night would be descending soon. I had dropped quite a bit of elevation down the ridge now, and if I were to climb back up I would have to climb a considerable way before there was a viable descent route to the valley. If I continued down the ridge however, it looked like I could find a much quicker route down to Rumbak. I decided to head down the ridge. Tomorrow I would come back and explore the ridge, I told myself; she would have to leave prints, and no matter how convoluted the trail they would eventually lead me to her den.

The next morning I awoke in Padma's home in Rumbak. Before dawn, I climbed up the stairway to the rooftop terrace. Stars were now beginning to show in the clearing sky and although the day would likely be clear and sunny, I could see that at least 15 centimeters of snow had fallen overnight. The previous day's spoor would be completely covered. If the snow leopard stayed in her den today, I would have no hope of finding her. She knew now that I was hunting her, and even though the only trophy that I wanted was a photo of her, she would undoubtedly follow the legendary evasiveness of her species.

Even if this leopard had not felt actually threatened by human beings, it seemed to me that she might relish the sport of eluding this one. I remembered the numerous pursuit games that more than one house-cat that had lived with me had invited me to join, and how much they seemed to enjoy these games. One thing that cats and at least a few humans can share is a sense of humor, and even some sort of sense of irony. Cats love to play pranks and I was beginning to wonder what short of joke this one was going to show me.

The sun was well up before I set out on the trail for Yurutse in the morning. I had been eschewing the predawn starts lately because of the extreme cold and because I had come around to the idea that the best time to catch a glimpse of a snow leopard is in the late afternoon. But today I was leaving much later than usual, perhaps somewhat despondent that the previous day's hot trail was now completely wiped out. The snow on the path was undisturbed except for a single set of tracks, headed uphill, which had been made earlier in the morning. About half way to Yurutse I encountered the source of the tracks in the form of a young monk, who, it turned out, was headed back down hill after performing a puja at the family shrine at Yurutse. The robe he was wearing seemed completely inadequate for the cold temperatures he must have encountered earlier this morning. His feet were shod in a pair of running shoes and his bare calves made direct contact with the snow at every step he took.

After we greeted each other I asked him if he was cold.

"No," he replied.

"Tummo?" I asked.

"Yes," he said with a grin.

"Ah."

When I reached Yurutse, I found that Yangchan was the only occupant of the one-house village. Rinchen and his wife had gone to Leh for a few days and the rest of the family were probably gone for the winter. I found the sixty-two-year-old woman on the roof terrace wielding a shovel and surrounded by large mounds of snow that she had already moved that morning. She was pretty well done clearing the roof when I arrived and took me downstairs to make me tea.

After tea I set off for the crest of the ridge again. There were numerous blue sheep tracks in the snow but no signs of cat prints. When I reached the crest of the ridge I could see through the binoculars that there was a herd of sheep just below the tumble of rocks that I thought might contain the leopard's lair. Maybe she was having lunch delivered to her doorstep today, I thought. I dropped down the slope of the ridge until I came to a knoll where it steepened sharply. Turning my body to face inward, I began to kick a step in the snow with the intention of climbing down the slope. On the first kick the face avalanched immediately. The slide went right down to a thin layer of ice on the frozen ground beneath the snow, and when I tried to kick a step in this I found it to be as hard as stone. The steep slope was smooth, and although I could probably slide down to the saddle below without serious injury, climbing back up here without an ice tool would be problematic. I thought about the ice axe that I had left in Leh.

I spent the rest of the day watching the ridge with my binoculars waiting for the leopard to jump out of concealment and get her meal. But I figured that this was unlikely now. The wind blowing down from the pass would have carried my scent and alerted her to my presence.

During the next two days it snowed more and avalanches came down frequently, several even across the trail between Rumbak and Yurutse. I still went up to the ridge but it was getting hard to break trail and avoid the danger of slides. On November 18 I made to the crest of the ridge for the last time in 2009. I sat there beneath the deep blue Himalayan sky and evaluated the options. The avi danger was getting high and if I were buried in one, there would be no one nearby to dig me out. My toes were cracked and bleeding from the long days in mountain boots. I had lost at least 6.5 kilograms. I was exhausted. I decided to quit the search for this season. On my way down on the trail from Yurutse to Rumbak in the late afternoon I saw that there were no other human tracks on the trail except for the ones I had made that morning. There were some animal tracks however. One set came from higher up, crossed my path and then went up again. I looked at them closely. There was a distinct print in the centre of the widest portion of one of the boot marks I had left that morning. It was the size that a large dog's paw would leave. I looked at it closely. It was very clear. There were no signs of the claw marks that a dog or wolf would leave. This animal had retractable claws. Here then was the prank. I smiled. This mark in the snow in the middle of my own boot print was a kiss off. But it was also an invitation. I turned to look up the slope.

"I'll be back," I said.

That evening I used the single sat phone in Rumbak to make a call to Leh. The village had only had this phone for a few months. Shortly after they first got the phone, I learned, a village elder had been badly injured in an accident and a call was made on the new phone. A military helicopter arrived promptly and took the injured man for treatment to the army hospital in Leh. The airtime rates for the use of the phone were cheap compared to what I was used to, and I concluded that the service must have been heavily subsidized by the Indian government. This was the government that had an army stationed in the territory equivalent in numbers to considerably more than half the permanent population—a situation that would normally be considered absurd overkill for an army of occupation even if faced with an extremely hostile population. But the Ladakhis were not hostile at all. Gifts in the form of infrastructure projects were being showered on them everywhere. This sat phone was somehow cheap enough that the parents in the village could afford to regularly call their kids who were attending a government-funded high school in Leh and living with relatives there. The Indian government considers Ladakh a very strategic area, and they do not want to have any of the problems with the populace that they have experienced for decades just over the Himalayas in the predominantly Muslim portion of Kashmir. I suspect that before they put any soldier on a plane for Ladakh they tell him, or her, "Be nice, be nice, be nice, or you will be in deep, deep, shit."

When I got hold of Dawa at the hotel on the phone, I asked him to send a taxi up toward Jingchan in the morning to pick me up. I stressed to him though to tell the driver not to attempt to drive more than half way up the 16-kilometer road as the villagers had told me that there was heavy snow above that level, and I did not want the car to get stuck.

In the morning I set off on the trail to Jingchan and then continued further on the road. On the way I encountered a motor cycle laden with two riders. The bike was skittering around in the heavy snow and I saw both riders tumble from the machine more than once while they were in my view. About an hour after I saw the bike disappear around a corner, it reappeared with a single rider; the passenger had evidently been dropped at the trailhead at Jingchan. But soon after the rider disappeared around another corner, I came upon him stopped and jumping repeatedly on the stalled machine's kick-starter in an attempt to get it going again. After a brief conversation I could tell that the rider was not very mechanically versed, and so I helped him pull out the spark plug with the aid of the small tool kit he carried. The plug was fouled, and after cleaning it up a bit I tested for a spark. There wasn't one. I checked all the electrical connections that I could find and tested for a spark again. Nada. There was nothing else that I could do. We replaced the plug and I left the rider futilely jumping up and down on the kick-start again.

After turning the next corner, I could see my taxi coming down the road in the distance. He was right on time. When he pulled up I could see that there was another occupant in the car in addition to the driver. This turned out to be a sort of assistant to the driver. As soon as the driver stopped the vehicle, he attempted, for the sake of experiment, to get it going again but only succeeded in getting one of the wheels spinning hopelessly in the snow.

The assistant pointed at the other rear wheel. "Not working," he said.

"That's because of the differential," I said.

"No, just loose, we fix," was the reply.

The two young men then got out a jack and raised car far enough so that most of the weight was off the wheel that hadn't spun. Then they both kicked at the suspended wheel furiously with their feet. They were pleased when, after lowering the car, it was once more able to move forward. I was a bit stunned trying to figure out what I had just witnessed and had to conclude that the spline shaft on that side must have been worn sufficiently so that the wheel was periodically disengaging from it and consequentially the whole drive mechanism. I could see when the car moved forward that the wheel had somewhat of a wobble.

Although Ladakh is a culture quite separate from the rest of India, one of the characteristics that Ladakhis do share with the mother country is the reluctance to fix stuff until it is completely inoperable. Obviously, by Indian standards, this vehicle was not at that point yet; all you needed to keep it going was a jack and an assistant to help you kick the wheel back on when it started to fall off.

I told the driver that there was a man stranded a way further down the road and that we should go pick him up. When we arrived at the scene, the motorcyclist was still jumping up and down on his machine, but with flagging strength and enthusiasm and now seemed just about ready quit this useless endeavor. At first the three young men tried to pick up the bike and fit it into the car's trunk. I could see that this was obviously not going to work, so when they gave up on that I figured we were ready to take off, and the motorcyclist was going to have to come back with a truck some other day to retrieve his machine. But then the assistant driver procured a nylon rope from somewhere in the car—a new plan had been devised—the motor cycle was going to be towed. I was a bit dubious of the efficacy and safety of this plan, but reminded myself that this was the Mahayana, the Great Vehicle, where no one, or their motor cycle, got left behind.

We set of with the rider perched on his machine and the towrope attached to the headset below the handlebars. The bike skittered wildly in the snow and the rider wiped out and went tumbling every few minutes or so. Fortunately he was landing in the soft snow and so was not injured, but he seemed to be getting exhausted and very cold. As he was picking himself up from the last fall, his fourth, the assistant began to speak to the driver loudly in Ladakhi while climbing out of the car. This is the end of this craziness then, I thought to myself. But no, that was not the case at all; apparently the assistant had decided that the rider was having way too much fun out here and wanted to have a try. So the motor cycle owner climbed into the car, glad to warm himself, while the assistant driver mounted the bike. Then we were off again. Several times during the journey down the snow-covered road I thought that the assistant would lose it as the bike snaked and banked, but he always managed to recover control. He just would not give up, no matter how much the bike bucked around. I watched him out the back window; he must have been freezing out there with no hat and without gloves, I thought. But he gave no sign of it. For the whole ride, he wore a huge, ear-to-ear, grin.

THE PARIKSHIT PALACE
NOVEMBER 2009

It was now late November, and Leh was a cold place. I was sick again and shivered with fever chills. Consequentially for the last two nights before my flight, I stayed at the luxurious Grand Dragon, the only place in Leh that still had real hot showers at this time of year. It was certainly a treat. I would normally never stay here, not just because of the high price, but also because of the clouds of dust near the center of town where the hotel was located, which would have set off my allergies. But now with all the snow on the ground that was not an issue.

I had a bit of trouble locating the Grand Dragon. I kept asking locals for directions, and it was perhaps because of my feverish condition that I kept misunderstanding and wandering in circles. After and hour I found myself standing in the snow at the spot that I started at—feeling no closer to my goal and, in my vulnerable condition, cold and exhausted. A middle-aged Kashmiri was eyeing me while standing in the doorway of his shop. I was waiting for the pitch. He was surely going to invite me into his shop to get warm and then sell me stuff. I was practically the only tourist left in Leh and he was almost the only Kashmiri to keep his shop open here at this time of year. He must be really hungry, I thought to myself.

"What are you looking for?" he asked.

"The Grand Dragon," I replied wearily.

He began to give directions but must have seen my eyes glaze over because he stopped suddenly in mid-sentence and turned to lock up his shop.

"Come, I will show you," he said, turning back toward me and then striding off down the road.

I followed him knowing that it was one of the techniques of sales to make the client feel indebted. After guiding me to the hotel he would surely try to bring me back to his shop and sell me stuff. Feeling that I was just too sick and weary to deal with a Kashmiri sales pitch right then, I decided that when we reached the destination I would just hand him a hundred-rupee note and then walk off. End of relationship. Service paid for. I fumbled in my pocket to have the note ready.

"There," he said as we came to a halt and he pointed at a building, "the Grand Dragon."

I reached into my pocket, but before I could pull out the note he nodded to me and then turned and walked off briskly in the direction of his shop.

I pulled my hand out of my pocket without the note. "Thank you," I shouted. He kept walking away. So quick to judge I had been. I felt suddenly small.

It was minus 20°C at the airport the morning I left Leh. When I stepped off the plane in Delhi one a half hours later the temperature there was already climbing toward its afternoon high of plus 32°C. Normally, I hate the climate and the pollution of Delhi, but now, at least for the first few hours after arriving, the warmth was a balm.

I checked into a hotel in the Karol Bagh section of Delhi, which is a popular shopping area for locals. Outside my window I watched a fourth-story addition being added to a building. The bricklayers were working skillfully, but the construction materials consisted solely of bricks and mortar. There was no sign of any rebar or any other kind of reinforcement. Did I mention that India is being subducted under Asia? When even a medium-sized earthquake inevitably shakes this city, construction methods like this will cause many casualties. In 1993 an earthquake measuring 6.4 on the Richter scale struck the Latur district in southwestern India and killed 30,000 people. The next year an earthquake measuring slightly higher on the Richter scale struck Los Angeles, a much more densely populated area than the devastated district in India, and twenty people were killed. Falling bricks killed many of the people in the Latur earthquake in the early hours of the morning as they slept. Ironically the poorest people there, who lived in straw huts, were largely unscathed. So much for the three little pigs' school of engineering.

On another subsequent visit to Delhi I would come to stay in a hotel called the Parikshit Palace. This appellation seemed odd, because as I said before if there is one English word that Indians understand and use, it is the Anglo expletive for fecal matter. Soon after checking in to this place I went to take a shower in my room. When I finished I drew back the curtain to find that the entire bathroom was flooded. As I stepped into the bedroom, which was fortunately dammed off with a substantial floor sill, and began to dry myself, I noticed that the flood was slowly draining away— undoubtedly through the floor and onto the ceiling of the room below. I called the lobby and after a time a couple off young men showed up with a bucket and mop.

"Do you want me to change rooms so that you can get a plumber to fix this," I asked.

"No, only small leak," one of the young men replied as he began mopping.

"But it needs to be fixed or it will affect the ceiling of the room below." I said.

"No, is no problem," he came back.

"But it will cause mold," I ventured.

"No mold. No problem."

Sure enough, when I checked in the same hotel some two weeks later, preferring to face the devil I knew, I suppose, having encountered much worse in India, I happened to get the very same room. And when I took a shower, the floor flooded again. This time I did not bother to call anyone.

I recently looked up the hotel on a popular travel info website. There was only one review. It was in Italian and entitled, "Un Disastro Totale." First time to India, I guess.

But the Parikshit Palace is a kind of microcosm of greater India, a place where so many problems, large or small, are ignored. Much has been written about how India will be the world's economic superpower in a few decades time. These writers must be observing an India in some parallel universe. Their view may come about because the depth of corruption and inefficiency in the country is simply unfathomable to them. There have been suggestions that India could surpass China or the US in industrial output in a few decades. But what it would take for India's infrastructure to merely catch up to China, even if the latter stood still for the next fifteen years, is hard for me to imagine. One just has to walk out into the street in pretty well any city or town in India and look at the disorderly tangle of electrical wiring overhead to catch a glimpse of one of the reasons why. This mess is part of an electrical grid system that fails regularly all over the country. Every viable business that wants to have a system of scheduled production must have back-up diesel-powered generators, or be hooked up to a private power station. The irregular flow of power for many industries in India greatly affects the quality and the price of the products they put out. This is one of the reasons that, outside of the garment industry, call centers, and software development outsourced by multinationals, India produces relatively few products that are competitive on the world market. Efficient transportation is also lagging in many realms, although the country is presently in the process of an ambitious and long-needed upgrade to the national highway system. The rail system, a legacy of the Raj, is well run, but its capacity, even being the largest in the world, is enormously strained.

Much the country's infrastructure is jury rigged together; it is a Rube Goldberg contraption, much of which would have to be torn down and rebuilt from scratch to work properly, and I fear that the country may be running out of time for that. The real crisis that India will face in the next decades is a water crisis. A great deal of the water for irrigation vital to agriculture comes from aquifers that are being wastefully depleted much faster than nature can replenish them. The water table throughout most of India has dropped drastically—even in just the last decade. A World Bank report estimates that 60 percent of the country's ground water blocks will be in critical condition by 2025. Add this problem to the decreasing water flow in the great northern rivers, like the Indus and the Ganges, due to the shrinking glaciers in the Himalayas, and there is a recipe for disaster that could lead to mass starvation. Already in Delhi, where it is estimated that 40 percent of the water pumped into the city is lost through leaky pipes, there are fights over water every day. And unfortunately India's largest export, at least indirectly, continues to be water, mainly in the form of cotton textiles and rice—both produced from highly water-intensive agriculture.

India is not the only country that will face a water crisis in the coming years. The exploitation of peak water that a number of countries are arriving at now will make the concept of peak oil seem trivial in the decades, and perhaps in as little as a few years, to come. China is another country where the cracks are beginning to appear—quite literally. A number of cities in northern China are having ever-accelerating problems with cracking pavements due to the collapsing land as a result of the draining of aquifers. And as the drills go deeper and deeper to exploit a diminishing resource, more concentrated levels of arsenic and other toxic minerals are coming up with the precious water. Fresh waster scarcity will be a huge problem for much the world, but India, I believe, will be the canary in the mine.

Someday in the not distant future, even Americans might have second thoughts about pulling up water that has been stored in fossil aquifers since the last ice age to water their lawns and fill their swimming pools with this non-renewable resource. But then maybe they won't. Not until the hose runs dry. Then we may only wonder what they were thinking.

The vaunted demographics that are supposed to carry India into a future of unlimited prosperity are in reality its greatest impediment. While it is true that India has a growing middle class, its numbers are still relatively small in proportion to the vast majority of the population that lives at or near a subsistence level and therefore consumes resources at a per capita fraction of what populations in the first world are used to. About 65 percent of Indians earn less than 50 US cents per day, which translates to $2.00 a day when adjusted for purchasing power parity (PPP). In India, the second most populous country in the world, most people still do not have access to a toilet. I don't mean a flush toilet, but just a hole in the ground. The Indian government has announced that it will end poverty by 2020, which is defined by the World Bank as less than $1.25 per day after purchasing power adjustment. This is a noble aim, as about 30 percent of Indians still live below even this line, and one wishes that the fulfillment of this goal were possible within such a dysfunctional system. It is questionable, however, whether the majority of the population of one and a quarter billion could ever be raised to the standards of the middle class, under any system of government, without quickly straining the land's resources to the breaking point.

Behind the high wall of the Himalayas, Ladakh is, despite its harsh environment, somewhat of an island in this swelling ocean of overpopulation—with less than one hundredth of the population density of India as a whole. Although Ladakh has a proportionally smaller middle class than the rest of India, it also seems to have no extreme poverty. This is despite that fact that Ladakh has no high-tech industry, no large-scale manufacturing, and an even more unreliable power grid than most of the rest of the country. What Ladakh does have is a cohesive and relatively egalitarian social structure, higher social status for women compared to the rest of the country, and a seemingly continuous history of small families. This last tradition has been vital for the region's sustainability. Putting the sudden brakes on population growth, as China has done, albeit out of dire necessity, will skew demographics so that a smaller population of young people will end up taking care of many old people. Halting or reversing population growth suddenly has its own downside, although the consequences are not likely to be nearly as terrible as the alternative of unchecked growth.

India is by no means a country of stupid people. There is much highly intelligent writing in the Indian papers, and schools are churning out graduates well versed in high-tech skills. But it is somehow a country of stupid polices that foment in a culture of corruption at every level of government, from high politicians down to the lowliest traffic cop. I have witnessed a policeman being bought for the equivalent of what would have been less than 50 US cents. I heard a young Indian once ask an American if corruption was as prevalent in his country as it was in India. The American's answer was thoughtful, and perhaps only partly tongue in cheek.

"In America, corruption is largely confined to the highest corporate and political levels. It is not accessible to the common person. Here in India, corruption is much more accessible to the people, and consequently your system is more democratic."

India is indeed the world's largest democracy, and the pandering of power-hungry politicians to the narrow and short-term interests of an uneducated, and highly manipulated, rural population, which still makes up the majority of the country, is likely a contributor to the chaos, and an impediment to constructive long-term planning of infrastructure. The centralized planning of the autocratic government of China may just have a huge advantage in this regard.

Although India is the home of much profound spiritual and philosophical thought, it is also a place of numerous shameful, but appallingly common, practices; the infanticide of female babies and the forced marriages of young girls to older men, and their consequent rape, being among them. Indian women have a lot to be angry about.

Walking out of my hotel in Karol Bagh, I stepped into the chaos of Delhi. I was immediately accosted by young men hawking their outstanding and guaranteed services, which included shoe repair and ear cleaning. The shoe repair guys were the most persistent; one of them followed me for more than a city block, insisting that he could make my ratty sneakers like new. After I told him, "No, thank you," politely but affirmatively at least a dozen times, I finally stopped and turned to confront him.

"You don't understand, 'no thank you,' do you?" I said. "Do you understand, fuck off, then? FUCK OFF!" I shouted this last expletive.

The young man backed away and then turned and walked in the other direction. I felt satisfied that I had blown off some frustration, but at the same time was somewhat ashamed that I had been rude to someone who had so far fewer advantages in his life than me, and was just trying to survive.

After a few more blocks I entered one of the stations that serviced the newly opened metro line. I was impressed by the cleanliness and orderliness of the station after the chaos of the street outside. I could have almost believed that I was in Europe or Hong Kong. A large billboard featured a picture of a young couple in bed together, looking very pleased with themselves and each other, advertised a brand of flavored condoms. This was so different from the India that I had once known that I pulled out my camera with the intention of taking a picture. I was immediately stopped though by a security guard who told me that this was, "not allowed."

Boarding one of the spiffy transit cars, which had been constructed by Bombardier, an international corporation with its origins and corporate headquarters in Canada, I soon arrived at the station near Connaught Place. This was the centerpiece of the city, the location of a variety of exclusive shops featuring international brands, and the business headquarters of a number of larger Indian firms. It was also the location of the prestigious American Express office, traditionally situated in the most high-end commercial part of every major city in the world.

But what I found here during my first visit to this place in twenty years truly surprised me. The facades of almost all the buildings, arranged in concentric circles and originally constructed in the early 1930s, were crumbling everywhere I looked. I concluded that this was likely due to the extreme air pollution, which was eating at the concrete and stone of the city as well as its inhabitant's lungs and hearts. There was now a frenzy of construction activity down here to try and repair this mess before the advent of the Commonwealth Games, which the city was hosting in less than a year's time. But what shocked me was that the entire center of the circle, previously a grassy park, with approximately the area of a football field, was now occupied by a shantytown of construction workers and their families. Most workers on large projects in India are generally paid so poorly that they cannot possibly afford rents in a city and consequently live in shanties. But this scene here was astounding. There were shacks only a few yards from the American Express office, in an area that apparently has the fourth most expensive office space in the world. I saw a boy trying to modestly wash his body by a water faucet while keeping himself wrapped in a towel while hundreds of people walked by. I watched young women dressed in colorful saris carrying tubs of sand and concrete on their heads. There were young children playing in the middle of this construction site, and slightly older children working in it. The whole thing was the consequence of decades of neglect and a lack of preventive maintenance that is one of the unfortunate hallmarks of the mindset of greater India. And now there was a mad dash here to try to repair the decay of years before a flood of visitors and media came to see it. I felt that I was gawking at India with its pants down, and it was not a pretty sight. At the very least the government, which can afford to maintain a standing army of 1.3 million troops as well as equipping another two million plus reservists, could have provided trailers with rooms, dorms, and sanitary facilities for these workers and their families— and a schoolhouse trailer for the children. It may be though that in the world's largest democracy, itinerant construction workers are unlikely to get chance to vote, and are therefore of little consequence to the politicians. Disgraces like the Connaught Place shantytown therefore need to be held up to the rulers by the national and international media.

India is a country of much dysfunction. Some Western visitors find it hard to love India; those that do, though, love her deeply no matter how much they hate so many things about her, and no matter how many harsh words they write about her. Some of us are, at heart, forever smitten by her. I loved India even as a child, long before I ever went there. India is, after all, the source of the world's profoundest ideas.

Indian philosophers and, later, mathematicians were the first to realize the value of emptiness, of nothingness. We take the application of this idea for granted now without realizing that it came from a deep philosophical concept. It was represented long ago in India by Shiva's forward-facing open palm. Its application in mathematics is the zero, which the Arabs are sometimes mistakenly credited with inventing. It did come to Europe by way of Arabia, but was conceived in India. By the fifth century AD Indian mathematicians had taken the concept of void, or emptiness, represented by the Sanskrit word, Sunya, and devised a symbol for it to use in their number system and calculations. This single concept has shaped our world profoundly. Imagine doing rocket science with Roman numerals. Our modern technology, computers, GPS, what have you, could not exist without the applied concept of emptiness.

This is by far not the only deep idea that India has given us. The origins of the science of yoga are hidden in the far past, but ever since the sage Pantanjali wrote down his sutras over 2000 years ago, we have had a document that is a key guide for the understanding of the human mind and emotions. Buddhism, which in the last decades has come to have great influence in the West, had its origin in India, and is itself, to a great extent, an amalgam of older Indian philosophies.

I gave my daughter an Indian middle name, Devi, which means goddess—or Goddess. A *devi* can be a sort of female angel, but Devi, Goddess, is the female aspect of the immanent divineness within all being, all existence, and even emptiness—from which all creation springs forth.

RISHIKESH
NOVEMBER 2009

I arrived in Rishikesh on November 24. This holy city, whose name means "place of the sages," is located on the upper Ganges where the foothills of the Himalayas rise abruptly from the northern Indian plain. It had changed a great deal since my last visit twenty years ago. What I remembered as the serene city of ashrams was now the city of noisy motorbikes. The enclave known as Laxman Jhula is separated from the main part of the city by the Ganges, and connected to it by two pedestrian bridges. During my last visit there was only one hotel on that north side of the river, in addition to a number of ashrams. Now there were numerous hotels there as well as more ashrams.

Rishikesh first came to world attention in 1968 when the Beatles came to visit their guru, the Maharishi Mahesh Yogi, official sage to a number of Hollywood stars, and the founder of the Transcendental Meditation movement. During the famous Beatles retreat here, Ringo Starr and his wife were the first to bail from the Maharishi's ashram after only ten days. Lennon and Harrison lasted for almost two months, but then apparently left somewhat disillusioned, in part, it seems, because of the guru's sexual impropriety. Lennon later recounted in a *Rolling Stone* interview that when his spiritual master asked why he was leaving, he replied, "Well, if you're so cosmic, you'll know why." He later wrote a song called "Sexy Sadie" that mocked his former guru. Lennon originally titled the song, which is on *The White Album*, "Maharishi," but Harrison persuaded him to change it.

When I was a teen I had friends who preached the Maharishi's Transcendental Meditation (TM) with evangelical fervor, and some of us were frequently admonished by his enthused new followers for our drug and alcohol use. Ironically the ringleader of this local chapter of the worldwide cult was the same person who had once sold me my first tab of LSD.

A hard core of us imbibers, skeptics, potheads, and even some who practiced meditation without screaming banners, soon formed a counter cult to TM. It was based on the over-consumption of cheap red wine; the return to the world of which, after residing briefly in the gut, was declared to precipitate cosmic consciousness. In the course of all-night house parties, as soon as someone was heard retching in the backyard, we would rush out and congratulate them, welcome them to the initiated, and shower them with generous libations of the sacramental liquid. The originator of this mock cult was the same person who had given me one of my first books on yoga, at age fifteen. He was only a few months older than me but his inquiring mind and intolerance of anything that smacked of pretense made him an interesting friend, and someone who set me on the road to many of my own inquiries.

In retrospect, the point of our mock cult, if there was one, is that so many roads lead simply to escapism, whether that escape comes from reaching the bottom of a wine bottle or gazing long at your navel. This is not to denigrate the practice of meditation, which is the method of liberating the mind from its ceaseless, and sometimes pernicious, churning. Meditation can be the vital rest stop on the road of thoughts; it is the temporary letting go of all thinking, even critical thinking. But don't you have to learn critical thinking before you can let go of it? There are no answers without questions. Maybe not even without the right questions.

Method acting is a good example of letting go at the right time while practicing an art. A truly great method actor, like Dustin Hoffman or Daniel Day-Lewis, will get so far into the character he is portraying that he will become that character. He will forget that he is on a set. He will forget about the script. But he has to learn the script before he can forget it.

This may be the essence of attainment in all art, sports—whether flying a helicopter, skiing, making a splatter painting, meditation, whatever. If you never turn your mind off and let go, you will never get to the "zone." If you turn off your mind without ever engaging it though, then you may just be a fool. Putting on a pair of skis for the first time and pushing off onto a 40-degree icy slope with obstacles below will likely get you seriously injured or killed, no matter how much you empty your mind. But if you have been consciously practicing and thinking about steep skiing technique for years, then you can do this without hurting yourself, but likely— only—if you do have emptiness of mind. Now is the time to not think about technique; you have learned all that. Trust your body; you have trained it. Focus your mind, but without thought. This is the dynamic meditation achieved in a long-practiced sport or art.

But will the mindless repetition of a secret mantra given to you by a guru help you find higher consciousness? That may depend on the questions you have asked. Or the questions your guru has helped you ask. These are the places that your mind has been, and the passages that are behind you may determine were you are going. Simply having an empty mind is not the same as achieving emptiness of mind.

As yet though, I hadn't found any personal gurus who had helped me sharpen my questions; they just wanted to tell me stuff. A real teacher helps you discover, a poor teacher just fills you up with stuff. But people like to be stuffed; they don't like to pay to be hungry.

So here I was in Rishikesh, in the place that is often called the world capital of yoga. But yoga is so many different things to so many different people. It is one of the seven classical systems of Indian philosophy. It is a scientific system of psychology and introspection. It is a path of moral conduct. It is a system of enhancing awareness and a way of cultivating concentration, through meditation and other techniques. And yes, yoga also has an aspect that incorporates various body postures called asanas in order to promote body awareness and physical health, so that the mind can become calm and focused enough to engage in the other aspects of yoga.

Traditionally yoga consists of eight limbs, or practices, of which the practice of asanas is one. In the West it is predominantly the practice of this one feature that has become most associated with this ancient philosophy. To many people in North America, in fact, yoga has come to mean a stretch class. To quite few people, it is, as well, the practice of a fashion statement. Contemporary American yoga-chic has greatly enriched the executives and shareholders of the highly successful corporation, Lululemon, with its chain of yoga apparel stores. How is it that yoga, the art of detachment, and the seeking of the otherworldly, became so worldly—that the asanas that were formulated to strengthen the body so that the mind could sustain meditation, have become a tool to enhance vanity? Yoga is a Sanskrit word that means *to join*. It is derived from the same root word in the Indo-European ancestral tongue as the English word yoke. Yoga then means to join body, mind, and spirit. To some it means union with the all. With God. And what does Lululemon mean? I won't go there.

Here in Rishikesh there are also a number of successful gurus cum marketers, some of whom live in lavish homes and are chauffeured in fancy cars. Most of those here that are dressed as holy men though are wandering sadhus, homeless and dirt poor.

Sadhus come in many forms. Some are retired businesspeople or civil servants, who have finished their worldly careers, have raised their families, and have now forsaken possessions, to wander and seek spiritual wisdom and enlightenment. These are somewhat more rare these days, but they still exist. Another much larger group just want to escape the craziness of the Indian system, especially the confines of the caste system, and choose to become what we could consider hash-smoking, hippie dropouts; but in India they have an occupation that is quite respected. Another group dresses up lavishly and makes a living, sometimes quite a good one, hustling tourists and posing for photos. This last type is actually rare in Rishikesh, and I have never been accosted by aggressive holy men there, as I have in some other places. The real hustle in Rishikesh seems to take place in the higher echelons.

On my second day in Rishikesh, I overheard a conversation between a pair of young Western women.

"Swami came up to me today and spoke to me," said one.

"Oh, what did he say?" the other responded.

"He said, 'I see you coming back to Rishikesh many times. I will see you often in the future,'" she replied somewhat breathlessly.

"Oh, he has such insight and vision. You must feel blessed."

Yes, Swami does have insight, I thought to myself. He's not short on marketing skills either. This guru will likely help lighten this little gopi's burden of worldly earnings over the repeat visits he is priming her for. The lucky girl even seems like a good candidate to be chosen by her guru, in keeping with contemporary Indian tradition, for the privilege of presenting her yoni to her master's sacred lingam. He may tell her it is a special gift. I would call it being fucked both ways.

I stayed in the Hill Top Guest House, actually a very cheap hotel, which was only part of what made it, for me, the best hotel in Rishikesh. Located up river, and as the name implied, it is up on a hill, away from the noise and bustle of the town. It has a rooftop terrace with a small vegetarian restaurant. All restaurants in Rishikesh are vegetarian, as it is a holy city, where no meat or alcohol is consumed. The rooftop was a great place to watch the sunrise, and as it is my habit to rise before dawn, I was up there every day to watch it. I never did attend a formal yoga session in Rishikesh, in part because I couldn't imagine another setting that would have matched the rooftop, with the view of the sunrise, temples, river, and mountains. This was the perfect place to perform morning asanas in solitude, which being who I am, I often prefer for some things. And there was the cool air of the early morning up here. I have in the past ended up in stuffy yoga studios wishing I was outdoors—or at least that there were some open windows. The other reason that I never went to a yoga class in Rishikesh is that although I greatly enjoy the aura of this ancient sacred place, I am wary of its hype. I am sure that there are some great teachers in Rishikesh, but I guess that I was just afraid of encountering more disillusionment in the process of looking.

I found an exercise barbell on the rooftop, which I began to use to try to restore some of the muscle mass that I had lost in the nearly two months I had spent at high altitude. After breakfast at the German Bakery across the river, I would go for a hike in the hills, visiting villages accessible only by foot, or would hike up-river where there was virtually no habitation, and swim in the Ganges. These hills, if they stood in another part of the world where they were not dwarfed by the nearby Himalayas, would be called mountains.

By coincidence three of the small group of late-season tourists that I had met at the Oriental Guest house in Ladakh were staying at the Hill Top here. One of them, a young man named Ian, was another Brit who had purchased an Enfield in India and was touring the country with it. There was a Canadian couple staying here who worked in Jasper National Park in the summer, he on a fire watchtower and she as a ranger, and then spent the rest of the year in the Himalayas. I once wrote a fictional short story that featured a couple that worked at similar occupations in Jasper Park in the summer and then spent the rest of the year in the Himalayas. It was interesting to meet my characters in the flesh. The woman had gained a bit of weight since I had created her in the parallel universe of my mind, but otherwise they were pretty close. The weight gain may have been due to hash smoking. One night I saw her sitting cross-legged in the rooftop restaurant holding a spoon and bent over an enormous tower of Hello to the Queen. This is the name of the most decadent dessert on earth, made up of heaps of layers of chocolate cake, ice cream, banana, and gooey sauces. It is served all over the Indian subcontinent to stoned tourists.

Walking downstream near dusk one day I came across a group of about a hundred people seated on the sandy beach of the riverbank before a very fat, almost naked, man reclining on his side on a blanket and propped up with cushions. I couldn't help but be reminded of Jabba the Hutt in Star Wars. The large man was giving some kind of lecture in Hindi to the crowd, which was made up of Indians. I don't understand Hindi, so I couldn't understand what he was saying, but I had no trouble hearing it even from a distance as it was amplified by a sound system. His speech sounded pedantic, aloof, and condescending. Well this guru certainly hadn't succumbed to the vanity of his physical form, gotta give him that. As for his other appetites though…I guess I would just have trouble trusting anyone who looked like Jabba the Hutt.

The Diamond Cutter Sutra is so named because only a diamond is hard enough to cut another diamond—and only a mind can cut another mind—for good or ill. A good teacher can leave a legacy of polished gems, a bad one, a trail of fettered or even shattered minds. There have been many scandals involving spiritual teachers, both in the East and West in the last decades. Many, many young, vulnerable women have been severely damaged by their rapacious gurus.

One of the most accepted etymologies of the word *guru*, is "One who lifts the darkness." It was once a noble word, with a noble history. But for me, from what I have seen, read, and heard, it is a word that has been defiled, perhaps beyond hope of redemption. I personally would have serious misgivings of any teacher who would presently accept that title. In many cases "one who lifts skirts" might be a more suitable appellation for these guys.

And why is the guru business, and business is what it is in many cases, such a boys' game anyway? Just like investment banking and stock trading, it is largely a testosterone-driven sport, and so is the salesmanship of being a guru and collecting the all-important client base. Perhaps there are really holy men out there who can look into your inner self and understand you at first meeting, but psychopaths and sociopaths often have the uncanny ability to do that too. Since the spectrum of psychopathic behavior is many times more common among men than among women, maybe it's time we started to seek out more women as spiritual teachers. They are not likely to be led by their dicks either. The Dalai Lama recently threw a stone at the male hierarchal mold when he announced that he believed that the next Dalai Lama could be a woman.

I have seen gurus in India literally worshiped by their followers. I believe that this can be unhealthy for both the teachers as well as the students. If the teacher is perceived to have a god-like status, the burden of expectation could engender a neurosis or even a psychosis in the teacher. This is perhaps the reason behind the mad acts of the so-called "crazy wisdom" gurus. Drug and alcohol addiction is also not entirely uncommon among spiritual teachers who crack under the strain of living up to the expectation of something that they know they are not. Of course if the teacher is a psychopath then there is no problem for the teacher since psychopaths generally perceive themselves to be above other humans and are perfectly happy to be worshiped. Problem for the students though. There are, of course, exceptions; the Dalai Lama had tremendous expectations placed on him from a very early age; he not only lived up to all of them, but also managed to remain humble through all of it. I am sure that there are many other Tulkas who have managed to do this.

My mother-in-law, Ani Migme Chödrön, who has been a Buddhist nun for twenty-four years, advises her students not to fall for star power when looking for a teacher. This is good advice. The best sales people are not necessarily the best teachers, and thoroughly corrupt people sometimes have uncanny charisma and power over others. The master flim flam artist, Sai Baba (the second), once had the standing prime minister of India as a devotee, in addition to having a network of ashrams in 126 countries.

Personally, perhaps because I like to keep things simple, if I was shopping for a spiritual teacher one of my criteria might be to choose one who has the wisdom, like the great spiritual teacher Krishnamurti, not to accept the title of "guru." This method of shopping would have some advantages. For one thing I suspect that it is harder to lie about being humble than it is to lie about being fabulous.

There is an old Buddhist saying that goes, "If you meet the Buddha on the road, kill him." This simply means that ultimately each of us has to be our own master, our own guru. Most of us though, need some sort of roadmap, advice, and, most importantly, the fellowship of like-minded people on the way. But we shouldn't swallow bullshit just because we are lonely. There are teachers who tell their disciples that they can indulge in the habits that they preach against because they are special, or even that they are above earthly matters, so it does not matter how they behave. It's heartbreaking how many people fall for nonsense. Perhaps this is mob madness. Spouting wisdom is easy, living it is much harder. Every student in any field should always be asking the teacher, "Show me, show me, show me. Have the courage to move on if you are lied to. Listen deep down inside to your inner guru; she will never abandon you; she is always there.

I had been looking at the Royal Enfield that the owner of the Hill Top hotel had parked out in front of his building. He offered to rent it to me for a reasonable fee. I was tempted. My motor cycle skills were rusty though, and I would be driving on the other side of the road. I remembered how hard I had to concentrate while driving in the UK. Not to mention—this was India. I put myself in the saddle and tried out the controls.

"The front brake isn't working," I told the owner who was standing nearby.

"Oh, you never use the front brake. You just need a back brake," he replied.

"Yeah, I saw a couple of guys go off the road on a scooter a couple of days ago. I saw the rear wheel of the scooter lock up and put the bike into a skid. I guess that they didn't use their front brake either. Or they didn't have one. They were quite badly injured."

I got off the bike. "I'll think about it," I said.

That evening I heard that a young Brit, not Ian or Adrian, had lost control of his Enfield on the road just on the other side of the river. He had slammed headfirst into the front of a truck. He was dead. I stopped thinking about renting this Enfield.

On my last evening in Rishikesh, I went to pay my tab at the Hill Top restaurant. The two young men who cooked, served, and ran the place had provided me with excellent meals over the last five days. Since I was recovering from my weight loss in the high mountains I was eating about five meals a day, at least two of which were at the Hill Top. But that evening I got into a dispute with the boys over the bill. It went something like this.

"This bill can't be right. You must have made a mistake," I said to them.

"No mistake," one of them came back.

"No, it can't be right."

"Too much?"

"No, not too much, too little. I have been eating like a pig here for five days. You have charged me too little. This is only a little more than twenty dollars. It can't be right."

"No, it's right."

I insisted that the boys add up the tab again, which they did, and it came out the same again. So I paid the tab and added a 50 percent tip.

The next morning I left for the long trip home.

Part Two

THE RETURN
MAY 2010

The cabin lights in the plane were turned off. Helen was asleep beside me, as were most of the passengers, or at least they were trying to sleep in the economy class seats around us. Quite spontaneously I reached out and pulled up the blind covering the window beside me. I don't know what I expected to see; we were not even near any land, and it was dark—although the dawn that was chasing us, as we were flying west, must now be getting nearer. I saw that there was a faint reflective glow off the wing, and floating just above its tip there was the crescent moon next to the morning star, the planet Venus. It was mid-May, the same month, as the story goes, that the Buddha saw these two celestial bodies in this configuration, just before the dawn that brought not only the light, but his enlightenment. The crescent moon and the morning star are the ancient symbols of the goddess—she who shows the way. It was a nice omen. I closed the window shade and tried to sleep.

The morning of the next day we arrived in Leh. I was pleased to be able to bring Helen here with me. Over the years we had seldom had a chance to travel together, as one of us usually seemed to have a commitment to our respective businesses when the other was free. But now I was sort-of-retired, and Helen had managed to get a month away from her work commitments. Besides being pleased that I had my spouse and favorite companion in adventure along, I also figured that I had brought my best asset for finding the ghost cat. Helen, professional cartographer, amateur botanist, bird watcher, and all around keen observer of the world, was much better at finding stuff than me. It seemed she could always find things in our cupboards much quicker than me, even things I had put away there.

Helen is short and muscular, her hands rough and powerful, a climber's hands. Her favored headgear is a ball-cap and she wears no make-up. With a single, brief (minutes) exception, I have never seen her in a skirt or dress, and in her mid-fifties, her stomach is as flat as a granite sheet. Helen's mother is a Buddhist nun who lives in a monastery in Canada. But Helen is as down to earth as her mother and I are unworldly. She is the anchor that keeps me from floating off into the ether.

Every spring Helen travels almost right across Canada to visit her mom in Nova Scotia. The monastery is perched on an escarpment on the tip of Cape Breton Island. It is hauntingly beautiful place; I have visited there once. But there are no mountains, only hills, so Helen and I do sort of feel out of our element there. It's not that I don't appreciate the ocean; I worked on it as a seaman and beachcomber for years in my youth, but I have gotten used to having steep inclines around me where I live and mostly travel to—so that every day I have something to charge up, and get charged up by. Helen loves her mom and loves to visit her, but monastic life does not really suit her, to say the least. She is therefore fit to be tied every May or June when she returns from Nova Scotia, and I have to take her into the mountains right away for a few days to get her calmed down.

Helen's path of yoga is definitely Karma yoga, the yoga of action, of doing stuff. One of the few times I have seen her sitting on the back porch with a book in her hand on a sunny summer day, was when she had wiped out on her mountain bike that morning and had ice packs on her black and blue leg. One night Helen described her own Eightfold Path for me. It was the way, she told me, to escape the wheel of daily existence and reach a place of higher being. The next day, just before she was off to join her girlfriends in the Nevada desert for a climbing trip, I asked her to write this wisdom down for me. It goes like this:

Right Conditions
Right Route
Right Plan
Right Map
Right Companions
Right Attitude
Right Gear
Right Beer

Maybe it is because Helen is so well grounded that she doesn't need to torment herself looking for deeper meanings. Some evenings she spends time in her garden digging in the soil. I frequently entreat her to wear gloves when she is engaged in this activity, but she seems to love the feel of the dirt in her fingers. A writer, maybe it was John Fowles, once said that all art is a failure because no art could ever achieve perfection. A true artist could never be satisfied with his or her achievement because it would always fall short of the vision. The only way to nurture perfection, and be completely satisfied with the product, he said, was to be a gardener or a farmer because only nature could achieve perfection.

One day I was at home doing some improvements on the house we lived in at the time. It was our first house in Squamish and we had bought it primarily as an investment with the intention of reselling it. I'm not really one of those guys who gets a huge amount of pleasure out of working with my hands, even though I've been reasonably competent at it. My dopamine and serotonin satisfaction centers don't seem to work that way. Even when I worked as a sculptor, it was the conceptual part that I enjoyed most. But stuff needed to be done, and besides, Helen, I knew, like many women, could get turned on when seeing her guy in a tool-belt, fixing stuff. One of my projects that day was to install a lock on the patio door that would enable a secure opening for the cat to get in and out. I was in the process of drilling a hole in the aluminum frame of the door when the drill bit suddenly caught and stopped, momentarily transferring the motor's torque onto the doorframe. I heard a crack and saw a single hairline shoot across the pane of glass. Then there was another and another. The cracks kept propagating for about twenty seconds, and then a tiny piece of glass fell to the floor. It fell right out of the center of the pane where I could see there was a tiny hole. The rest of the glass was still in place, although it had fractured into at least a thousand pieces among a web of iridescent cracks. I waited for the whole thing to come crashing down. It didn't. I stood there stunned. It was beautiful.

A couple of days went by during which time I expected the glass to fall down at any moment, but it still didn't. On the third day I announced to Helen that I was going to try to preserve this extraordinary thing.

Helen was silent for a few seconds and then said, "Honey, I'm not sure if you understand what people are looking for when they shop for a house."

"Well I would think that they would appreciate special features that came with the house, like a special piece of accidental art."

Helen sort of sighed and then said, "Well, if you think so."

That day I went to work in my studio in Burnaby and at the end of the day loaded some supplies that I would need for the preservation project into the car. On the way home I drove by Murrin Park and saw that my favorite bouldering traverse was dry. Pining for a quick and strenuous workout after the long drive, and having my climbing shoes and chalk bag in the car, I figured another fifteen minutes would not make any difference if the lattice was now still standing near the end of the third day.

When I arrived at home I saw that the amazing glass structure was still together. I got my equipment out of the car. My plan was to first coat both sides of the glass with some quick curing artist's fixative applied from an aerosol can; this way I would not have to touch the delicate structure. After several coats of this I could move on to applying coats of epoxy with brush and roller. When I got inside the house, I laid out a drop-sheet in front of the glass. I dared not take a deep breath. I put on my respirator. Picking up the can of aerosol fixative, I aimed it. I swear that I was a second or so away from pushing the button when the whole thing came crashing down.

I stood there holding the can of fixative that was now pointed at the outdoors.

When Helen came home and I told her what had happened she said, "Well, Honey, maybe this is a lesson to teach you that you have to learn to embrace impermanence."

It is not often at all that Helen sounds like her mother, the Buddhist nun. I suspected that she was relieved that we were now going to get a new, and conventional, patio door.

As soon as we had dropped off our bags at the Oriental Guest House and had a quick tea, we climbed up to the Shanti Stupa. Helen and I are both addicted to exercise; we are like a pair of raptors, birds, who even when sort-of-tamed, need to be released from their tethers and allowed to fly each day, or otherwise they go into quick physical and mental decline. We joyously inhaled the cold, thin, dry air of the morning and the high desert on our climb up the stairs. Then we lay on our backs on the stone terrace below the Stupa and looked up at the impossibly blue Himalayan sky.

I have learned that I can make it to Leh from Vancouver in about thirty hours, if I make all the connections. If. This time we had missed all of them. There was a four-hour delay in Vancouver due to a bomb scare. Before we boarded the plane it was obvious that we were going to miss our connection in Hong Kong and subsequently our flight to Leh. Helen began to get a bit anxious.

Don't worry," I told her. "This isn't Air Canada—or, God forbid—United."

Sure enough Cathy Pacific rearranged all our flights including the one with the Indian Airline from Delhi to Leh. I'm not sure how they even knew about it. In addition they put us up in five star digs in Hong Kong and we got the day to tour the city, which Helen had never seen before. Then they had a representative meet us when we stepped off the plane in Delhi and drove us to another five star hotel and picked us up again before dawn for our flight to Leh. They paid for all our meals. And this treatment was for economy class tickets. We could have quite a different experience if we had traveled over the Atlantic instead of the Pacific, even though the distance and fares from Vancouver to Delhi are about the same either way. Suffice to say that all the airlines that are currently rated five star are based in Asia or the Middle East.

We were tired though, for the stay in the hotel in Delhi, nice as it was, lasted only a few hours before we had to catch the early morning flight to Leh. All the flights between Leh and Delhi take place in the early morning because the cooler the air the denser it is, and therefore the greater the saving on fuel for the big climb over the Himalayas, We would try to stay awake for as long as possible the day of arrival in Leh to adjust to the time difference, but by mid-afternoon, drained by the traveling, the jet lag, and the thin air, we both passed out on the bed.

The next morning we went to Thiksey Monastery. Just before I left Leh the previous fall, Punzo, the manageress of the Oriental, had advised me on buying insurance there to better my chances of finding the snow leopard.

She had told me, leaning closer, and lowering her voice, "I don't know if you believe in this…but…um…if you want to see Shan, you should…you might…um…go to the Gompa and make a puja."

Several more Ladakhis, including my regular driver, Lobsang, had made the same suggestion. So here we were, in front of the enormous statue of the Maitreya Buddha, the future Buddha to come, placing some rupee notes on the altar and lighting incense sticks and butter candles.

The next day we went into the mountains. It was a day trip as we were in need of acclimatization. I took Helen to the site of a ruin on a spectacular perch above a desolate canyon about a two-hour hike from the town of Stok. I had previously visited this ruin, quite an extensive complex running the length of a narrow ridge. Once again I wondered at the work of hauling, stacking, and mortaring together the many thousands of stones that made up the structure. I wondered also why it was built here as I looked at the infertile expanse all around. It was not on a trade route either; there was a much easier way to get into the Rumbak valley than the high pass, the Stok La at the end of this canyon, and all the drainages that led down to this riverbed were inhospitable and uninhabited. I could only conclude that this construction was intended as a last redoubt, in warring times past, for the people of Stok.

I had hiked up this canyon the previous fall with a young mountaineer, Andy, who was doing volunteer work in Leh. Our ostensible purpose on that day hike from Stok was to wander up the valley and keep a sharp eye out for snow leopards. But then we got competitive, as guys will do, and charged all the way up to the old Stok Kangri base camp at over 5000 meters (16,400 ft). By the time we got back down to this canyon we were in the dark, in a storm, with snowflakes swirling in the light of our headlamps.

When I learned that Andy, who had the partial disguise of a thick beard, was only twenty-four, I was stoked that I had been able to keep up with him. And I was pleased that Helen and I had been able to come up here today with without difficulty after so little acclimatization for the altitude. I was sixty years old now, and often felt like I could cheat the physical decline of aging. But whenever I lulled myself in to believing that, another part of me knew that I was in denial. Helen and I enjoyed our bodies, and each other's, so much, but we both knew that couldn't last forever. I remembered the time that I had broken my leg badly, and I was in a cast for six months. I hiked for miles on crutches every day, until, even with gloves on, my hands were blistered and bleeding. When I graduated to a walking cast, I cut enough of it away so that I could ride my mountain bike. I beat my fists on the walls frequently. I was in a rage of despair, not just because my one-man mountain guiding service was now out of business, cutting off my income when my partner was pregnant with my child, but with the realization of how much in the body, the person who had believed himself to be a being of the mind and spirit, really was.

Chasing around in the mountains was healthier for people like us, with obviously wacky neural chemistry, than inactivity, but sooner or later we would have to slow down. One of our choices in dealing with this inevitability was to push the limits of risk to the point where we were unlikely to live long enough to have to deal with the decline of our bodies. I had one friend who went out on a virtually suicidal attempt on an unclimbed face that was continually swept by avalanches. It was just before his thirtieth birthday. He wasn't a dark person, but actually one of the most cheerful and energetic people I have ever met. He certainly wasn't broodingly self-destructive. However, like a samurai, he seemed completely prepared to die on any climb he went out on. Perhaps he is carrying on in some parallel universe, having accomplished a feat that might not be duplicated for a hundred years. Or ever. But science and philosophy seem to be pointing to the idea that an infinity of parallel universes does exist. In which case there would be no way to escape the inevitable decrepitude of the body, since "you" would just carry on somewhere else. But even if I could completely accept that idea intellectually, it went against the nature of my emotions. There have been few times in my life, although they have been memorable, when, at the height of an adventure, I was cheerfully prepared to die. Besides, I still have a daughter to look out for in this universe.

The alternative for Helen and I was that we would have to change our focus to some realm of the mind or spirit. I guess that enjoying the body is like a drug; it's hard to quit, or even cut back. And enjoying the body means different things to different people. For some it might be TV, soft cushions, and popcorn. Helen and I didn't even have TV at home. We have a garage climbing wall, books, computers, gym equipment all over the house, heaps of outdoor adventure equipment, and each other. Our idea of outdoor enjoyment frequently involved significant cold, pain, and fear. We sometimes remind each other that, "It doesn't have to be fun—to be fun." But it was fun, and I did not want to give it up. This is what Patanjali, in the Yoga Sutras he wrote some 2500 years ago, called attachment to sanskaras: conditioned memories of pleasurable or painful events in the past, and the consequent projection of those kinds of events into the future, arousing desire or aversion. Buddhism, which in its fundamentals is a school of yoga, has a similar concept and word, sankhara. We cling; we cling to our memories of pleasure and pain. I needed to find a way to let go. I felt I needed a sign to show me the way.

Helen called to me and pointed to a patch of snow amidst the ruins. I went over to her and looked at where she pointed. The print was clear. It was perhaps two days old. It had been made by a snow leopard.

Some ten days later Helen and I were exploring the ruins of the fortress at Markha. We had come over the Ganda La a couple of days previously and had only met two other Western trekkers since then. They had attempted to get over the 5200-meter (17,060-ft) Gongmaru La pass, which was also our objective, but they had turned back because they felt that there was too much snow. We were looking down at another group of trekkers now camped in the field down below the ruin. They were with guides, ponies, and cooks. We had spoken with them about a half hour before and found out that their intention was also to cross the Gongmaru La in three days time. I was pretty certain that they would not be able to do this with their horses. Deep consolidated snow is dangerous for horses, especially if they are carrying loads. The terrain can have holes hidden under the snow, and if a horse stumbles and falls with a lower leg trapped in the snow, it can easily snap a bone. And what can be done then? Go back down to a village and possibly bring back an antique firearm? Or a big knife? Or club the animal to death with a rock? I doubted if the guides were going to subject their animals to much of this kind of risk.

Helen and I, though, were used to traveling in snow. The only thing we normally feared about it was the potential for avalanches. There was little chance of that here now with the mostly consolidated spring snow. And the snow would be a meter deep at most here in this high desert, not 3 to 5 meters like we were used to back home. We had made arrangements with one of the locals in Markha to carry our gear on his ponies up to a high pasture, called Nimaling, below the snowline. We had promised to pay him double the going rate for a day on account of the fact that he would have to leave his farm at the height of the planting season. On the other hand he had agreed to travel double the distance of a normal trekking day for this fee.

We had spent the last ten days clambering around in the Stok range looking for the elusive ghost cat. We had been over another high pass called the Stok La, and we had explored the ridge above Yurutse where I had chased the cat last fall. This ridge, like most of the others, was now decorated with a variety of spring flowers. Not enormous stands like we have in our alpine regions back home, but individual plants blooming here and there in stark contrast to the desert harshness. But all the cat sign on the ridge was quite old. We had gone back and scouted the canyon where we had seen the print in the ruin as well, but found no more sign. I thought about climbing the 6120-meter (20,080-ft) Stok Kangri, as Helen and I had never been that high together, but thought that we should leave that for a couple of weeks as there did seem to a lot of relatively fresh snow at that elevation and we would have to trudge in it for a considerable distance compared to our planned jaunt over this pass. I had proposed this Markha valley trek to Helen as she had never done it, and there were virtually no other tourists there this early in the season.

"What about the snow leopards though?" she asked. "Aren't we supposed to be looking for snow leopards?"

"Let's put snow leopards away for a while," I said. "You don't want to spend your whole time out here sitting on ridges looking for snow leopards. You have to go back to your job in a couple of weeks. I can stay and pursue my obsession. It's my obsession, not yours. Let's just go for a trek and have fun. The snow leopard trail seems to have gone cold anyway."

"Are you sure?"

"Yes, I'm sure."

The next morning we set off early, leaving most of our gear with the pony man, who told us that he would leave in an hour and catch up to us later in the morning. After about three hours we came to Hankar and spent some time exploring the fortress up on the pinnacle. We kept a sharp eye out while we were up on the heights there watching for the pony man—no sign of him though. We decided to push on instead of waiting for him.

We followed the trail into a canyon and along the banks of a small stream, the Nimaling Chu, a tributary of the Markha River. About a half an hour above the village we stopped at the stream to refill our water bottles. The water seemed clear and clean here but we would purify it with tablets nevertheless because so much of the wildlife here was infected with the giardia parasite and stream contamination from animal feces was inevitable. I had a small amount of the some sterilized water left in my bottle that I was about to finish off when I noticed that there was some sediment in the bottom of the transparent plastic bottle. I was thirsty for a sip but I knew that Helen, who generally drank less water than me, still had more water in her bottle that would enable us to quench our thirst for the time being until the thirty minutes that it took for the purification pills to take effect had passed. But when I turned to Helen, I saw that she was also dumping the water out of her bottle, in imitation of my procedure, I supposed.

"No," I shouted, as I watched the water that I wanted to slake my thirst with spill on the rocks. I immediately regretted raising my voice though.

Helen looked startled. She put her hand on her chest. Oh no, what have I done? I thought to myself. Helen suffered from tachycardia, a chronic heart condition characterized by sudden bouts of a racing arrhythmic heartbeat. These bouts were sometimes set off by a sudden shock. I put the water bottle down, stepped toward her and put my arms around her.

"I'm sorry," I said. "Come and sit down on this boulder."

After she was seated on the boulder I rolled out one of our foam sleeping mats for her to lie down on. It took about ten minutes for Helen's seizure to subside, which was lucky as they had been getting worse lately and could last for hours. We both knew that there was some risk in going out to remote areas with her condition, but she was determined not give up her adventurous lifestyle because of it. Helen had been waiting for several years for surgery to correct the affliction and was likely to be able to finally receive it in the following months after her return from India.

We continued on the trail for the rest of the morning arriving at the seasonal pasture called Thachungtse just after midday. We were now getting hungry and regretted entrusting our packed lunches to the pony man. We sat down in the sunshine with our backs propped up against a low stonewall and ate the last of the snacks that we had brought.

"Are you sure that this guy is going to show up?" asked Helen.

"Yeah, I'm sure."

"Well, where is he? He should have caught up to us by now."

"Ladakhis are not good time keepers, but they are not dishonest."

"Are you sure? What is to stop him from just keeping all our stuff and selling it."

"Well there are some cultures where the locals would be indifferent or even respect such behavior, but this is not one of them. If this guy ripped us off he would be completely disgraced in his village, even the whole valley, even back to relatives and associates in Leh. It's unthinkable. I have never heard of such a thing here."

"He could have had an accident," ventured Helen. "What time do you think we should start to head back if he doesn't show? We're going to get pretty cold up here at night without our sleeping bags."

"Okay, how about if we wait until three and then start to head down. We can walk the trail to Hankar in the dark with our headlamps."

We settled down to wait. There was an unusually large herd of blue sheep, about eighty in number, on the south-facing slope of the ridge in front of us. The juveniles, true to form, had gathered in a group of about ten at the top of a steep gully. They were getting ready to practice their snow leopard evasion tactics. There was one animal, which appeared to be the leader, standing at the edge of a short vertical drop at the entrance to the gully. He (or she?) was staring fixedly down the steep rocky slope. All of the group were now as still as statues. Then the leader jumped. The other animals followed in quick, but orderly, succession. They hit the loose rock below the vertical drop and cascaded down the gully in breathtaking bounds. It seemed as though their legs, instead of breaking their descent upon each landing, were rather uncoiling like springs and propelling them to even greater velocity. It almost seemed as though free fall velocity was not enough for these animals to escape their, for the moment, phantom, but fearful predator. We could hear a loud series of clatters as a cascade of dislodged rocks followed the animals down the gully.

"Holy shit," breathed Helen, who had never watched this performance before, although I had tried to describe it to her. "Unbelievable," she added in a gasp as the animals hit the debris fan at the bottom of the gully.

The animals finally began to decelerate as they reached the flats at the valley bottom. A group of about a half a dozen mature males had interrupted their grazing to watch the juveniles' performance. A few of the animals that had participated in the gully charge now wandered over to them. The two groups stood face to face, staring at each other for about half a minute. Then the elders went back to grazing and the younger animals reassembled and began to climb back up the slope.

"Wow, what a show," said Helen. "Do you think that the older dude was saying, you showed good leadership skills there kid. I'm proud of you?"

"Well there did seem to be some looking for approval from the younger ones and there seemed to be acknowledgment from the older ones…maybe." I grinned at Helen, glad that she had gotten to see this display.

I looked up the slope and saw that two of the juveniles had balked and remained at the top of the gully—future meals for the ghost cat.

In another half an hour or so the group had reassembled at the top of another gully. I fumbled with my camera to figure out the how to use the movie function. I had intended to take only still pictures with this camera, but it occurred to me now I had to try to record one of these incredible performances and I did manage to capture the tail end of the second gully charge here on video. After this second descent the animals took a break to graze. The ascents and gully drops were obviously at a cost to the youngsters, both in the expenditure of calories and the time taken off from grazing, which seemed especially dear considering the sparseness of the vegetation in this desert landscape. Evolution had apparently, though, deemed the investment in this dangerous and energy costly activity worthwhile to enhancing the odds of individual survival. Once again I saw the specter of the ghost cat, the harsh coach that had pushed these animals to develop this extreme athleticism.

At two o'clock we were relieved to see the pony man, Tashi, show up with his two horses. After unsaddling the horses he began to look for bits of fuel to make a fire in order to brew up some tea. Not wishing to waste time with gathering sparse twigs and dung, I told him that we would use our gas stove to heat some water. Asking him why he took so long he sheepishly told us that we had traveled much faster than he had anticipated and said that we were very strong. Once we finished lunch we reloaded the horses and as Helen went to put on her daypack Tashi gestured to her to throw it on one of the horses. She did so, but I told him that I preferred to carry mine when he offered this service to me. We pushed on for about two hours at a fairly quick pace, as we wanted to get to the campsite before dark. The two-hour delay waiting for the pony man had cost us. I would have just skipped the tea and grabbed a quick bite but Tashi had seemed determined to have tea. Perhaps he needed the rest.

We climbed higher, breathing deeply in the thin air. In my mind I kept seeing the blue sheep charging down the gully. I had seen the grace and power of the snow leopard reflected in the prowess of these animals as they performed their remarkable rehearsals for the confrontation with their adversary. These creatures just didn't seem to stumble. It was like extreme skiing or unroped solo climbing— you fall, you die. But here, instead of a few outstandingly talented and outrageously brave individuals, a whole species, with the exception of a few balkers, participated in an extreme sport activity. The balkers, I supposed had their own survival tactic, but it did not seem to be as successful as that of the audacious in the passing on of genes.

And behind this spectacle of the gully charge was the specter of the ghost cat. She was the coach and harsh mentor that had endowed these animals with their athletic grace. I hadn't seen her, but in this way, I had. The landscape reflected her too. The ungrazed growth of grasses and other plants sometimes just below the crests of ridges and along the slopes certain of gullies was vital to the reseeding that was the base of the whole ecosystem here. These slopes were ungrazed because they were easy ambush sites that predators, mainly the snow leopard, would have been able to take advantage of. This is a vital principle in ungulate, predator, flora relationships. In North America some entire ecosystems have been restored with the reintroduction of wolves.

Overhead a lammergeyer circled. Its broad wings were motionless as it was being lifted effortlessly on the late afternoon thermals. This bird, also called the bearded vulture, was dependant on the snow leopard, lynxes, and wolves here for its living. It was the bone breaker, the final scavenger that feasted on the nutritious marrow after all the other predators and carrion eaters had had their fill. Even though it is a vulture, it is a beautiful and graceful bird to watch in flight. Perhaps for this reason, in Persia, it is considered lucky to have a lammergeyer's shadow pass over you—as had just happened to me.

Was I going to get lucky and see this ghost cat someday? Did it matter? If I could really practice Buddhism, it shouldn't. I looked toward the snow-capped shoulders of Kang Yaze to my right. To the left the late afternoon sun was highlighting the otherworldly contours of the ancient raised and folded seabed, the Sea of Tethys, which tens of millions of years ago had supported an ecosystem much different than this one. The monument of its passing was this stunning mountainscape. The sky was a deep blue infinity. And I was here with my partner. What more could I want? The bird continued to soar effortlessly overhead. *Let it go*, a voice inside me said. That voice had been whispering quietly for days. Now it had grown louder. There was a thought that kept bubbling to the surface, one that I had kept pushing down for a long time. Now I finally let it rise. I confronted the truth that I had been trying to avoid—that this obsession with the snow leopard was no longer a metaphor for a spiritual quest. It may have been when it started twenty-five years ago. But now I simply wanted a picture of the ghost cat for my wall. I wanted a trophy for my sustained my efforts. How shallow I had become, I thought to myself. I was a raging furnace of desire, and it seemed that the longer that I looked for her, the more the flames were stoked. I had always thought that this quest would teach me something. But now I faced the truth: I had learned nothing. If looking for the snow leopard was any kind of meaningful metaphor, and not just a trophy hunt, then there was only one conclusion. There was only one lesson for me to take away, and now I had to finally embrace that lesson as a first step.

In the Japanese Zen parable of the monk looking for the animal on the mountain, his finding it, after many signs, is a symbolic affirmation of his spiritual advancement. But for me to see my animal now would only be the affirmation and consummation of my greed. My pretense of "student of Buddhism," with no commitment to the practice of Buddhism, was a dodge. I was a fraud. She had truly revealed my inner world to me by teasing me with so many signs, but never revealing herself.

I looked down at the camera bag that I wore on my hip like a gunfighter, ready for a quick draw and an action shot with the telephoto camera. The bag that was bouncing on my hip at that moment was out of focus in my vision though because of the expensive distance-vision prescription glasses I was wearing. I had worn them everyday during my last two trips to Ladakh, even though they were not ideal for walking in the rough terrain as they made everything within about 2 meters out of focus to my eyes. I wore them because I believed that they would enhance my chances of seeing a snow leopard. For a moment I felt like I was standing outside of myself, looking down at this foolish being.

Somewhere along that climb below the Gongmaru La, I did let it go. I don't think that it happened in one particular moment. It was perhaps more like a string of moments where my desire fell away drop by drop and was replaced by a feeling of contentment with being in the world, this world, at this moment, exactly as it was. Besides, I had been pretty happy to be here for the last two weeks with Helen. This was so different from my long past of solitary wanderings. Helen's keen eye gave me a new perspective, and her joy in observing this world was contagious. It wasn't all about the reaching the summit, or seeing the snow leopard. I believe that it was in part, the sheer pleasure of her company, that allowed me to face, and then put aside, the insatiable craving that had been forged in my solitudes. The solitude that I had mistakenly thought would be the release from craving.

A chill wind began to blow up as we climbed towards the entrance to the broad valley where we planned to camp. It was near dusk when we stopped to unload the horses. Helen immediately went to pull her down jacket out of the daypack that had been loaded on the pony. I went to pay Tashi. He looked quite exhausted but I knew that he would be able to ride one of the unloaded horses back down to a lower elevation where he would likely camp. As I handed him the money that we had agreed on, plus a tip, he told me that he had secretly not believed that we would be able to do this trip in a single day and had fully planned on two.

"You are very strong," he said. "I did not believe you. Very strong man. Strong woman."

As soon as he left I turned to Helen. She was sitting on a boulder huddled in her down jacket. This was not like her at all. Normally she would be unpacking and organizing camp. I went closer to her and squatted down. I saw that she was shivering.

"You're chilled. Why didn't you put on your down parka sooner."

"It was on the pony. I didn't want to stop."

I pulled the stuff sack that contained Helen's sleeping bag out of her pack, and after shaking out the bag to restore its loft placed it over her shoulders and wrapped it around her. Then I inflated her air mattress and placed it on one of our foam insulation pads. Then taking the sleeping bag from her shoulders I laid it out on the mattress. I heard her teeth chattering as she climbed into the sleeping bag, still wearing the down parka.

"Hang on, Honey," I said to her. "I'm going to fill our bottles from the stream and then I'll make tea. We'll get you warmed up."

Helen drank two cups of hot tea but it took almost an hour before she stopped shivering. In the meantime a figure had appeared walking towards us out of the gathering gloom of the approaching night. It turned out to be an elderly man clad in layers of wool and leather. His face was as weathered as I had ever seen. I had heard that there were two elderly shepherds that lived up in this high pasture for about half the year. I had noticed a dwelling across the meadow, which appeared to be typical of stone and dung constructions that the shepherds used here in the highlands.

"Julay," I said to the shepherd in greeting.

"Julay," he replied.

We stared at each other for several seconds before he spoke again.

"Gya," he repeated.

"What?"

"Gya," he repeated.

"Hamago," I replied, which meant that I did not understand.

"Gya rupee," he said, holding out his hand.

Ah! *Gya* was the Ladakhi for one hundred. He wanted one hundred rupees for camping in his meadow. After paying him his fee, I headed off toward what looked like an outhouse that I supposed was provided with the camping fee. Before I passed over the threshold of the entrance to the small tumbledown shack, I turned on my headlamp. As I stepped inside I looked down to see a piece of wood with a nail driven through it. The rusty spike was pointed upwards and I could have easily stepped on it. In a shithouse! Yikes! The feces-dipped pungi stake was a deadly weapon used against the Mongols in the thirteenth century by the Vietnamese and, in the twentieth century, resurrected from the guerrilla warfare manual of great general, Tran Hung Dao, to be employed against Japanese, French, and American troops. A single puncture though the skin could result in an agonizing death. I picked up the board and banged the nail out with a rock.

I returned to our camp to find Helen out of the sleeping bag and on her hands and knees, vomiting. I helped her clean up and get back into the bag. I took the thermometer out of our first aid kit and it soon confirmed what I already knew—she had a fever. Shortly after that Helen ran to the outhouse.

"I think that you may have giardia," I said to her when she returned. "We have the drugs to treat it."

"No, I don't think it's giardia," she replied. "I've had giardia before and it doesn't feel quite the same. I'll hold off on the drug."

The drug was Tinidazole, not at that time legal in Canada, even with prescription, but available at Asian pharmacies and carried by all veteran Himalayan travelers. It usually worked within twelve hours compared to the twelve days or so it took the drug that was legal in Canada to have effect. But it was strong medicine that likely nuked friendly and unfriendly parasites in your system alike, which was why Helen was reluctant to take it without a surer diagnosis.

She was up a number of times during the night and couldn't seem to keep much fluid down. I was worried as dehydration could have serious consequences at this altitude. The temperature dropped to about minus 20°C. We were in the open, layered in our parkas, sleeping bags, and bivi bags. The clear sky was loaded with stars in the way that is only seen from the highest places on earth.

THE GONGMARU LA
JUNE 1, 2010

Consider yourself lightly; consider the world deeply.
MIYAMOTO MUSHASHI, THE BOOK OF WALKING ALONE

At dawn I pushed my arms back into the sleeves of the oversized down parka and lit the stove while still comfortable and warm in the half bag and bivi bag. Helen had suffered a bad night, but seemed to be sleeping soundly now. We would have to make a decision this morning whether to begin the long trek down the valley that would take several days, or to attempt to climb the remaining 450 meters (1475 ft) over the pass. Once we were over the pass at 5200 meters (17,050 ft) it would be a downhill walk all the way to the road-head in about two days.

By the time Helen stirred a couple of hours later, I had downed a couple of cups of coffee and a bowl of porridge. I made her tea, but she did not want any food. We were still undecided about our plans. When the sun hit our campsite at about 9 a.m., Helen climbed out of her bag and stood unsteadily.

"I want to give the pass a try, Honey, but I don't think that I can help you pack up," she said.

"That's okay, Baby. Just sit down, keep warm, and conserve your strength."

It took me about another hour to get everything packed up. I took most of the food cooking supplies in my pack. I placed the camera with the compact telephoto lens in the bottom of Helen's pack.

"You're packing away the Nikon?" asked Helen.

"I'm putting away a symbol of my craving?" I responded.

"Oh…Jeez," came from Helen, sitting on the boulder, huddled in the parka. "I guess my mother would approve. But remember that after twenty-five years without a beer, she still wants one sometimes."

"Yeah, well, maybe this is a start."

When both the packs were loaded, but before I closed the lid of mine, I unzipped the pocket on the underside of the top flap. From there I took out the spare pair of sunglasses I kept there. I placed the case that contained the prescription photochromatic glasses in the pocket and zipped it up. I completed the symbolic ritual by putting on the non-prescription sunglasses. Then we set off toward the Gongmaru La. I remember thinking to myself that perhaps one day I might see a snow leopard still, but I felt now that if I ever did it would be on her terms, when she was ready to show herself to me. Perhaps when I was ready. That morning, I felt that it was she who would know.

After half an hour of a slow pace, it was evident that Helen was struggling. The burden on her body caused by thin air and the weight of the overnight pack were exacerbated greatly by her illness. I began to see that in this situation no amount of willpower would get her to the pass.

"Put down your pack," I said to her. "Just take your down jacket in your daypack and leave the rest. I'll come back down for it."

"Are you sure you can do that?"

"Yes, I feel strong today."

It took us almost another two hours to reach the pass at our slow pace. The wind was gusting from the Himalayas to the west when got there, but we only had to drop a short ways down the lee side to find respite from it. I wolfed down a bar, and then made sure that Helen was bundled up and sitting on an insulated pad before returning to the crest and starting back down the other side. It took me another two hours for the round trip. I felt pretty good the whole time, except when I got to a final steep section just below the crest. There I began to feel a pain in the middle of my chest at the end of every intake of breath. This was unusual for me, at least since I had quit smoking twenty years before. The pain was minor, but it worried me. I'm sixty years old, I thought to myself; what if I have a heart attack here? How will Helen get out of here in her condition without me? What will she do?

By the time I got to the crest again, the pain was gone. I ran down the slope to Helen's waiting spot and showed up panting.

"How are you doing, Honey?" she asked, obviously concerned that I had over-exerted myself.

"Great," I answered, gasping, putting down her pack. "Mind if I go for another lap?"

I grinned. She laughed. I was so happy to be able to be her white knight.

We picked up our packs and began the descent. The snow was knee deep in places on this side and coming up this way certainly would have been extremely exhausting. We stopped a couple of times to check the map and compass as we did not want to get off route this late in the afternoon. We quickly dropped below the snowline and came to the top of a steep-sided canyon. We could see on the map that the trail ran along the right hand wall of the canyon for a ways. We debated whether we should enter the canyon and walk to its exit in the remaining light or camp here. It did not seem like there would be any good campsites in the canyon itself. We decided, somewhat spontaneously, to keep going. We walked through the canyon for some time, at a couple of points descending to the rocky streambed and then climbing again to the trail built into the right-hand face. At one point we were walking along the narrow track that fell away steeply to the stream about 30 meters below. I was enjoying the security of being able to place my feet without the distortions of the prescription distance glasses that I had worn every day previously and had now packed away. I could still see quite well, I thought, though features in the distance did not quite as sharp as with the other glasses.

Tomorrow we would arrive at the road-head. Although I did not know it then, tomorrow would be the last day of trekking for us on this trip. Although I had planned to stay over here for the summer once Helen returned home, after tomorrow Helen's bouts of tachycardia would become much more frequent, and I would have to take her home in person, as she would be unable to travel on her own. Her surgery in Canada would be entirely successful, and she would be out rock-climbing five days after having it. But today would be our last day together in the realm of the snow leopard. Dusk was now only an hour away.

Perhaps it was my previous season of visually scouring the landscapes of Ladakh day after day that trained my eye, so that I was alerted by my peripheral vision to the movement near the bottom of the canyon. I turned my head. I heard a stone tumble and saw something moving with extraordinary speed up the near vertical face on the other side of the canyon. It was a sleek and agile animal, and even with my less than perfect vision, I could see that it had spots. It was a snow leopard.

I reflexively reached into my breast pocket for the point-and-shoot camera that I had been using to take snapshots of our passage over the pass and down the canyon. Now I squatted down and began to take snapshots of the cat, about 140 meters away; she was ascending the crumbling rock face with astonishing agility. While I was working the camera with one hand, I was motioning to Helen with the other. She came and knelt down beside me.

"What are you looking at?" she asked quietly, and then almost immediately blurted out a breathy whisper, "Oh my God…"

The cat reached the rim of the canyon wall and then slowed to a more leisurely stride, seemingly quite unthreatened by us now, with the gulf of the ravine between us. I suddenly found the Nikon with the telephoto lens thrust into my hand; all around Helen there was a jumble of stuff sacks and other gear that she had unloaded while scrambling to find the camera that I had placed in the bottom of her pack. I shot a quick round of pictures through the telephoto and then putting down the camera, pulled the compact binoculars out of my other breast pocket. By this time Helen already had her own binoculars out and then I heard another "Oh my God."

I raised my binoculars and followed the cat walking along the top of the ridge. Then, to my astonishment, two more snow leopards came into view. The three cats greeted and nuzzled each other and then all three turned to look toward us.

"It must be a mother and two almost-grown cubs. I've never seen a picture of this in the wild," I said.

"You better take it then," replied Helen.

I raised the camera that I had buried in her pack a few hours before.

SUNRISE
JUNE 2010

I awoke the next morning at our campsite at 4000 meters (13,125 ft). We had walked for several hours into the darkness by headlamp before we had found this flat, sheltered spot near a stream. Although there was ice in my water bottle, the air felt positively balmy here after spending the previous night 750 meters (2460 ft) higher, below the glaciers of Kang Yaze.

The snow leopards had posed for us for some forty minutes while we watched them with binoculars and took pictures. We left them, as dusk was approaching, wanting to get out of the canyon before dark. As I began to set up the stove now to make coffee, I contemplated what we had seen. Once the burner was lit, and the pot with water set up, I picked up the Nikon and looked through some of the pictures in the preview screen. This time it hadn't been just a dream. I thought about all the years that I had spent looking for her, believing that she was a solitary being like me, and then when she finally showed herself to me, she was with her family—

and I was with my spouse. The cats had been overt in their displays of affection with each other. She, the mother, was not completely the loner that I had expected all these years, one day, to meet—loner to loner.

I had so long been looking for her. She, the animal, the metaphor, the goddess, had melded into an inseparable shape shifter, continually eluding, but always beckoning. Now I had seen her— in one of her guises, at least. But discovery often seems to unlock yet more questions and more mysteries. For some people, it is the embracing of simple answers to the unanswerable that gives them solace; for others, perhaps the few, it is the unanswerable depth of the mystery itself: the experience of gob-smacking awe that we feel in the presence of Mystery's diffused and scattered lights and the tidbits of clues that rain down to us daily from an infinite sky. As the seer/poet who composed Exodus has Yahweh tell Moses:

> "But you may not look directly at my face, for no one may see me and live." The Lord continued, "Look, stand near me on this rock. As my glorious presence passes by, I will hide you in the crevice of the rock and cover you with my hand until I have passed by. Then I will remove my hand and let you see me from behind. But my face will not be seen."
>
> *Exodus 33:20*

Humanity's universal search for a transcendental meaning has raised some interesting and beautiful monuments in the realms of art, literature, philosophy, and religion. But those are all, after all, people-made things and of this world, even if some of the folks who created them do seem to have moments of otherworldly inspiration. But for most of us meaning isn't some secret to be found by finally overturning the right stone. We ultimately find meaning by doing what can make life meaningful: doing useful things, treasuring sublime moments, having convictions and the courage to practice them, and perhaps above all, caring for others.

I looked over at Helen, who was still sleeping. Dawn was breaking over the mountains of Tibet to the east.

Part Three

Soon after returning home in 2010 my old back injury flared up; with one leg partially paralyzed, I was crippled to the point where I could not go to the mountains for the whole summer. "Go back to India—you will heal," Helen told me. That worked. I ended up climbing 6150-meter (20,175-ft) Stok Kangri in Ladakh before I returned home again.

My daughter had a severe crisis in late 2011. In early 2012 we went for a walk together—around the Himalayas—a walk that lasted for most of the two and a half months that we spent in Nepal and India.

On May 3, 2013, I found myself once again stepping off the plane in Leh. I felt that there was still something unfinished here.

CHASING THE LIGHT
JUNE 2013

Buddhism has been in my consciousness for a long time. My earliest memory of an association with it was of a brass statue of the meditating Buddha that I had convinced my mother to purchase for me at a second-hand store. I was perhaps seven years old. I am not sure what attracted me to it; perhaps it was the look of serenity on the figure's face; maybe it was because the figure seemed somehow human and otherworldly at the same time. I looked at the statue every day.

The great Viennese psychotherapist, Alfred Adler, stated that one's earliest memory should be paid especial attention to, for in it was a key to the individual's secret life goal. My earliest memory is of sitting in my parents humble kitchen in post-war Vienna, and listening to the sound of the wind wailing in the stove pipe that ran through the ceiling to the roof. I don't know why I perceived that sound to be so mournful, but I remember feeling such sadness that it felt like my heart would break. It seemed like I was trying to remember something forgotten, something huge. I could not have had many memories at the time; we left Vienna when I was three and a half. But that was what made me so sad—I was so new, but I wasn't. There was so much that was lost.

I spent a lot of time reflecting on the process of memory when I was quite young. I was always aware of my mortality, even though I know now that young children are not supposed to be. I knew that the Russian soldiers who occupied our portion of the city had the power of life and death over us. They were the bogymen of my childhood. I remember being chasing by them in my dreams, and I remember, once, being chased for real, my mother clutching my hand, as they pursued us through the woods where we had been picking mushrooms. I knew that memories were vanishing things; I equated the loss of memories with death and tried desperately to capture and hold them. One memory that I especially treasure goes back to that same kitchen in Vienna. My father had just explained to me that we were going to leave for a new land called Canada, where we would have to learn a new language called English. He said that he was beginning to study this language. I asked him to teach me. He looked around the room—I suppose looking for an object he knew the name for in the new language. He pointed toward the ceiling at the bare illuminated bulb hanging there. "Light," he said. "Light," I repeated. I had learned my first word in the exotic tongue of the faraway land. I clutched the new memory like a precious stone. I knew that this was something special.

Children are not supposed to be philosophical, but when my daughter was three I received a phone call from her mother.

"Your daughter," she began, emphasizing the first word, "is sitting here going, 'I don't want to die. Why do I have to die?'"

When I read and hear that young children are not supposed to have such thoughts, it seems strange to me. She did. I did. When she was very young, a number of people called Maxine an "old soul."

One of my friends was convinced that my daughter had been her teacher in a past life.

Being a skeptic, I actually don't believe in reincarnation after death in the most literal sense, but yet the wind in the stove pipe memory haunts me still. And when I examine my deep fear of death, I find that what I fear, perhaps most, is waking up again, struggling to remember, but having lost it all again. It takes so much of a lifetime, it seems, just to acquire just a little wisdom. Why do we have to throw it all away? Maybe I should write a note to myself, and others, just in case reincarnation is real. Maybe that's kinda what this book is.

FACING THE DRAGON
MAY 2013

What is to give light must endure burning.
VICTOR E. FRANKL, PSYCHIATRIST, PHILOSOPHER,
HOLOCAUST SURVIVOR, BODHISATTVA

I awoke again as I had done a number of times during the night and squirmed my body around in the sleeping bag, so that I could maneuver to press the stud that would activate the light on my watch. It was 1:30—still three and a half hours till dawn. I had previously never had much trouble sleeping at high altitude, but now, camped at 4800 meters (15,750 ft), I was experiencing Cheyne-Stokes syndrome, also called periodic breathing, a kind of apnea, where you characteristically stop breathing as you fall asleep and then wake up gasping for air. My case was not extreme, but it was enough to disturb sleep. Although I carried drugs that would help with these annoying symptoms, I was so used to acclimatizing easily and naturally that it had not yet occurred to me to use them.

It was my sixth night in a row camped out, alone and in the open, at high altitude. Although I was getting a bit old to be doing a solo vision quest, I figured that I had at least one more solitary wandering in the high mountains in me. I had left Leh almost a week ago, and assured by the weather forecast that there would be clear skies for at least five days, I had eschewed, as is often my habit with a good weather forecast, to bring a tent. That first night, at 4500 meters (14,765 ft), it stormed—and snowed almost a foot.

I had encountered a Himalayan wolf on my way up to my first camping spot and having always felt a special kinship with wolves this had pleased me. There were also fresh snow leopard prints in the snow. I set up camp on a ledge set into a steep slope near the spot where Helen and I had seen the snow leopards three years before.

When it finally stopped snowing that first morning—well after dawn—I began to dig out my stuff. Where had I left the reading glasses? The stove? Did that mound of snow over there contain my boots? At least I had the foresight to put them in a plastic garbage bag. As I huddled in the claustrophobic bivi bag waiting for it to stop snowing, while getting my face pelted with flakes every time I looked out, I thought of the storms and flights of arrows that Mara had sent to test the Buddha's resolve after he had seated himself at the immovable spot. In the morning I was briefly tempted to pack up and flee down the mountain. But only for a few moments—this was not a vacation—I had wanted to feel a bit on the edge up here. This was, after all, near the world's boundaries, the maximum altitude that humans could survive long term. La Rinconda, a mining town in the Peruvian Andes at 5100 meters (16,730 ft) was the highest long-term settlement in the world. Beyond that altitude, humans could not survive for anything like a normal lifespan; the human body, above this line, no matter how fit, is slowly dying.

The day before coming up here, while slicing up a chunk of yak cheese in my hotel room for part of the trip's provisions, I had lost my mindfulness and cut my finger while making the last slice. This was unfortunate, as I knew that wounds were slow to heal at high altitude, and sometimes showed little sign of healing at all until after one descended to lower elevations. I pulled off the bandage to inspect the wound on the third day out. The gash had opened considerably and was oozing and inflamed. I wished now that I had brought some antibiotic ointment. I decided to try an ancient, but little known, battlefield treatment that is sporadically recorded as far back as Pharaonic Egyptian times. The only scientific study that I have ever encountered on this unusual remedy was done by the Collage of Pharmacy in Bangalore. Their results were rather astounding. So were mine, it would turn out. But I had to overcome some cultural conditioning before I could bring myself to whizz on an open wound.

After it stopped snowing that first morning and I got my stuff dug out, I sat in meditation. There were many distractions. Although withdrawal from the world is supposed to be easier when you are older, it seemed that in some ways it was the opposite for me. Although I felt largely at ease being alone in the mountains, the one thing that I missed was…I guess you could call it female energy. After seventeen years of living with Helen, I was used to seeing her every day, even though I had sometimes traveled without her for a couple of months at a time. I seemed to make women friends easily wherever I went and was used to the company of women; being without them was somewhat like being without oxygen. I was much more of an ascetic monk when I was in my twenties, but I have always bonded easily with women—much more readily than with guys. Now when I tried to meditate and focus on my breathing and empty my mind, pale, naked breasts kept floating into my inner vision. In the legend of the Buddha seated at the Immovable Spot, it is recounted that Mara also attempted to distract the sage with these sorts of visions. Siddhartha though, apparently had a much more disciplined mind and heart than me.

The next night it snowed only about 5 centimeters and after that it was clear skies. But Mara wasn't done with me yet. On the fourth night he unleashed his demons.

When one first starts sleeping out alone in the mountains or forest, every sound in the darkness is an imagined threat. But I was way past that years ago. There was nothing in the external environment that I really feared here in the night, although I was just a little wary, at this campsite, of potential rock fall from above onto the ledge I was camped on. Consequently I had built a little barrier of stones to offer some protection for my upper body. The day before I had seen a pie plate-shaped rock, but with considerably more mass than a pie plate, come spinning, cartwheel like, past my campsite. I saw the buzz-saw teeth on its rim as it went by. I figured that it could just about take a leg, or and arm, or a head, right off. Or it could come down and open the chest of a sleeping man—and expose his beating heart. Nice one, Mara. But I actually wasn't that concerned about stone fall, knowing that almost all the rock fell during the heat of the day and rarely during the sub-zero night.

No, I wasn't really worried about dangers out there. But what was buried in my head was altogether another matter. These were Mara's real demons—the ones who come to show you the dark depths of your own soul. The fourth night is the traditional climax night for the ritual vision quest that native North American youths underwent as their right of passage. Well, I wasn't a youth anymore, which meant that I had had more time to collect and conceal so much mental stuff over the years. It all rose to the surface on that fourth night. The demons came. They danced before me. They were dressed as my failures, the consequences of my greed, my lust, my fear, my sloth, my addictions. I couldn't take it. I resolved to flee back to the distractions of civilization in the morning, but that thought, the idea that I would live the rest of my life subsumed in those distractions, led me into even greater despair. I cried out. I howled like a wolf. Curled in a fetal position, I begged the god I did not believe in for mercy.

The day before I had had my first encounter with other people in four days. They were a British couple with their two children, accompanied by a local guide and his assistants, and they had ponies to carry their gear and their youngest child. They were the first party to come over the Gongmaru La (5200 meters; 17,060 ft) this year. I found out in conversation that the guide was Rinchen's father, and actually the family head at Yurutse. I was surprised that, in all the times I had been at Yurutse, I had never met him. He said that this was because his income, derived from working away from his home, was vital to the family's revenue. He looked up toward my campsite and said that it was not a good spot because of rock fall, and he suggested that I move my camp to what looked like a flat spot on the ridge on the other side of the canyon. I told him that I had climbed up there already with that thought in mind, but found that there was in fact no flat spot up there, only a sharp ridge. We were having this conversation seated in the bottom of the canyon, which had a number of level spots; but you generally don't camp in the bottom of canyons in Ladakh with its notoriously unpredictable flash floods. I knew that a number of unwary trekkers had met their demise in this way.

I had climbed up toward the Gongmaru La the morning before, and found to my dismay that I was inexplicably weak. Gasping for breath, I made it to only the 4900-meter (16,075-ft) level. On the way back down to my campsite I was so dizzy that for a while I was convinced that I could be having a cerebral edema, the most dangerous form of high altitude sickness, where your brain literally gets crushed to a pulp by the pressure of fluid. But I didn't have a headache and I could easily balance on one leg so that diagnosis didn't make sense. What the hell was going on? I finally came to the conclusion that it must be the antihistamines that I had been taking to combat the dust in Leh and that I had continued to take up here as a sleep aid. That diagnosis turned out to be correct; I found out later that antihistamines could indeed have adverse effects at high altitude. Three years before, when I had been in Ladakh with Helen, I had had quite a bad reaction to fleabites that I had acquired while spending the night at the homestay in Skyu. Helen and I both searched our kits for antihistamines, but found none. When we returned to Leh, Helen told me that the antihistamine tabs had mysteriously turned up in her first aid kit just where they where supposed to be and had apparently been all along. She could not understand why she had not seen them when she had searched. I was mildly peeved with her over this, but realize now that, had she found the medicine, I would probably not have made it over the Gongmaru La, and certainly would have been unable to do the relay carry when she was sick, and consequently we would not have seen the snow leopards.

I finally got to sleep during the night of the demons but awoke again sometime after midnight. A song was playing in my head. It was "The House of the Rising Sun."

> There is a house in New Orleans
> They call the Rising Sun
> And it's been the ruin of many a poor boy
> God, I know, I'm one
>
> Mother, tell your children
> Not to do what I have done
> To spend your life in sin and misery
> In the House of the Rising Sun

It wouldn't stop. It was as if it was being fed into my brain from somewhere else. "Yes," I shouted into the night, "I am a sinner, I am a gambler, and I have wasted much of my life."

Then, in a few seconds, the song faded away.

The next morning, I awoke at dawn, made coffee, put on my boots, packed my day bag, and although I had resolved for a few moments during the night to go down in the morning, I now planned to ascend. But as I looked down into the ravine, I noticed something strange—fresh footprints in the snow that filled the bottom of the gully. I immediately climbed down to take a closer look. They were human footprints. I remembered checking the gully for prints just before dark, in case I had missed any wildlife wandering by. I was sure there were no prints down here at dusk. I was leaving no marks now myself in the hard morning snow. That meant that the prints were made after dark, but before the temperature dropped enough to harden the snow. This was inexplicable because the prints were headed down the gully and the only entrance further up the drainage, just before a sheer headwall with a waterfall, was a steep slope that would be difficult to climb down in the dark. Why wouldn't whoever had left these prints just come down the trail instead of climbing down into the gully? Had I scared them with my howling? When, a few days later, I told my friend and local outfitter, Tashi Gonbo, in Leh, about this strange event, he told me that the prints had been left by a Belung Pa. This was a race of beings, he explained to me, which lived in the mountains apart from humans. They ate the flesh of people who were foolish enough to wander alone in the heights.

"Have you ever seen one?" I asked.

"No," he replied, "You see one, you're dead."

Tashi sometimes enjoyed pulling my leg, but he seemed serious about this and began regaling me with stories of locals who had mysteriously vanished in the mountains and were assumed to have been eaten by the Belung Pa.

"Um, do the Belung Pa wear shoes?" I asked, remembering the prints.

"Oh yes," replied Tashi. A bit different then from the Bigfoot, Sasquatch, or Yeti, I supposed. So, let me see now…I had frightened some Grendel creature enough with my existential despair that he hadn't even wanted to try to get a taste of me and took a hazardous detour to avoid getting close to me? That made no sense at all, but then either did anything else.

Two and a half hours after leaving camp, I was standing on top of the Gongmaru La. It had not felt difficult. In the clear air I could see down to the summer pastures of Nimaling, now still mostly covered in snow. Above the hanging valley of Nimaling was the majestic summit of Kang Yatse. To the west were the summits of the Himalayas.

After spending about an hour and a half on the summit of the pass, I began the descent back toward my camp. Arriving there, I packed up all my gear. But it was no longer my intention to return to Leh today. I was moving my camp to a higher elevation.

The moon had set. The sky was clear. The darkness overhead was spangled with star lights—from the orb of Betelgeuse to the fairy dust of the Milky Way. There is no simile appropriate to describe the view of the unfiltered night sky. We don't see it anymore in our lit-up cities. We hide from it. Perhaps we fear those lights as much as we fear the darkness. There's just so much—unimaginably much—stuff out there. Creation has no sense of economy. What was she planning to do with all this? The answer to that may be she made enough stuff to realize every conceivable possibility, even the most unlikely, as long as everything was put together following her rules, put in place, as far as we can tell, some baker's dozen and a bit trillion years ago.

The late sixteenth-century Italian philosopher, Giordano Bruno, conceived of the idea that the universe was infinite. For this blasphemous concept, and others, such as that the stars were all suns, and that they had their own solar systems, he was stripped, had his tongue bound, and was burned alive. By the Catholic Church, of course. But now, as far as science can tell us, the universe does appear to be infinite. Without boundaries. Without end. The observable universe, that which is theoretically, if not quite actually, visible from earth, is about 93 billion light years across, and it is still expanding, at a somewhat mysteriously accelerating rate, some 13.75 billion years after the event of its apparent creation, which we call the Big Bang. But this visible or observable part of the universe is not even a drop in the ocean compared to infinity, which, as far as we can tell, is the actual size of the universe. When scientists talk about the present size of the universe, they are usually talking about the merely *observable universe*; all the rest is too distant for the light to have reached us since the time of its beginning. Even many scientists seem to want to avoid this somewhat daunting reality, and therefore use the term "universe" when they really mean *observable universe*, which even with its billions of galaxies, each containing billions of stars, is likely a mere mote in the vastness of infinity.

But the existence of an infinite universe has some startling logical consequences concerning its nature. The possible number of different arrangements of atoms, the Lego blocks that form every visible thing, is unimaginably large, in a space that goes on theoretically, forever—but the variety of those combinations, even though unthinkably great, is finite. On this immeasurably grand canvas, there is a limit to the various ways the universe can put the blocks together—whether fashioning microbes, snow leopards, or galaxies.

That means that duplication is inevitable again and again and again. And that meant therefore that somewhere out there was another being who was an exact duplicate of me, on a planet exactly like this one, and he was right now, in the sense that there can be a "right now" in an Einsteinan universe where time is relative, fighting for his life in an avalanche like the one that almost killed me the year before. He may or may not survive his avalanche. But if the universe is infinite, then there would be lots and lots of duplicates of him—me—that would. In Western philosophy it is accepted that if there is a perfect duplicate of you, and you are extinguished, then the copy is you. That is actually the principle behind the idea of teleportation as featured in science fiction like *Star Trek*. Information is transmitted across a distance, the original is destroyed, and a duplicate is created at the other end utilizing that information. It would be an eerie way to travel—especially the first time. But then maybe I already had. Perhaps we sometimes fail to notice our own demise. Maybe sometimes death is neither a dark curtain nor a white light, but something too subtle for our ken. If the information of each of us was duplicated all over the universe then it should be impossible for me, or anyone, to die an accidental death—subjectively that is. There would alternatively be lots of places in the universe where I was being mourned for not surviving that avalanche. To be able to watch this funeral of myself in a galaxy identical to this one, the best-estimates calculation is that I would most probably have to travel 10 to the 10 to the 28th power meters—a very long ways to go, even if I knew which direction to travel in.

But one of the assumptions in all this is that given the right circumstances—a bunch of amino acids, lightning bolts, and so on—life, or at least its precursor, will arise. That is a widely prevailing assumption in modern science. But one thing we should consider is that maybe the genesis of life does not happen quite so readily. In three and a half billion years, about a quarter of the age of the universe, it seems that it has only happened once on earth. There is no right-hand wound DNA, although there is no reason why it should not work just as well for information storage as the left-hand version that every cell, everywhere, uses. An analysis of the genetic code says that we share a common ancestor with trees, flowers, birds, and all the creepy crawlies of the earth—even pond scum. Everything that lives on this planet is family. Life, as far as we can tell, only began here once. Fundamentalist Christians, no matter what other absurd anti-science assertions they make, may have gotten that part sort of right.

But then maybe not. We know that the earliest life was anaerobic, meaning that it did not require oxygen for growth. Oxygen is actually poisonous for anaerobic organisms. With the advent some 2.5 billion years ago of cyanobacteria, which through photosynthesis fix carbon and produce oxygen as a waste product, almost all the anaerobic organisms went extinct within a couple of hundred million years—as soon as the planet's remaining oxygen sinks, such as oxidizing minerals (red ochre again), became saturated. After the rise of the cyanobacteria and other photosynthesizing plant life, a new genesis would have been much more unlikely. Additionally the record of an earlier multiple genesis would likely not be recoverable. Scientists though, are still looking for it. Perhaps some simple microbe, an alien remnant of another beginning, still survives somewhere deep underground hidden from the volatile gas that slew its brethren eons ago.

There is another observation that implies that life, at least intelligent life, doesn't happen easily though. If life arises inevitably, the assumption is often made that there should be other civilizations out there—some more advanced than ours. But after decades of listening with radio telescopes for the electronic racket that a civilization, even one merely as developed as ours should make, we have encountered only silence. So we have to ask: are we alone?

It would appear that it takes an incredible amount of luck for a planet to produce and maintain a "just right" environment that is stable and friendly for life for billions of years, and also for that planet to avoid the extraterrestrial forces that could completely extinguish that life at any time. These events would include, but not be limited to, the planet being struck by giant asteroids. We know that this type of event has occurred a number of times here since the beginning of life on earth, and that such events were probably responsible for the sudden extinction of up to 80 percent of the species existing on the planet at the time of collision. These types of not-quite-terminal events during the history of our own planet created new niches, and so seem to have at times spurred on evolution, rather than inhibiting it. But we were lucky there. The rocks that hit us could have been bigger. Or a supernova could have gone off nearby and fried us. Or...

Our galaxy contains some one hundred to four hundred billion suns. A seemingly large number, but for a comparison to biological figures, it is a ballpark equivalent to the number of neurons in a human brain, and certainly a much smaller figure (by about three orders of magnitude) than the number of guest organisms hosted in a single healthy human's gut. The more that I learn about the complex relationships on this planet involving plate tectonics, carbon cycles, the magnetic field, cosmic rays, ocean plankton, and many other factors—that are all required to sustain life—the more I come to believe that a few hundred billion solar systems may not necessarily be enough scenarios for another successful experiment that produces intelligent life in this galaxy. But if the canvas of the universe is truly without end, what are the possibilities then? Will everything that can happen, no matter how remote the possibility, happen? And happen again and again? In mathematics, some infinite sets are smaller than other infinite sets, but they are still infinite.

But even if the multiple duplication of information is out there in the unfathomable vastness to make us all physically indestructible, what happens to the soul? Where does it go when I get snuffed in this tiny corner of the universe and infinite versions of me carry on like the endless reflections of mirrors within mirrors within mirrors? Buddhism teaches that there is no such thing as an individual imperishable soul—that clinging to that belief is merely the clinging to an illusion—that even the idea of a self is an illusion. Well, I was still doing a lot of that clinging—even though I had followed the difficult, but rigidly logical, argument for the Buddhist case many times. Maybe that was why I kept returning to these mountains. Here, at one time, I had been as close as I had ever come to experiencing that letting go—of being something that was not just me.

I had been reading a new translation and commentary on Pantanjali's Yoga Sutras up there in the last week. The philosophy of Yoga, like that of its sister Indian philosophy Samkhya, posits that the core of being is not intellect but pure awareness. It is only because intellect is so noisy and never shuts up that we identify with it so strongly as to who or what we are. But, says Pantanjali, if you can just teach your noisy mind to be still for a while, you will realize who you really are. Consciousness ceases in deepest meditation, as it does in death, but awareness does not. And that awareness permeates the universe. It is the light in the eyes of every sentient being. It is the Being, call it the Godhead, if you like, whom you see in your lover's eyes, in your child's eyes, in your worst enemy's eyes. But even if you can realize that your adversary is as much you as you, that may be no reason to lay down your sword—as Krishna has to keep reminding Arjuna in the Bhagavad Gita. Do your duty, play the game, assume the role. Remember that you are Divine, but then forget it. For the true sage, human existence, it may be, is a kind of method acting.

When I got back to Leh, I emailed Helen and told her that I had spent a week alone in the mountains.

"Did an Angel come down and talk to you?" she emailed back.

"Better than that," I replied, "a Demon."

SHIVA'S DRUM
MAY 2013

The radio in the antique and replica shop was tuned to Leh's only station. In addition to the static pouring from the speakers, the vague melody of a Ladakhi song could be heard. Wandering around the shop, I came across a bronze statue of Shiva as Nataraja, the cosmic dancer. The god in this form is represented as having four arms and hands. In his upper right hand there is a drum; it represents the beat that initiates and perpetuates creation. In Hindu mythology, the universe came into being with a vibration, the first sound, Om, Aum, or Ommmm, which continues to pervade all of existence.

Modern astrophysics, like Hindu myth, also uses the analogy of a sound to describe the very beginning of the universe. We call it the Big Bang, a term coined in 1949 by astronomer Fred Hoyle who actually didn't subscribe to the theory, and was therefore, some believe, making fun of the concept with this appellation. The name stuck though.

In 1964, two young scientists, Arno Penzias and Robert Wilson, at Bell labs, were trying to fine-tune a very sensitive antenna they were using for radio astronomy and satellite communication. They had cooled their receiver with liquid helium to suppress heat interference and had filtered out radar and radio broadcasting. No matter what they tried though, there was still a static hum that they couldn't account for and couldn't seem to get rid of. They were convinced for a while that it was caused by pigeon poop, and therefore kept cleaning their instrument thoroughly. But the hum would not go away. After eliminating pigeon shit as the culprit, they performed experiments and found that the source was extraterrestrial. Further investigation revealed that it came from outside the galaxy. And it came from every direction. Completely baffled they rang up some eggheads they knew of at the physics department at nearby Princeton University. The egghead who answered the phone was Robert Dickey, and it turned out that he and his team were working to find the precise thing that Penzias and Wilson were trying to get rid of.

After Dickey put down the phone, he famously told his team, "Boys, I think we've been scooped." Indeed Penzias and Wilson were the ones who received the Nobel Prize for what was perhaps, next to the interpretation of the red shift, the most extraordinary discovery in cosmology in the twentieth century—though they had no clue initially as to what they had found. What they had stumbled upon was the signature of creation, a broadcast from the very early universe.

In modern scientific cosmology the universe is believed to have been in the state of a hot plasma for the first several hundred thousand years of its existence. Tiny quantum fluctuations in the very early soup had been amplified by a short but extremely rapid expansion of the universe, called inflation, some 10 to the minus 36 seconds after its beginning. After inflation the universe continued to expand but at a much slower rate. The original fluctuations continued to be further amplified by energetic photons bouncing around in the plasma, and this activity produced harmonic waves, in essence sound waves at very low frequencies, with amplitudes millions of miles across. This continuous rhythm of sound waves, at first rising in tempo and then falling, like an Indian raga, created lumpiness in the cosmic soup. The lumps formed the seeds of stars and galaxies. I looked again at the Shiva statue holding the drum in the right upper hand. The left upper hand held a flame, the cosmic fire of creation, destruction, and transformation.

After the plasma cooled enough for proper hydrogen atoms to form, the universe suddenly became transparent. Now the photons that had been bouncing around in the plasma could take off on their long journey. Light could shine forth. These original photons still make up about 99 percent of the radiant energy in our universe, starlight only accounting for the remaining 1 percent. The primordial photons though, which were once in the visible light spectrum, have been traveling for an estimated 13.7 billion years, consequently they have been stretched by the expansion of the universe into the microwave spectrum. We're too late on the scene therefore to see these photons with our eyes, but we have actually been listening to them ever since the invention of radio—although like Penzias and Wilson, we initially had no idea what we were hearing. The static that I was listening to on this shopkeeper's radio was mostly interference from terrestrial radio sources and emissions from our sun and other stars, but about 1 percent of the static you hear on a radio is the cosmic microwave background radiation, the CMB. It is the remnant of the Big Bang. It is the hum of creation. Ommmmm.

I was still looking at the statue. Shiva's lower right hand was empty with the open palm facing out and downward. This was the hand gesture, or mudra, that represents fearlessness. I have read that this open palm gesture can, as well, represent the timeless void, which is unmanifest existence. It is the emptiness of being without boundaries or ego. But just as it is difficult to keep thoughts from appearing when we are meditating, science tells us that emptiness in physical space has a hard time staying truly empty. Because of what we call the Heisenberg uncertainty principle, the stuff of the universe has no certainty of being anywhere, or not anywhere, only a probability of existing in any place. Of course with large conglomerations of particles, there is a near enough certainty that, for instance, your spouse is not going to suddenly go poof in front of your eyes. With individual particles though we have no absolute certainty that they are going to do anything or be anywhere—only a probability. The same thing goes for empty space. It can't stay empty; virtual particles are continually popping in and out existence there, and energy fluctuations are always taking place. It is for this reason that when inflation took place, it blew up these tiny fluctuations, into irregularities large enough to eventually form galaxies, and later, trees, butterfly wings, people, and snow leopards. If it were not for these irregularities our universe would be a homogenous energy/matter soup, and we certainly wouldn't be in it. Shiva's empty hand then represents the void, *Sunya*, from which all creation irrepressibly springs forth.

Shiva's lower left hand was pointed toward his raised left foot. This symbolizes the transcendence of super consciousness, or enlightenment, over the flux of existence. His right foot was planted on a dwarf demon that represents ignorance. Around his waist was a snake that represents Kundalini or Shakti, the divine force of the goddess that permeates all.

The early stars in the universe were mostly composed of primordial hydrogen, which compressed under the massive force of a star's gravity was being transformed by fusion into helium. When all of a star's helium has been used up in the nuclear fire, the helium starts to fuse into heavier elements like carbon and oxygen. In a star that has more than eight solar masses this conversion eventually becomes runaway, and then all hell breaks loose—the star explodes, releasing more energy in a brief period than our sun will release in its whole lifetime. An exploding star like this, called a supernova, sometimes outshines the hundreds of billions of suns in the galaxy than contains it.

But in the destruction of the star, a new genesis takes place. During a supernova a variety of new, heavier elements are forged and seeded into space. The explosion also sends out a shock wave (once again the drumbeat), which helps along the process of pushing more free floating hydrogen atoms together to begin the formation of new stars. Since everything in the universe attracts everything else by way of gravity—everything that's close enough not to be overwhelmed by dark energy that is—a lot of this newly created stuff becomes the building blocks of new star systems. Only now however, in these second or third generation star systems, the universe has some cool new stuff to work with (rather than just the primordial hydrogen and bit of helium and lithium that were created shortly after the Big Bang) and new projects are possible.

Each living thing on this planet is one of those projects. The calcium and carbon of our bones, the oxygen in our blood, many of the vital elements that make up our bodies, were created in the forge of an exploding star, some five or seven billion years ago. A star that had come into being because of infinitesimally tiny quantum fluctuations that had become amplified into flutters of energy and matter, which then became the heartbeats of creation. I looked again at the statue's hands that held the fire and the drum, reflecting on the enormous amount of time and energy the universe spends to create a sentient being. A reminder to spend our precious time here wisely.

The Shiva statue was a nice piece. Although I am not really a collector of objects, preferring on my travels to acquire memories, images, and ideas, instead of the burden of stuff, very occasionally I do like to bring home some physical reminder of where I have been. I had on more than one occasion brought back Indian brass statues for profitable resale—and I had once injured my back hauling a suitcase full of the stuff around the world, which was perhaps a lesson. It certainly would not be practical to buy this large, heavy piece in Leh, as I knew that I would already be paying for overweight for my luggage when flying out of Ladakh, due to the camping, climbing, and cold weather gear that I would already be hauling home with me.

I stepped out onto the street, and temporarily blinded by the radiance of elemental transformation occurring some eight and a half light minutes overhead, pulled down the sunglasses that were perched on my forehead and placed them over my eyes.

CONVERSATIONS WITH STANZIN
JUNE 2013

One morning I went to Thiksey Monastery for the 6 a.m. puja. Butter salt tea was served during the ceremony to the monks and the few tourists seated on floor mats in the main temple. After about a half hour of watching and listening to the ritual, I wandered outside and toured around the building complex that made up the monastery.

I got into a conversation with a young monk named Stanzin. In the course of my questioning, he told me that he was twenty-three years old and had entered the monastery at age twelve. Unlike most of the monks, he had not been sent there by his parents at a very young age (the youngest monk at Thiksey at this time was two), but had wished to join the monastic community of his own choice. I learned that he, like a few other monks at Thiksey, had been sent off for several years to study Buddhist philosophy at a kind of university in southern India. I asked him if some of the kids who were sent to the monastery at an early age decided that they were not happy being monks when they got older and would choose to leave the monastery. He replied that this happened occasionally, but then added that the important thing to understand was that happiness is a state of mind, it was not about being in a certain place or having a certain profession. Unhappiness, he said is brought about by wishing that you were in a different place, always wanting different things, unhappiness was about being in a constant state of desire.

"I feel desire all the time," I replied, "I just spent a week alone in the mountains on a sort of retreat, but almost every time I sat in meditation I would see a woman's naked body."

"Yes, that is your attachment to desire."

"I don't understand how monks can live without women anyway. I love women. How can you do it?"

"You have to realize the impermanence of all things. All the things that you love, your wife, your daughter, will perish in a short time. When you see a woman's body during your meditation, you see the beauty of skin, but look deeper—see below the skin—see the blood, the snot, the excrement. See the decay."

I was familiar with this particular Buddhist visualization, which I called the bag of pus meditation. I had used it once to help overcome a doomed infatuation. But was the Buddhist monks' approach to celibacy really different than that of Catholic monks and priests? Having attended Catholic schools for nine years, I had experienced the horror show of repressed sexuality that existed there. I had spent one year in the charge of the now infamous Irish Christian Brothers, a Catholic teaching order. My experience with the brothers was that if you were one of their favorites you would be regularly groped. We kids called it "being fruited up." If you were not a favorite then you would receive frequent beatings. I got a lot of beatings. In fairness though, it is likely that various Catholic orders have different cultures; I did not sense the same predatory atmosphere during my short summer stay, at age eleven, with the Benedictines, as I did with the Christian Brothers.

Catholic celibacy, though, makes sense as a corporate policy. If priests were allowed to marry then they would own property, which they would then bequeath to their heirs. This would not be advantageous to the Catholic Church, perhaps the most ruthless corporate entity in history. Through the promulgation of its crusades, inquisitions, witch hunts, genocides, and through the terror of the many unspeakable tortures that it has inflicted on vast numbers of human beings, the Catholic corporation, through its long history, seems to have been primarily oriented towards a single goal—the enhancement of its own power. Imagine being burned alive for espousing, or just being accused of holding, an idea that deviated in the slightest way from Church doctrine. Pope John Paul II, to his credit, made a public apology for the many past crimes committed in the name of the Church—without offering a detailed list, of course, as that would be too horrendous and shocking. But the church continues today, with its stand against contraception, to pursue its own corporate interests—more Catholics, more revenue, more power—at the price of a vast increase in human suffering and against the long-term welfare of the planet.

Buddhism differs from other major world religions in that the words of its founder, as recorded in the sutras, actually invite skepticism, even skepticism of its own doctrines. "Test everything that I have told you for yourselves," were the words of the Buddha.

In practice, though, Buddhists can be as rigid in their doctrines as Christian fundamentalists. This seems to me to be particularly true of some Western Buddhists, most of whom have come from Christian or Jewish backgrounds, and who, spoon fed by their gurus, often seem content to merely have traded one set of catechisms for another.

The principle of free inquiry in Buddhism, even if not perfect in practice, is quite different than the "believe or burn" doctrine held by the Catholic Church, which for centuries, not content to let heretics get their comeuppance in the next life, roasted them in this one as well. This earthly institution claimed the right to pass judgment in the name of God. When a conclave of Catholic cardinals decreed in 1870 that the pope was infallible on matters of faith and morals when speaking *ex cathedra*, they automatically condemned all future popes to bear the sin of this hubris. That burden was perhaps too much for Pope John XXIII, who did attempt to reform the church, and who offered this statement: "I am only infallible if I speak infallibly, but I shall never do that, so I am not infallible." I must admit that I am amazed that a reformer like Pope Francis has now reached the highest level of power within the church. Did the cardinals really know who they were voting for? It is too early yet at this writing to tell how this will play out.

But what was going on here at these Buddhist monasteries? Was something being hidden? Buddhist monks were not supposed to drink alcohol but, in my wanderings around this monastery, I had a couple of times climbed up onto the highest flat roof, to get a good vantage point for a photo; there I had found a large pile of empty whiskey bottles. Was there a component of the apparent celibacy that was also being hidden? I didn't feel the powerful repressed sexuality here that I had often felt around Catholic monks and priests. The only time that I really felt a sexual atmosphere at a cloister in Ladakh was actually among young Buddhist nuns. But that hadn't really felt very repressed at all—more like playfulness and affection.

I was beginning to get the idea, in my conversations with Stanzin and other monks here, that the Buddhist monastic attitude towards celibacy was quite different than that in Catholic institutions. Celibacy in the Catholic Church was a kind of sacrifice. I remember one Catholic priest proudly describing his celibacy as "an open wound." Even the most famous of modern Catholic monks, Thomas Merton, in addition to his affair with a twenty-five-year-old woman when he was in his fifties, seems in some of his writings, to be strangely obsessed with women. Lawrence Ferlinghetti related that upon meeting Merton in San Francisco, the monk could not seem to stop gawking at passing women. The Buddhist monks here though, rather than regarding their celibacy as self-inflicted suffering, as the Catholics seem to, rather see it as part of their practice of attaining release from suffering—not necessarily in the next life, but in this one. My experience at Catholic schools had previously convinced me that institutional celibacy could never be anything except an unnatural and unwholesome perversion, but now I was beginning to see that perhaps it could be something different. I did not feel the atmosphere of deep neurosis here among the Buddhist monks that I frequently sensed among Catholic celibates. Although I still could not imagine celibacy for myself, in an abstract sense, I could see how psychological discipline, acquired at an early age, could lead to a life less bound to the needs of the senses. Few monks these days are solitary recluses who go off to meditate in caves for years at a time, as did the great founders of the modern Tibetan Buddhist orders, the saints of legend. For most monastics, the Sangha, the brotherhood, the company of the like-minded is a vital part of the monks' and nuns' lives. I had experienced some of the flavor of this when I spent time in a Benedictine monastery as a kid, and maybe even a bit later when I spent a short time in the military reserve. But on the whole I have never bonded as well with groups of guys as I have with women. I have a number of times found myself the only guy invited to a lesbian women's social event. It made me feel flattered—and at home.

The closest thing that I have known to membership in a Sangha, I suppose, is my bond with the climbing community. There, the purpose has something in common with that of the Buddhist Sangha: the mastery of mind, emotions, and body for specific ends. The big difference is that the climbing community is not dedicated to the liberation of all sentient beings, but to the gratification of the hedonistic desires of its individual members. But there are some climbers, actually many very high-end rock climbers, who go through a stage, usually in their youth, where they live in poverty, somewhat monk-like, sacrificing all worldly comfort in the single-minded pursuit of the perfection of their craft.

There are a number of stories of young climbers who, Buddha-like, made vows similar to those of Shakyamuni at the immovable spot. One of my favorite was of a young man who went to a famous climbing area in France called Verdun, in the middle of one summer and vowed that he would not leave until he had accomplished a *redpoint* on an extremely hard climb that only a few of the very best climbers in the world had accomplished. A *redpoint* is the linking of very hard technical moves, often with repeated falls on a lead rope, until the sequence is mastered, and the climber is able to climb the entire route without a fall. In the upper echelons of climbing, performance at this level requires extreme focus, visualization, and mind body control.

This particular young man spent the rest of the summer at Verdun, attempting over and over the difficult climb and failing again and again. The autumn came and still he stayed on. He was cold and hungry. Someone gave him a bag of potatoes. His sandals were broken and he had only his tight-fitting technical climbing shoes, which were not at all suitable for walking. Someone donated a pair of house-slippers that were much too large for him. The weather grew colder. Each morning he would shuffle out to the base of the climb in his oversize slippers, with his sleeping bag wrapped about him, for he had no cold weather clothes, recruit a belay partner from the few remaining climbers, put on his climbing shoes, tie into the rope—and try again. Verdun was his immovable spot. He knew in his heart where the achievement of his goal lay. Ascending the rock would come only when he had first transcended his mind. In the late fall, on a bitterly cold day, he got his *redpoint*. The next spring he became the first non-European male to win the World Cup, the top award in international climbing competition. If your goal is to beat the world—begin with yourself.

In the middle of my conversation with the young monk, Stanzin, at Thiksey Monastery, he turned the interview around.

"You tell me, now," he said, "what you think you know about Buddhism."

"Well," I began, "the obvious answer is the basic Buddhist idea that suffering is primarily caused by desire. Release from suffering is therefore about freeing ourselves from desire."

Stanzin nodded. Encouraged, I continued, "Well, one of the premises of Buddhism seems to be that there is no such thing as an individual imperishable soul. That which we call our mind, or our sense of an individual self, is largely an illusion. When we see the world and ourselves as we really are, then we realize that all phenomena, including what we think of as ourselves, can only arise interdependently. When we realize that we don't really exist in the sense that we thought, when we can let go of ourselves, then we can begin to let go of our attachments, desires, and aversions. First we need to let go of our ignorance. Like the three animals," I pointed to the Wheel of life Mandala painted on the wall beside us.

"Yes, the three animals," affirmed Stanzin, smiling. "You know quite a bit about Buddhism."

I felt pleased upon hearing this. But then he added, "You have done the easy part. Now you just have to do the hard part. You have to learn to practice Buddhism."

A few days later I visited Thiksey Monastery again in the early morning and once more found him sitting on the bench outside the main temple. He motioned to the seat beside him for me to sit down. Our conversation soon became involved enough with complex philosophical ideas that we came to the point where the language barrier was causing a significant impediment to the communication of my questions and his answers. Stanzin motioned and spoke in Ladakhi to a young layman standing nearby, whom he obviously knew. This man then sat down with us, and being more fluent in English than Stanzin, helped us out whenever we got stuck.

When I asked Stanzin how Buddhists could believe in the impermanence of all things and yet hold the belief that there is reincarnation after death, he gave me an answer that went something like this. "The Buddha meditated for many years to try to find the *imperishable individual soul.** He discovered in his meditations that it does not exist. Every moment is change. But change does not cease with death. You will continue to change after you die. What is you is both real and illusion. When you go down to the Indus today and put your hand in the river, you can say, "I put my hand in the Indus." And when you do that tomorrow, you can say, "I put my hand in the Indus," once more. But the river that you really put your hand in yesterday is all gone. The water that you put your hand in yesterday has flowed out toward the sea."

Stanzin pointed to another wall painting that featured a variety of animals. "Here is the most important thing for you to know about Buddhism," he said. "You see those animals? They are all different. But in the story of this painting the artist wants to show you that the animals are all friends. We are all different, but we are also the same. We must look into each other's hearts, and into ourselves, to know this. Then we will learn to have compassion for others. Learning philosophy without learning to open your heart, will do you no good."

I left the monastery, and arriving in the outer courtyard, started up the rented Enfield motor cycle I had left there. I listened to the

---

* Stanzin actually used the term "Atman" in this context several times, but this Sanskrit word has so many different meanings that I have used a substitution phrase in this edited conversation that is more precise in conveying what I believe to be, his intended meaning.

satisfying rumble of the engine, thinking about what Stanzin had told me as I steered the bike down the road to the dusty plain and the way to Leh.

THE SUMMIT
JUNE 2013

I switched off the headlamp and waited for my eyes to adjust to the dark. The moon had gone down with the sun and would rise again only with the dawn. The darkness was almost complete. Only gradually did vague shapes begin to appear, looming above, in the gloom. It was 3:30 a.m. and I was lost somewhere on a steep snow and rock face of 6150-meter (20,1750-ft) Stok Kangri, the highest mountain that can be seen from the Leh valley. I had left Base Camp at just after midnight, about thirty minutes after another party, two Brits and a German, accompanied by two local guides, had departed on their own summit bid. After their headlamps disappeared over the first ridge, I did not see them again until they returned to camp.

My eyes had now fully adjusted to the darkness, but I still couldn't make out much of the terrain around me. What I could see though, with a clarity beyond anything I had ever experienced before, was the immense band of the star-spangled Milky Way, spread out against an unimaginably black void of sky. Lost or not, it was certainly worth it to be up here on this moonless night to see this.

My crampons bit securely into the hard surface of the snow. The pitch was at about the limit of what I could manage using French technique. If it got any steeper I would have to switch to more strenuous *front pointing*, also called German technique. Although I felt secure on the solid snow, I had to keep stopping to catch my breath in the thin air of 5500 meters (18,045 ft). But where the hell was I anyway? I had climbed this mountain twice before, going back to 1985, and I thought I knew the way, but this stygian darkness was so complete that I had lost my orientation. I continued to push a route up on the steep snow, sometimes scrambling short sections of rock with my crampons still on, until I came near what I thought was the crest of a ridge. But now a series of vertical stone towers stood like sentinels to block my way—these kinds of structures are appropriately called *gendarmes* in the climbing lexicon. I had to climb down several hundred meters on my front points, and then traverse several hundred more before I found another line up a broad gully of steep snow. It was now 4:30 a.m. and beginning to get light. It appeared that there was a series of gullies above me that might continue to the summit. It looked doable but quite technical and would be extremely strenuous. But I didn't remember the face being this steep on my other ascents. The last one, in the fall season, some two and a half years ago, was basically a walk up a snow-free ridge. The first one was somewhat more technical, up a permanent snow/ice face that has since been devoured by the ravenous appetite of global warming. But neither time did I recall seeing all these rock buttresses and separated snow gullies that were now coming into view in the dawn light. By 5 a.m. it finally became apparent to me where I was. This was not the south face where I was supposed to be at all. I was actually on the steeper east face. A glance at a compass, which I had left in camp, would have told me that sooner; but perhaps because I was so sure that I knew the way, I had not even thought to include it when I packed my gear for this climb the afternoon before. It was normally a piece of equipment that I never went into the mountains without.

There was a route above that would probably go, but not for me, considering the amount of energy I had expended climbing up and down in the dark, and considering the time of day. Although the temperature was still sub-zero now, in another two hours it would rise suddenly and the hard layer of surface snow would weaken so that every step would likely send me post-holing knee deep into the unconsolidated snow beneath. It was also way too late now to get around to the normal route on the south side. I began to descend to the flat glacier at the base of the face.

After crossing the glacier, part of the south face came into view, and I could now see the other party near the summit ridge. If they made it to the top, they would be the first ones this season.

A number of parties had attempted the climb this year, but none had yet succeeded, some reportedly turning back only a hundred meters from the summit. Having heard, during the past weeks, about all the groups that had retreated, I had decided to come up and "see what all the fuss was about," as I had written in an email to Helen. Now, feeling whipped by my own hubris, I wished that I had visualized the exact route more carefully, instead of assuming that I would find the way as I had done twice before. Both those times I had started the climb under the light of a full moon. This was much different. And I had not brought a GPS to Ladakh because the maps available here were not accurate enough to be useful for that kind of navigation. The only really accurate maps here were in the hands of the military, and they were closely guarded secrets.

The moon in Buddhism is a symbol for the path to enlightenment, the Dharma. The goal is reached through the Triple Refuge: the way, the teacher, and the fellowship. I had attempted this climb without the moon to light the path, without a guide, without companions. What would it have been like to come up here with a guide who really knew the way? I would have followed him, with the bright circle of light cast by my headlamp bobbing a few feet in front of me. I would probably not have turned off the light and allowed my eyes to adjust to the dark. Had I not gotten lost, I would not have seen those stars.

It was likely that the group near the summit ridge would make it. They were all experienced mountaineers, not just guided tourists, who would be prone to waste precious energy trying to master unfamiliar crampon techniques. I returned to camp at just after 7 a.m., resolved to try again the next morning. Feeling exhausted by my struggle on the east face, I was hoping that my body would recover during the day. Having not planned on this extra day though, I had not brought enough food to really carbo load again. Additionally I had come up to base camp too fast the day before. The trip from the trailhead at the village of Stok to base camp was, to my knowledge, never attempted by climbing groups in a single day; but I thought that I could get away with it because…well…I had done it before, and this way I would be able to hire a porter for a single day to carry the bulk of my gear to base camp and drop it there. A few days before, I had hiked up to base camp and returned to the trailhead in a single day to test my fitness, having recently recovered from one of those Asian drinking water illnesses. I had stopped for a rest at a place called Mankarmo, where most parties headed for Stok Kangri would spend a night before ascending further. There three young men were in the process of setting up a tea tent for the season where climbers and trekkers would be able to buy refreshments and food. When I asked them if I could get a cup of tea, they sheepishly told me that they had somehow neglected to pack a few things on the pony caravan that had brought their supplies up here. The missing items for the tea tent, it turned out, included the tea and the tent—also the cups, sugar, and the most of the food. They said that they were hungry themselves, having only biscuits to eat, and were hoping for the arrival of another caravan of supplies soon. Looking around at the stacks of boxes, I could see that what had made it up here were abundant supplies of soft drinks and bottled water.

Having not understood, when I was told that there was no sugar for tea, that here was actually no tea either, I told them that just powdered milk, which they did have, would be fine. A short while later they served me hot water and powdered milk in the truncated bottom half of a plastic water bottle. Fortunately I spied a small jar of instant coffee among their things, and I got one of them to add some of that to my beverage. One thing that the mountains have taught me is that things are not so much delicious because they are inherently delicious, but often because of where you are, how tired you are, how much in need of nourishment you are. The instant coffee in the improvised cup was truly, memorably, delicious—and energizing. No la-di-da barista could have made me happier. The boys did not want me to pay, embarrassed by the disorganization of their set up. But I insisted on paying, saying that since I was their first customer of the season, they had to accept my money for the sake of good fortune, both theirs and mine.

I had felt strong that day, so I figured that I could go up to base camp again now and sleep there for a few hours before the climb as long as I went up relatively slowly. It didn't quite work out that way though. The young Nepali porter that I hired was extremely fit and perhaps he wanted to show off how strong he was. Being competitive myself, and having him on my heels almost the whole time, induced me to walk faster than I intended; I arrived at base camp feeling quite light-headed and cursed myself for running down my physical reserves so carelessly.

After my misadventure on the east face, I was back at base camp and now would have the whole day to kill with no shelter from the merciless high altitude sun, having brought no tent for what was supposed to be a lightweight speed ascent. The two Brits and the German with their guides returned to camp at about 10 a.m., pleased that they had been the first to reach the summit this season. They were quite knackered, though, and spent most of the rest of the day in their tents, while being served beverages and food by their staff. The Brits had a tent for sleeping, one for dining, and one, shady and well ventilated, for lounging. The sun at this time of year is high in the sky for much of the day, and there was consequently no natural patch of shade. I tried several times to devise a shelter from the sun with my ground tarp and trekking poles—with little success. The day passed as I tried alternate sessions of napping and meditation, but although my body was tired, my mind was too restless to really settle down to either. It seemed like the light of the over-illuminated landscape all around me was seeping into my brain and keeping it ablaze. Finally, at a little after 7 p.m., the sun went down behind the mountains and I had respite from the high-altitude radiation. Now the temperature would begin to drop quickly to sub-zero.

I awoke to the chimes of my internal alarm at 10:30 p.m. after about two hours sleep. My body wanted more. Wrapped in my down parka and sleeping bag I was warm and comfy. Out there it was cold. My body said, "Stay here." Part of my mind said, "Come on, sit up," while another part said, "You need more rest—stay in bed." I dozed. Then a voice said, "This is your last chance; you have no supplies for another try; get up and go, or I will flog you for years, probably for the rest of your life, for missing this window because you were a lazy sloth." It was the voice of my personal Fury. Every climber has one of these. Needs one. I sat up and wiggled out of the top part of the sleeping bag and turning on my headlamp, lit the stove that was beside me. Five minutes later I was drinking hot black coffee and getting the morning caffeine rush that I love. I left my bivi site again just after midnight, like the morning before. There would be no other parties attempting the climb today, and I would have the mountain to myself. The last two days had taken their toll though, and I knew that I really needed a day's rest. A day that I didn't have. I was resolved, though, to push on as high as I could and make an honest effort today. I would soon see how well my body had recovered during the first steep climb, of about two hundred meters, right out of camp, to the crest of ridge. All the way up that first bit I waited for my reserves to kick in. They didn't. Nor did they for the rest of the climb. I felt exhausted from the get-go.

About an hour and a half after setting out I began to cross the flat glacier at the foot of the south face. The hazards here, I had been warned, involved crossing three streams that ran through trenches cut into the ice of the glacier. You had to jump over these streams, guessing at where your takeoff platform might not be so undercut as to collapse under you as you went to jump. The current and volume of the water in the streams was sufficient enough that I would be in serious difficulty if I fell in, particularly since there would be no one to assist me. At each of the crossings I searched with my headlamp to try to find a narrowing and probed the takeoff platform with my ice axe before committing to the leap. I couldn't help but think of the story of the young man who fell into one of these kinds of streams flowing over the surface of the North Saskatchewan Glacier in Canada. The current swept him into a sinkhole and down he went into the bowels underneath the glacier. I once hung off the end of a climbing rope looking down one of these sinkholes before I had heard the story, and tried to imagine what it would be like to fall into this abyss of darkness and cold. It never occurred to me, at the time, that such an experience could be survivable. I was certain that going over the edge here would be an abandon-all-hope type of event, like falling into the maw of a live volcano.

But the young man did survive. The sub-glacial stream, after keelhauling him across the stones embedded into the ice of the roof, spat him out, alive, at the foot of the glacier and into the swift current of the North Saskatchewan River, which then became yet another survival challenge in its own right. How long he was under the ice, I'm not sure, but in any case it was obviously not longer than he could hold his breath. Amazingly, I heard him say that he did not remember feeling fear at any time during the experience. He developed a lifelong fascination with water, though, after the incident and now works as some kind of hydrologist for the United Nations. His tale rang a bell deep within me. I marvel how archetypal this story is: the descent of the hero into the underworld from which there is no hope of return—and then—the resurrection. I believe that is why Joe Simpson's incredible return from the dead after the terrible events on Siula Grande in Peru, recorded in *Touching the Void*, struck such a chord with a general readership. It too was so much more than the telling of a climbing adventure—it was the Hero's Journey.

After leaping the three streams and crossing the glacier, I came to what, I now, correctly, assumed to be the south face of Stok Kangri. And an hour later, I stopped at rocky out cropping, which provided a flat platform protruding from the snow face. I was pooched. It felt like there was no more gas in the tank. After eating a bar and drinking some water, I waited for some of my strength to come back. That didn't seem to be happening though. It was starting to get light. I looked at my altimeter. It read 5500 meters (18,045 ft)—only half way to the summit. I would have to give up. I simply could not climb another 600 meters at this altitude, in this state.

Climbing to me, and I believe all real climbers, is not all about getting to the top; it is all about how you get to the top. The simplest style is the purest and the best. A couple of weeks previously I had been invited to go on an organized expedition to climb this peak. It was to take five days. It would have full service, meaning guides, cooks, sleeping tents, dinning tents, even a toilet tent. Imagine sitting up in your bag in the morning and having your coffee handed to you. I had never had this sort of experience before on a climb. I had been tempted to join, but then decided that I was not ready for this kind of pampering. Maybe when I was seventy or eighty, but not now. I had the soft life in the relative palace I lived in at home; being in the mountains should involve a certain amount of suffering and hardship after all. But now my hubris had caught up to me. Here I was sitting on this ledge, and I was spent. Consequently I would have to tell all the local guides whom I would meet on the way down and who would surely ask me if I had made the summit that I had not. I remembered how they had looked at me with respect in the last few days—like I was not just another tourist, but a peer. Now they would think that I was just a crazy man after all. I looked toward the summit and slowly rose to my feet. I could still put one foot in front of the other, I knew. How long I could do that before the day warmed up and the snow surface began to cave in, I didn't know. But there was only one way to find out.

At this altitude every ounce of extra weight could feel like a chunk of lead, so I decided to leave the daypack on the ledge. I rummaged through it for anything essential, taking out the water bottle and shoving it into one of the large pockets of my down parka. The temperature was still sub-zero, so I couldn't part with the warm jacket. I hesitated over the camera and wished that I had brought a smaller one; it felt like a brick in my hand. I decided to leave it; I already had summit shots from this peak.

After climbing another half hour I could see the descent footmarks left by the previous day's group. The snow this time of morning was still very hard and my crampons were hardly leaving any visible marks. The route that the other party had taken went up to below the southwest ridge and then followed a long traverse across the face under the ridge towards the summit on the east end of the face. I was going to take a more direct route up the face. The slightly steeper climbing did not worry me, as my crampons felt secure in the hard snow. I just kept putting one foot in front of the other, feeling confident using French technique until a short steep section near the summit, where it was expedient to switch to front pointing. I had to stop every few steps to take extra breaths, careful not to push beyond the zone of occasional mild dizziness into that space, where a loss of balance and the dropping of the ice axe would result in a rapid descent down the 900-meter south face. When my altimeter read 6000 meters (19,685 ft) the sun was up and I had taken off the down parka and tied it around my waist. Theoretically there was still 150 meters to go, but I was now counting on the altimeter reading 100 meters low, as the air was warming up and therefore air density would be increasing—even as oxygen molecules per given volume were decreasing and consequently breathing was getting even harder. I turned out to be right about the altimeter. At 6:51 a.m. I stood on the summit. To the north I could see the great pyramid shape of K2 and the Karakorum Range. To the west and south were the Himalayas. To the east was Tibet. Looking down the steep north face I could see a white pinprick that I knew was the one-house village of Yurutse. Rinchen and Agmo would likely be lighting the hearth fire and preparing morning tea there now. I sat down and leaned against a sort of Mani wall that was covered with snow and ice and festooned with half buried and shredded prayer flags. The morning was clear and bright; the planet, under a canopy of deep Himalayan blue, was laid out in vivid detail for hundreds of miles in every direction.

Each of us owns a unique string of shining moments, collected over the span of our lives. These gems are, by far, the most valuable possessions any human can ever hold. Now, when I bring up to the light my own assortment of shimmering recollections, I can see a pearl, which is the memory of the morning on that summit. And near the pearl there is a diamond—a vision of the unfiltered universe—that I saw on the night I was lost.

I could not linger here long as I knew that the sun would soon weaken the surface layer of snow. After about ten minutes on the summit, I started down. I did not encounter a lot of difficulty with the breaking crust that the party the morning before had described to me. This was probably because I was taking a more direct route. The descent was relatively uneventful except that during one of the stream crossings the takeoff platform gave way just as I pushed off for the jump. I kind of dove across the gap and ended up with my upper body sprawled on the far side, my cramponed feet dangling over the stream—while I hauled on the planted ice axe to pull myself to security.

I arrived back at base camp at about 10 a.m. The place was deserted until noon when two large parties arrived. By one o'clock I had packed up my gear and was ready to head down. Ominous signs of a change in the weather were evident by then, and indeed no one else was to make the summit for the next couple of weeks as this new storm cycle dumped a fresh load of snow. Shortly after beginning the descent, I encountered another group coming up accompanied by one of the young men from Mankarmo. His name was Kalima, and he was the one in charge of running the tea tent there, which had now been resupplied and was much better organized than on my first visit. He, of course, immediately asked if I had made the summit, and then gave me an exuberant high five. I told him that I was going to try to hike down to the trailhead and get to Leh tonight, but that I was too tired to carry my gear the whole way and did he think that there was anyone at Mankarmo that I could pay to carry it down. Kalima said that if I rested there for two hours he would be back down and would help me.

Kalima didn't actually show up at Mankarmo until four hours later, however, at which time it was too late to head down further. He apologized, saying that a storm had blown up at base camp and he had to spend a couple of hours helping this group set up their tents in the high wind. No worries though. The boys made me dinner and set up a brand new two-man spare tent they had for me to sleep in. I climbed into my sleeping bag just as the rain, which would be snow any higher up, began to fall on the roof of the tent. Then I fell into the deep sleep of exhaustion.

The next night in Leh, I was looking forward to another good sleep. Trouble was that now, at 10:30 p.m. there were two large Indian families congregating in the spacious hallway right outside my room, and they all seemed to be speaking at once in loud voices. Large groups of domestic tourists were a new phenomenon in Ladakh that was almost non-existent here when I last visited only a little over two years ago. What had effected this change was apparently the biggest blockbuster Bollywood movie of all time, a film called *The Three Idiots*, which featured Ladakh as a major location and even had the

Oriental Guest House, where I was staying, in the credits. Indian tourists, who usually stayed for five or six days, seldom went trekking, or even walking, taking taxis everywhere. For many it was an ideal place to get away from the killer pre-monsoon heat that hung over much of the sub-continent at this time of year. The domestic tourists generally conversed with each other at much higher volumes than Westerners or, for that matter, Ladakhis. Tashi told me that it was commonly said here that you could have five Indians or a hundred Europeans stay at your hotel for about the same amount of noise. Interestingly, when Ladakhis use the term, "Indian," they are talking about people from the other side of the Himalayas, and never seem to refer to themselves this way even though they are, citizenship-wise at least, Indian.

The exchange, when I went out to give the people in the hallway shit for keeping me awake, went like this.

"Excuse me but you're making a lot of noise. I have just come down from the mountains and I'm very tired."

"What mountain did you go to?" asked one man.

"Stok Kangri," I answered. What difference did it make what mountain, I thought to myself. I just want to go to sleep.

"Stok Kangri? How high did you go?" he now asked.

"Uh, the top."

"The top of Stok Kangri? Really? How many were in your group?"

"I was alone."

"But you had a guide."

"No, I was alone."

"You climbed it all alone? Really? All alone?"

"Yes."

"Weren't you afraid of getting lost?"

"I was lost."

"But you found your way?"

"Eventually."

I was about to add that I really wanted to go to sleep now, but he suddenly rose to his feet from the step he was sitting on in the hallway.

"May I have my picture taken with you?' he asked.

"What?"

Then another man asked, "Can I have my picture taken with you also?"

"Can my son have his picture taken with you? Devi, bring the camera."

"This is my daughter. She is fourteen. Can she have her picture taken with you?"

I posed for their pictures and ended up sitting on the floor with them in the hallway, telling stories and showing pictures for over an hour. These Indian tourists may have been noisy, but they sure knew how to toast and butter-up a raconteur.

AWAKENING
AUGUST 2013

I am sitting in a lawn chair in my driveway at home. It is a sunny late afternoon in early August. Across the street neighborhood children are practicing jumps on their mountain bikes on improvised ramps. There is a slight breeze that flutters the string of prayer flags strung over the entrance to our garage. I tell myself the flags are working for me, sending prayers to heaven and gaining me merit while I sit here and enjoy a ginger beer at ease in my chair. Do I actually believe this? Well, no. I fly the prayer flags because I think that they are beautiful, and also because I love the metaphor of the Avalokitesvara Bodhisattva, whose mantra is printed on the flags, and who, because of his infinite compassion, has forgone Nirvana and returned to the world to save other sentient beings. Every time I see the flags I am made aware of this sublime metaphor, which reminds me to try to have empathy for others and to treat my neighbors with kindness.

The flags also remind me of a faraway place. A place that I had to go to again and again. If the purpose of travel, work, play, Buddhism, and Yoga is to know oneself, these engagements can, and should, also lead one to forget oneself. I don't know what happened to me on the night of the dragon, below the Gongmaru La, but I have felt different ever since. It was so unlike the bliss-like transformative experience that we imagine someone having by going alone to meditate the high Himalaya; it was instead a descent into the deepest pit of despair. But it was transformative nevertheless. My life has changed. The world looks different.

I imagined, since my teens, that India would hold some secret revelation for me. I traveled there seven times looking for it. It happened only when I finally let go of every expectation. Just like when I let go of the expectation of finding the snow leopard, and then she showed up—the night of the dragon I let go of all expectations. But although I felt at peace the next morning, I had no idea then how much I had been changed. I had been looking all those years, but now I know that I was also running away. It wasn't until I nailed myself to the immovable spot and let Mara, or the dragon, or whatever it was, come to me that it happened—although I still have little clue what happened.

That which is called Buddhism is not Buddhism—therefore it is called Buddhism. This passage from the Diamond Cutter Sutra is one of the more important pieces of wisdom that I have come across. Obtuse as it sounds at first reading, it is not really some complex riddle, unfathomable to the occidental mind; it simply means that true reality is beyond the ability of words to describe, but that, since words are all we have, they will have to do. But we should not forget that words are an imprecise description of reality; they are merely shadows of reality—not even that. All the world's religions started off with the visions of seers and poets who saw far beyond the effable. To try to recreate intimations of their visions they used the language of metaphor. Their followers took their words, and in the case of pretty well every single religion, turned them into dogmas. The words that were originally intended as signposts were taken to represent the destination itself.

Buddhism is a little different this way. Although religious faith and even superstition has crept into some of its practice today, its founder, Siddhartha, tried to be very precise in explaining what he had learned in his vision. And it may be that he held a lot back because he did not want it to be misinterpreted. Unlike the founders of every other religion he did not offer even the intimation of a vision of the ethereal, numinous, or cosmic. He refused to discuss cosmology or life after death, but he stated that he had discovered in his mediations that there was no such thing as an individual imperishable soul. What he offered was a science of introspection, psychology, and self-help. He also offered a somewhat counterintuitive but very logical way of looking at the world and ourselves. He expounded that the things in this world arise in interdependence of each other and that all things, including ourselves, are in a constant state of flux. Our sense of an independent selfhood itself is rather an illusion. I don't think that it would be incorrect to state that this point of view comes closer to seeing the things of the world as events, rather than static objects. From this perspective then the term "human being" with "being," read unconventionally as a verb, comes closer to expressing the Buddha's view of human existence.

I feel that I am a somewhat different person today than when I began the search for the snow leopard almost thirty years ago, or even since I began this book three years ago. Events have changed me. Those events were largely the result of my own actions and thoughts, although I foresaw few of their consequences ahead of time. I suppose that this is what is meant by reincarnation and Karma. This is the esoteric interpretation of those two terms, but most Buddhists believe that an individual's Karma and reincarnation carry on after physical death. This can, on one hand, be interpreted on a purely secular level: we all make ripples in the pond, which propagate and spread ever outward. Sometimes even the smallest gesture of kindness can change another's life, just as a gesture of indifference, as Albert Camus pointed out, can extinguish one.

On the other hand, there is an interpretation of reincarnation that intimates that there is some unnamable energy that is literally transferred to some other realm, or even body, after death. This is where science leaves off in Buddhism, which is otherwise an empirical philosophy. But who is to say? Having had the fun of spending part of my adolescence growing up in a haunted house, I know that there are things that are unexplainable. I don't believe in ghosts; that's just a word, but the sea captain who built that house definitely left something of himself behind. That it was something mostly sad engendered my empathy and curiosity, seldom my fear. Many Buddhists believe that attachments can persist after death. I wish that I could have freed him, it, whatever it was that got left in that house. There are mysteries better left unnamed, for perhaps they are unnamable.

Helen comes out to the driveway and takes a seat beside me. She spreads out a map—eager to plan our next mountain adventure. I tell her that her garden is looking great. She is pleased. We wave together at a neighbor, who waves back. I take another sip of my ginger beer. It burns my tongue in a way that an endorphin junkie appreciates. I am back among the world's distractions, but they are no longer distractions. They are the purpose. Life's precious moments.

INDEX